CHILD PSYCHOLOGY

**CITY OF BIRMINGHAM
POLYTECHNIC LIBRARY**

AUTHOR   HARVEY. G.

TITLE   CHILD PSYCHOLOGY (1975)

SUBJECT No. 155.4077

BOOK No.   062594

P39970-B1(C)   0471358010

CHILD PSYCHOLOGY

GERALDINE HARVEY

John Wiley & Sons, Inc.
New York • London • Sydney • Toronto

Editors: Judy Wilson and Irene Brownstone
Production Manager: Ken Burke
Artist: Carl Brown
Composition and Make-up: Susan Garcia

Library of Congress Cataloging in Publication Data

Harvey, Geraldine, 1936–
    Child psychology.

    (Wiley self-teaching guides)
    Bibliography: p. 73, 128, 191, 280, 281.
    Includes index.
    1. Child study. I. Title. DNLM: 1. Child psychology.
WS105 H34c
BF721.H268   155.4   75–19149
ISBN 0-471-35801-0

Printed in the United States of America

75 76 10 9 8 7 6 5 4 3 2 1

Preface

What is child psychology? Briefly, it is a scientific discipline dedicated to the better understanding of children and their development. Child psychologists study many areas of development—physical changes, cognition, perception, and personality, to name a few.

In fact, one of the most difficult tasks in writing an overview of child psychology is defining the limits of the field. Child psychology draws from many disciplines: physiology, sociology, biology, and other specialized areas of psychology such as personality, learning, and perception. Essentially, it integrates whatever these fields have to tell us about children and their development. However, child psychology is a field by itself, with its own goals and research questions, and this book will try to give some idea of the scope of those goals and questions.

Another reason child psychology is so difficult to define is that the field has changed markedly in the past few years. In the past decade alone, thanks largely to the work of Swiss psychologist Jean Piaget, there has been a new surge of interest in cognitive development and the thinking processes of children. Children's thought is no longer seen as an incomplete replica of adult thought. Parents, teachers, and psychologists are now trying to understand the differences between children's thought and adult thought. When adults understand how children view the world, they can communicate with children more effectively.

Children's language is also being looked at—and listened to—from a new perspective. Psychologists have demonstrated that children of four understand and can use most of the complex rules of grammar. Language acquisition has become a very important area of study as psychologists continue to revise much of their thinking about how children acquire language. "The development of language" is treated as a separate chapter in this book, to reflect its new importance.

Finally, child psychologists have become increasingly aware of cultural stereotypes that may have, in the past, influenced our ideas about children and their development. Increasing cross-cultural research as well as input from minority groups and women's groups have led psychologists to be more cautious in interpreting age, sex, or "class" norms. Many old assumptions are currently being questioned, such as the supposed "superiority" of middle class (or even Western) modes of thought, the inevitability of certain boy-girl differences, or the "impossibility" of raising children's level of intellectual functioning. As these assumptions are questioned, new research is generated and often further questions are raised.

In order to reflect the contemporary view of child psychology, this book is organized according to the various areas of child development; each chapter deals with a specific area of development. Child Psychology is not intended to be a complete course textbook. Rather, it aims to give an overview of the entire field of child psychology. As such, it can stand alone as an introduction to child development or it can be used in conjunction with any of the standard college textbooks currently in use. Because it is an overview of the field, this guide cannot include much of the fascinating detail from studies of children. However, at the end of each chapter are suggested readings, so readers can follow up on areas of particular interest. It must be remembered, however, that the eventual object of study is the total child, and that child is a complex interaction of emotional, intellectual, and biological factors. Even if we were able to discover everything there is to know about all areas of development, we would not fully understand any given child. The motto of parents, educators, and psychologists ought to be: "Understand children as much as possible; enjoy them thoroughly."

Geraldine Harvey

Somerville, Massachusetts
March, 1975

How to Use This Book

Child Psychology is specially designed to help you teach yourself the basic concepts of child development. In this self-teaching format, the material is presented in numbered sections called frames. Each frame presents some new information and then gives you a problem or question which asks you to apply that information. After you have answered, you should compare your answer with the book's answer, which follows the dashed line in each frame. If the answers agree, read on. If not, review the previous frames to be sure you understand the correct answer before you go on. This format allows you to move at your own pace—as fast or as slow as you want—while insuring that you fully understand each major concept.

Each chapter includes behavioral objectives which outline what you will learn in the chapter. At the end of each chapter is a Self-Test to help you evaluate your understanding of the material in the chapter. The answers following the Self-Test include frame references for review, if a question poses any difficulty. At the end of the book is a comprehensive Final Exam, divided into chapter sections, with answers and frame references for review. If you wish, you may take the chapter Self-Test before reading a chapter, and then after completing the chapter, take the chapter section of the Final Exam, to measure how much you have learned.

Child Psychology may be read independently or as a supplement to a course text. The Cross-Reference Chart indexes chapters in the book to corresponding chapters in some standard texts in child psychology. Chapters 2-6 are followed by specific suggested readings, and a general list of further readings appears at the end of the book.

Other Textbooks in Child Psychology

The cross-reference chart on the following page indicates the pages in some of the popular Child Psychology texts corresponding to each chapter in Child Psychology. Below is a bibliography of the texts in the chart.

Jersild, Arthur T., Telford, Charles W., and Sawrey, James M., Child Psychology, 7th Edition (Englewood Cliffs, N.J.: Prentice-Hall, 1975).

Johnson, Ronald C., and Medinnus, Gene R., Child Psychology: Behavior and Development, 3rd Edition (New York: John Wiley & Sons, 1974).

Kennedy, Wallace A., Child Psychology, 2nd Edition (Englewood Cliffs, N.J.: Prentice-Hall, 1975).

LeFrancois, Guy R., Of Children: An Introduction to Child Development (Belmont, California: Wadsworth Publishing Company, 1973).

McCandless, Boyd R., and Evans, Ellis D., Children and Youth: Psychosocial Development (Hinsdale, Illinois: The Dryden Press, 1973).

Munsinger, Harry, Fundamentals of Child Development, 2nd Edition (New York: Holt, Rinehart and Winston, 1975).

Mussen, Paul H., Conger, John J., and Kagan, Jerome, Development and Personality, 4th Edition (New York: Harper & Row, 1974).

Papalia, Diane E., and Olds, Sally W., A Child's World: Infancy Through Adolescence (New York: McGraw-Hill, 1975).

Stone, L. Joseph, and Church, Joseph, Childhood and Adolescence: A Psychology of the Growing Person, 3rd Edition (New York: Random House, 1973).

Watson, Robert I., and Lindgren, Henry C., Psychology of the Child, 3rd Edition (New York: John Wiley & Sons, 1973).

Weiner, Irving B., and Elkind, David, Child Development: A Core Approach (New York: John Wiley & Sons, 1972).

	Jersild	Johnson	Kennedy	LeFrancois	McCandless	Munsinger	Mussen	Papalia	Stone	Watson	Weiner
Chapter 1	1, 2, 6	1, 2, 14	2, 7, 8	1, 5	1, 2, 3	1	1, 2	2	4	1, 2, 7	1
Chapter 2	2, 5, 6, 7, 9, 20	3, 14	3, 4	9, 10, 11, 12	1, 6	1, 2, 3, 4	4, 7	2, 3, 4, 5	1, 2, 3, 4, 5, 7	3, 5, 6, 10, 14	2, 3, 4, 5
Chapter 3	6, 7, 16, 21, 22	4, 6, 13, 14	2, 4, 5, 6	2, 5, 6, 7, 10, 11, 12, 13	1, 5, 6	1, 5, 6, 7, 8, 9, 11	2, 6, 7, 8, 11	2, 3, 4, 5	4, 7, 9	3, 7, 11, 14	2, 3, 4, 5, 6
Chapter 4	2, 5, 6, 7, 8, 10, 11, 12, 13, 15, 16, 17, 18, 21, 23, 24	4, 7, 8, 9, 10, 12, 14, 15	2, 6, 7, 9, 10	3, 4, 6, 7, 9, 11, 12, 13	1, 7, 8, 9, 10, 11	1, 9, 10, 11, 12, 13, 14	2, 5, 9, 10, 11, 12, 13	2, 3, 4, 5	3, 5, 6, 7, 8, 9, 10, 11, 12	4, 6, 8, 10, 12, 13, 15, 16	2, 3, 4, 5, 6
Chapter 5	13, 14, 19	4, 5	6, 8	10, 11	1, 4	1, 6	6, 7	2, 3, 4	5, 7, 9	7, 9, 11, 14	2, 3, 4, 5, 6
Chapter 6	8, 10, 11, 12, 14, 15, 18, 23	8, 10, 14, 15	1, 6, 8	7, 12, 13	1, 7, 11	1, 9, 12, 14	3, 4, 9, 12, 13	1, 2, 3, 4, 5	3, 8, 11	7, 12, 13, 15	2, 3, 4, 5, 6

Contents

CHILD PSYCHOLOGY

CHAPTER ONE
Introduction to Child Psychology

The growth and development of a child is a complex process involving physical, emotional, and intellectual changes. A child's development is affected first of all by innate tendencies and predispositions. For example, genetic factors determine, at least in part, whether a child will be small or large, early- or late-maturing, slow or quick to respond. However, a child's development is also affected by many environmental factors—culture, family, social class, and peer group, to name a few.

These genetic and environmental factors account for individual differences among children. However, the similarity of behavior among children of the same age is often very striking. In the course of development, all children go through certain stages; development basically follows the same pattern, regardless of differences in temperament and abilities.

Child psychologists are interested not only in individual differences but in these common developmental trends in children. They ask the following questions:

What individual differences exist in children?
How do these differences develop?
How do children change over time?
What causes these age changes in children?

In this chapter, we will look at some of the ways in which psychologists study these questions—the methods used to study children's development. We will see that psychologists are increasingly interested in studying general trends in development and in attempting to explain them. We will also look at some of the areas of development in which child psychologists are currently working.

OBJECTIVES

After completing this chapter, you will be able to

- discriminate between maturation and experience as they affect children's development;

- discriminate among the five areas of development generally studied by child psychologists;

- identify the factors involved in the learning process;

- identify and recognize examples of the four common methods used in studying child development;

- identify the factors in an experiment;

- discriminate between an observational study and an experiment.

WHAT IS CHILD DEVELOPMENT?

1. Child psychology is concerned with all areas of a child's behavior and development. Development is defined as the process of behavior changes over time. Probably the developmental process that comes most readily to mind is the sequence whereby a child crawls, sits, stands, and in that one dramatic moment, takes his first step. We call this whole process motor development. Similarly, when we study the changes in a child's speech patterns over time, we call this process language development.

   Obviously, experience plays a large part in determining the course of development. Children learn to speak different languages because they experience different language environments. A child growing up in France speaks a language different from that of a child

   growing up in England. This demonstrates that _____ plays an important part in a child's language development.

- - - - - - - - - - - - - - - - -

   experience

2. If you think about it, you realize that most children learn to talk at about the same age and that there are certain regularities in children's speech at various ages—size of vocabulary, length and type of sentences, and so on. A 14-month-old child does not speak in long, grammatically correct sentences, regardless of the opportunities

for language learning. What do you think might account for this?
(In your own words.)

dumb Parents. Lack of habits

The child just isn't old enough or mature enough. A child has to be
a certain age before he or she is able to put all the words together,
pronounce them, and think long, complex thoughts. A 14-month-old
is physically and mentally too young to do this.

3. In children's development, then, __maturation__ also plays an important
part. Maturation is described by child psychologists as the gradual
unfolding of genetically programmed sequences within the organism.
In the area of motor development, we find few striking differences
among cultures or among individuals. Children crawl, sit, stand,
and walk at pretty much the same age, regardless of their families
or cultural environments. Would you say that motor development is
more dependent on experience or on maturation? Explain your

answer. _____

_____

- - - - - - - - - - - - - - - - - - -

Maturation, since motor development varies little among cultures
and individuals, it probably depends more on maturation than on
experience.

4. When we observe any developmental change in a child, we can assume

that it is the result of some combination of _____ and

_____.

- - - - - - - - - - - - - - - - -

experience; maturation

5. Match the following:

_____ (a) development

_____ (b) maturation

_____ (c) experience

(1) that part of development that is
affected by the environment
(2) the process of behavior changes
over time
(3) the gradual unfolding of genetically programmed sequences within
the organism

- - - - - - - - - - - - - - - - -

_____

(a) 2; (b) 3; (c) 1

6. Child psychologists have disagreed over the years as to what part
    maturation plays in a child's development. Arnold Gesell, in the
    1920's, believed development to be mostly a matter of maturation.
    In a 1929 study, Gesell and Thompson trained one of a pair of identi-
    cal twins in stair-climbing, while the other twin was given no
    training. Thus the maturation level was the same for both children,
    but the children had different levels of experience. When the "trained"
    twin was able to climb stairs, both twins were tested on stair-climbing
    ability, and they performed equally well.

    (a) Which of the following statements summarizes the results of this
         study? (Check one.)

    _____ (1) Training in stair-climbing had an effect on later develop-
                  ment of the skill.

    _____ (2) Training in stair-climbing had no effect on later develop-
                  ment of this skill.

    (b) What do you suppose the researchers concluded from this result?
         (Check one.)

    _____ (1) Experience is very important in the development of motor
                  skills.

    _____ (2) Experience plays a small part in the development of motor
                  skills.

- - - - - - - - - - - - - - - - -

    (a) 2; (b) 2

7. During the 1920's, the concept of "reading readiness" was introduced.
    It states that until children develop certain perceptual and motor
    skills, they are not "ready" to learn to read. "Reading readiness"

    emphasizes the importance of _____.
                                     experience/maturation

- - - - - - - - - - - - - - - - -

    maturation

8. The early child psychologists thought that a child's motor development
    was almost wholly maturational, that experience played no part. The
    evidence available today, however, suggests that they may have over-
    stated the case and that experience does indeed have an effect on motor
    development.

Read the studies below. Check the ones which suggest that experience has an effect on motor development.

_____ (a) Dennis and Dennis compared the ages of walking in two groups of Hopi Indian children. One group spent their first few months almost continually on a cradleboard; the other group was reared in much the same way, but without cradleboards. The two groups showed no difference in the ages of walking.

_____ (b) Cross-cultural research shows that Ugandan infants, who are never left alone by their mothers and who receive massive amounts of stimulation, are weeks and even months ahead of European children in psychomotor development.

_____ (c) Burton L. White at Harvard has shown in a number of experiments that infants who receive extra amounts of stimulation (handling or enrichment of the child's visual environment) begin to reach for objects earlier that children who have not received such extra stimulation.

- - - - - - - - - - - - - - - - - -

(b) and (c) indicate that experience has an effect on motor development.

9. In the 1940's and 1950's, child psychologists became more interested in how children's behavior changed as a result of experience. They were interested in learning, particularly social learning. Some of the questions they asked were:
     What kind of child-rearing practices cause a child to show aggressive behavior?
     What makes a child dependent?
     What situations cause frustration in children?

Which of the following research questions would be of interest to a psychologist interested in the effect of experience on development? (Check one.)

_____ (a) At what age are babies first able to smile?

_____ (b) What causes some babies to smile more than others?

- - - - - - - - - - - - - - - - - -

(b)

10. Most of the child psychologists in the 1940's and 1950's were behaviorists: they believed that a person is the sum of all his or her past experiences and learning. Little attention was paid to the effect

that maturational levels might have on a child's behavior and development.

Which of the following statements would probably be made by a behaviorist? (Check one.)

_____   (a) Development is a "process of maturation meeting a process of education."

_____   (b) An infant is a "blank slate"; environment alone determines how the child will develop.

_____   (c) A child's maturational level determines developmental level.

- - - - - - - - - - - - - - - - -

(b)

11. Most psychologists today view with equal regard the influence of maturation and experience on children's development. They consider themselves _interactionists_. That is, they take the position that children develop new abilities through experience with their environment; however, children's modes of _perceiving_ and _reacting_ to the environment change with age according to certain innate maturational principles.

Look back at the three statements in frame 10; which statement would you say was probably made by an interactionist? _____

- - - - - - - - - - - - - - - - -

(a)

12. Which of the following would you say is the fairest statement of the interactionist position? (Check one.)

_____   (a) Maturation is more important than experience in children's development.

_____   (b) A child's development is produced by experience acting in combination with the maturational level of the child.

_____   (c) Children's development can be summarized as the result of all their past learning and experiences.

- - - - - - - - - - - - - - - - -

(b)

AREAS OF DEVELOPMENT

13. In studying children's development, psychologists have generally felt that they could investigate separately the following five areas of development:

    Motor development: increase in muscular control and coordination
    Cognitive development: thinking, conceptualizing, reasoning
    Perceptual development: integration of sense impressions—sight, hearing, and so on
    Personality and social development: habitual ways of behaving with others
    Language development: growth of language skills

    When we study the way a child learns to draw logical conclusions, we are concerned with what area of development? _____

- - - - - - - - - - - - - - - - - -

    cognitive

14. Many psychologists are interested in the relationship between frustration and aggression in young children. They are interested in what area of the child's development? _____

- - - - - - - - - - - - - - - - - -

    personality and social

15. When a psychologist studies how well children understand and reproduce various grammatical utterances, what area of development is being studied? _____

- - - - - - - - - - - - - - - - -

    language

16. Control of large muscles, as in hopping and skipping, comes before fine motor control, used in printing and stringing beads. This fact would be of interest to someone studying what area of development?

    _____

- - - - - - - - - - - - - - - - - -

    motor

17. Children improve with age in their ability to pick out simple figures embedded in more complex figures. What area of development does this involve? _____

- - - - - - - - - - - - - - - - - - -

perceptual, or cognitive

18. There is considerable overlap among these areas of development. For example, a child's inability to reproduce the sound "daddy," while representing a stage in language development, could be due to a deficiency in _____ development.

- - - - - - - - - - - - - - - - - -

motor, or cognitive

19. A three-year-old and a ten-year-old use the word "more." Research has shown, however, that the three-year-old and the ten-year-old have different understandings of what the word means. This demonstrates the overlap of what two areas of development?

_____, _____

- - - - - - - - - - - - - - - - - -

language; cognitive

20. Four-year-old children have trouble copying complex figures (for example, a star). This is considered due to problems with eye-hand coordination. What two areas of development are involved in this skill? _____, _____

- - - - - - - - - - - - - - - - - -

perceptual; motor

21. Children gradually develop the concept that "dog" refers not just to their own dog "Spot," but to all animals that have four legs, fur, and a tail, that are pets, and that bark. This process involves picking out and understanding many similarities and differences. What areas of development does this conceptualization of "dog" illustrate?

_____; _____

- - - - - - - - - - - - - - - - - -

perceptual; cognitive

22. As a review, match the following:

_____	(a) personality and social development	(1)	increase in muscular control and coordination
_____	(b) perceptual development	(2)	integration of sense impressions
		(3)	growth of patterns of interactions with others
_____	(c) language development	(4)	growth of language skills
_____	(d) cognitive development	(5)	changes in the processes of thinking, conceptualizing, reasoning
_____	(e) motor development		

- - - - - - - - - - - - - - - - - -

(a) 3; (b) 2; (c) 4; (d) 5; (e) 1

23. As boys and girls develop, they become increasingly different in their reactions, abilities, likes and dislikes, and so on, beyond whatever differences they may have been born with. It could be said, then, that there is actually a sixth area of development, the development of _____.

- - - - - - - - - - - - - - - - - -

sex differences

24. The final chapter of this book treats the development of sex differences. Are there any innate perceptual, cognitive, motor, language, or personality differences? How does the socialization process contribute to these sex differences? These questions are receiving increasing attention by child psychologists, and we will take a critical look at some of their current research and thinking in Chapter Six.

EXPERIENCE AND LEARNING

25. We have seen that a very important part of child development is experience. New experiences cause new behavior. Say that a child is playing on the floor with a toy and a kitten comes into the room. The child smiles and starts to crawl toward the kitten.

In this example, what is the specific experience that causes the new behavior (smiling and crawling)? _____

_____

- - - - - - - - - - - - - - - - -

the kitten, or the sight of the kitten

26. Psychologists try to determine very precisely what experiences produce what behaviors. If they are able to specify an event in the environment that causes a specific behavior to occur, they use the terms stimulus and response for the experience and the behavior, respectively.

In the example of the child and the kitten:

(a) What is the stimulus? _____

(b) What is the response? _____

- - - - - - - - - - - - - - - - -

(a) the kitten, or the sight or presence of the kitten; (b) smiling and crawling toward the kitten

27. If the child repeatedly smiles and crawls toward the kitten whenever the kitten comes into view, we say that the child has learned to make a specific response to a specific stimulus. In other words, what is learned is the connection between a stimulus and a response.

In the example of the child and the kitten, what is learned?

_____

_____

- - - - - - - - - - - - - - - - -

the connection between the stimulus (sight of the kitten) and the response (smiling and crawling toward it)

28. Let's take another example. One day, Noah's aunt comes to visit. When he sees her come through the door, he runs and gives her a kiss. Pleased as she is with this greeting, she gives him a crisp new dollar bill. After that, whenever his aunt comes to visit, Noah gives her a kiss and she, in turn, gives him a crisp new dollar bill. In this example:

(a) what is the stimulus? _____

(b) what is the response? _____

(c) what is learned? _____

_____

- - - - - - - - - - - - - - - - -

(a) the sight of his aunt; (b) giving her a kiss; (c) the connection between the stimulus (sight of his aunt) and the response (giving her a kiss)

29. (a) When psychologists try to be very specific about a behavior, what do they call it? _____

(b) When they try to be very specific about an experience, what do they call it? _____

- - - - - - - - - - - - - - - - -

(a) response; (b) stimulus

Note: All learning situations are not this simple. Obviously, there are situations in which it is difficult to identify exactly the stimulus and/or the response. In addition, some learning situations involve establishing connections between two stimuli, or between a stimulus and an internal process, or between two internal processes. Sometimes a child just "makes a new connection" in his head ("Aha! X equals Y") without making any overt response. The issue of "What is learned?" is still a very current and controversial one.

30. In many cases, we may want to increase the probability that a behavior will recur whenever the stimulus is presented (that is, we want to strengthen the stimulus–response connection). An event that increases the probability of occurrence of a response is called a reinforcer. In frame 28 Noah learned to give his aunt a kiss when she came to visit. What is the reinforcer for that behavior?

_____

- - - - - - - - - - - - - - - - -

the crisp new dollar bill

31. Psychologists do not agree on whether a reinforcer is necessary for learning. Learning does seem to take place more quickly, however, if a reinforcer is used.

Let's say that two children are trying to learn a spelling list. One child is given a piece of candy every time a word is spelled correctly; the other child is not. Both children eventually learn the list, but the child who was rewarded with candy learns more quickly.

What does this example show? (Check one.)

_____ (a) Reinforcers are necessary for learning.

_____ (b) Reinforcers have no effect on learning.

_____ (c) Reinforcers help learning take place more quickly.

- - - - - - - - - - - - - - - - - -

· (c)

32. Teachers and parents have always known that certain rewards—praise, a gold star, money, a new bike—have an effect on children's behavior and can be used to promote learning. Children might, in the normal course of events, learn to pick up their toys after playing with them. Parents know, however, that rewarding this behavior with cookies makes it much more likely that the behavior will be learned.

In the example above:

(a) What is the stimulus? _____

(b) What is the response? _____

(c) What is the reinforcer? _____

(d) What is learned? _____

_____

- - - - - - - - - - - - - - - - - -

(a) toys lying on the floor after play; (b) picking toys up; (c) cookies; (d) the connection between toys lying on the floor after play and picking them up

33. Something that follows a response and increases the probability that a child will repeat that response is called a _____.

- - - - - - - - - - - - - - - - - -

reinforcer

34. Another factor in learning often referred to by teachers is <u>motivation</u>. It is said that a child is "highly motivated" to learn. This usually means that the child is eager, interested, and somehow receptive to learning. Would you say that motivation is a factor in the environment or <u>within</u> the child? _____

- - - - - - - - - - - - - - - - -

within the child

35. In the preceding examples, we could observe the stimulus, the response, and the child's behavior. Can we observe a child's motivational state directly? Why? _____

_____

- - - - - - - - - - - - - - - -

No, because it is something within the child.

36. Since motivation cannot be observed directly, it can only be inferred from observing the child's behavior. When a teacher says that a child is highly motivated, what behavior is the teacher probably referring to? _____

- - - - - - - - - - - - - - - - -

that the child acts eager and interested in learning

37. When teachers use the word "motivation" in this way—to refer to how actively or eagerly children pursue goals—they are referring to <u>level</u> of motivation. There are also different <u>types</u> of motivation. Teachers and parents have long been aware that children learn for different reasons. Some children are excited just by seeing the results of their work; some learn in order to please the teacher or their parents; still others learn in order to compete, to do better than anyone else.

    (a) When we say that one child learns best when given a lot of praise, while another child learns best when competing with others, we are referring to _____ of motivation.
    level/type

    (b) When we observe that some children appear more eager to learn than other children, we are making an inference about _____
    level/type
    of motivation.

- - - - - - - - - - - - - - - - -

(a) type; (b) level

38. We have seen that <u>level</u> of motivation is inferred from a child's behavior. <u>Type</u> of motivation is inferred from what things are reinforcing to the child. If praise is reinforcing to a child, we infer that the child is motivated by a need for praise. If food is a reinforcer,

what can we infer is the child's motivation? _____

_____

- - - - - - - - - - - - - - - - -

hunger, or a need for food

39. What would be the reinforcer for a person who is motivated by thirst?

_____

- - - - - - - - - - - - - - - - -

water, or liquids

40. The subject of learning is a complex and controversial one, which can only be touched on briefly here. One excellent summary of the learning process, particularly as it relates to children and their development, is given in Chapter 2, "Theory in Developmental Psychology," <u>Child Development and Personality</u> by P. H. Mussen, J. J. Conger, and J. Kagan (New York: Harper & Row, 1974).

METHODS OF STUDY

41. So far, we have established that child psychology is the study of children's behavior and development (changes in behavior over time). We have seen that these changes are a result of both maturation and learning, and we have looked briefly at some of the factors involved in learning. Now we turn to the question of how psychologists study behavior and development.

Generally, child psychologists want to <u>describe</u> and <u>explain</u> development; however, the methods for describing and explaining development are quite different. Gesell and others observed and charted age changes in motor development—crawling, sitting, walking, and so on. Were they interested in describing or explaining the behaviors?

_____

- - - - - - - - - - - - - -

describing

42. When we attempt to explain a behavior, we try to tell what caused it.
When we say that a child is unaggressive, inactive, and unoriginal,
we are describing the child's behavior or personality. When we say
that overprotective parents produce unaggressive, inactive, and unoriginal children, are we offering a description or an explanation of

the children's behavior? Why? _____

_____

_____

- - - - - - - - - - - - - - - - - -

Explanation, because we are saying that a certain type of child-
rearing causes a certain type of behavior or personality.

43. Which of the following psychologists are attempting to describe
behavior and which are attempting to explain it?

_____ (a) A psychologist obtains test scores on two groups of
children to find out why one group learns faster than
the other.

_____ (b) A psychologist obtains test scores from several hundred
children and records how scores increase with age.

_____ (c) A psychologist attempts to find out what causes some
children to be more well-coordinated than others.

- - - - - - - - - - - - - - - - - -

(a) explain; (b) describe; (c) explain

44. Both descriptive and explanatory data are important in child
psychology. Descriptive data allow us to make generalizations
about what is normal behavior or development, and what is not
normal. However, we often want to know why a certain behavior
develops so that we can control or modify the behavior. (For
example, if we want children to grow into less violent or less
aggressive adults, we must understand what causes aggressive
behavior.) For which of the following questions do we need explanatory data, and which require only descriptive data?

_____ (a) Does violence on television cause children to exhibit aggressive behavior?

_____ (b) What causes anxiety in children?

_____ (c) Is my child mentally retarded?

_____ (d) Is it normal for a seven-year-old to require a nap in the afternoon?

_____ (e) What effect does language development have on a child's ability to reason?

- - - - - - - - - - - - - - - - - -

(a) explanatory; (b) explanatory; (c) descriptive; (d) descriptive; (e) explanatory

45. Let's look at the tools and methods used in describing behavior. When we describe what is normal behavior for children of a certain age, we are using an age norm. An age norm is information about what a lot of children are like at a given age.

(a) Which of the following is an age norm? (Check one.)

_____ (1) a description of a baby's first steps

_____ (2) a description of how well 100 babies walk at a given age

(b) Why is the other one not an age norm? _____

_____

- - - - - - - - - - - - - - - - -

(a) 2; (b) 1 is not an age norm because it is a description of only one child.

46. When child psychologists look at changes in age norms over time, they are studying age trends. The study of age trends is at the very heart of child psychology because it allows us to make general statements about the process of development itself. Let's say that a psychologist obtains age norms in the amount of television watched by three-, five-, seven-, and nine-year-olds. The psychologist then compares the norms to see if there are any systematic changes from year to year.

Is this psychologist studying age trends? Explain your answer.

_____

- - - - - - - - - - - - - - - - -

_____

Yes, the psychologist is studying changes in age norms over time.

47. Age trends are changes in _____ _____ over time.

- - - - - - - - - - - - - - - - - -

age norms

48. Which of the following are age trend studies?

_____ (a) Forty 5-year-olds are observed during nursery school play for evidence of aggressiveness and dependency.

_____ (b) A psychologist observes children's reactions to frustration under various conditions.

_____ (c) The sentences of three-, five-, and seven-year-olds are recorded to note changes in length and grammatical construction.

_____ (d) It is found that children of three cannot copy a triangle, but by age six, most of them have this ability.

- - - - - - - - - - - - - - - - - - -

(c) and (d) are age trend studies. The others do not study how behavior changes with age.

49. To study these age trends, child psychologists often make use of a longitudinal study—an observation of the same group of children over a long period of time. If the 40 five-year-olds referred to in frame 48 were observed systematically by a child psychologist over a period of 10 years, the research method would be described as a

_____ study.

- - - - - - - - - - - - - - - - -

longitudinal

50. Suppose a psychologist wanting to study the development of problem-solving ability in children observed a group of 50 children each year for 5 years on certain problem-solving tasks to see how their ability changed with age.

(a) Is this a longitudinal study? _____

(b) What is the age trend or developmental change being studied?

_____

- - - - - - - - - - - - - - - - - -

(a) yes; (b) the development of problem-solving ability

51. Obviously, such a study is very time-consuming, and in this case, inefficient, since the observer is interested in very small, specific bits of behavior. In the above case, the psychologist might instead observe five different groups of children, each group at a different age, on the same problem-solving tasks. This approach is called a <u>cross-sectional study</u>.

(a) In a cross-sectional study, are the children the same in all the groups? _____

(b) Would the study necessarily have to take 5 years? Explain.

_____

_____

_____

- - - - - - - - - - - - - - - - - - -

(a) no; (b) No; since each group represents a different age, they could all be tested simultaneously. The psychologist would not have to wait for a year before each re-test.

52. An observer interested in developmental changes in memory wanted to know how children of three different ages—4, 8, and 12—perform on a recognition memory task. Which of the following is a cross-sectional study to observe this, and which is a longitudinal study?

_____ (a) The observer gives the task to the same group of children at three different points in their development (ages 4, 8, and 12) and notes how the scores differ.

_____ (b) The observer tests three different groups of children, a 4-year-old group, an 8-year-old group, and a 12-year-old group, and notes how the scores differ.

- - - - - - - - - - - - - - - - - -

(a) longitudinal; (b) cross-sectional

53. Which seems the most appropriate type of study in this case? Why?

_____

_____

- - - - - - - - - - - - - - - - - - -

Cross-sectional study, because it is more efficient and less time-consuming.

54. Two psychologists studied a group of institution-reared children at four ages—when they were 3, 6, 8, and 12 years of age. They observed and interviewed children, gave them IQ, personality, and language tests. Is this a cross-sectional or a longitudinal study?

_____

- - - - - - - - - - - - - - - - - - -

longitudinal

Note: Generally longitudinal studies are done when a psychologist is interested in a wide range of behaviors and not just one small bit of behavior. (In addition, a rather large research grant is usually helpful.)

53. How would you change the longitudinal study described in frame 52 to make it a cross-sectional study? _____

_____

- - - - - - - - - - - - - - - - - -

Study four different groups of institution-reared children, a 3-year-old group, a 6-year-old group, an 8-year-old group and a 12-year-old group.

54. The two kinds of observational methods used to describe age trends in development are _____ and _____.

- - - - - - - - - - - - - - - - -

longitudinal; cross-sectional

55. What is the difference between them? (In your own words.)

_____

_____

_____

_____

_____

- - - - - - - - - - - - - - - -

_____

A longitudinal study is an observation of one group of children over a long period of time. A cross-sectional study is an observation of several groups of children, each group representing a different age level.

56. So far, we have been talking about descriptive data. To explain rather than simply describe a behavior, we need a particularly well-controlled observation called an experiment. In an experiment, the experimenter manipulates one variable (the independent variable) and observes whether, and how, another variable (the dependent variable) is changed. For example, a psychologist might suspect that babies smile more at their mothers than at strangers. The psychologist might observe the reactions of two groups of babies to a caretaker: in the first group, the caretaker would be the mother; in the second group, the caretaker would be a stranger. Amount of smiling could be observed and measured under both conditions. The two variables are: presence or absence of mother, and amount of smiling.

(a) Which is the independent variable in this case? (Remember: the independent variable is the one the experimenter manipulates or controls.) _____

(b) Which is the dependent variable? _____

_____

- - - - - - - - - - - - - - - - -

(a) presence or absence of mother; (b) amount of smiling

57. Suppose an experimenter wants to know if a child learns better from one kind of textbook than from another. One group learns the material from one book, one group from another; a standardized test is given to find out how much material was learned under the two conditions. Variables are: score on test, and type of textbook.

(a) Which is the independent variable? _____

(b) Which is the dependent variable? _____

- - - - - - - - - - - - - - - - -

(a) type of textbook; (b) score on test

58. The factor that is controlled by the experimenter is the

_____ variable. The factor that depends on the experimenter's manipulation or intervention is called the

_____ variable.

- - - - - - - - - - - - - - - - - -

   independent; dependent

59. Let's look at the following experiment: a manufacturing firm claims that their baby "crawler"—a machine that babies can lie on and pull themselves across the floor—helps babies learn to crawl. A group of babies who do not yet crawl use the crawler for three months, and at the end of that time they can crawl remarkably well. The manufacturer claims the experiment proves that the baby crawler "helps babies learn to crawl." Do you see anything wrong with this

experiment? _____

_____

_____

- - - - - - - - - - - - - - - - - -

   There is no way of knowing that it is the crawler that caused the babies to crawl. Perhaps they would have learned to crawl during those three months even without the crawler.

60. What the manufacturer must do is to compare his group of babies with a group of same-age children who do not use the crawler. Only if there is a significant difference between the two groups can one be sure the crawler had any real effect. The group that does not use the crawler would be called a control group. A control group is a group that does not receive the treatment that is being studied.

In testing the effect of the Head Start Program on children's language development, one group of children attends Head Start classes and one group does not. Which group is the control group?

_____

- - - - - - - - - - - - - - - - -

   the group that does not attend Head Start classes

61. In an experiment to test the effect of vitamin B on children's growth, the group that does not get the vitamin B would be the _____ group.

- - - - - - - - - - - - - - - - -

control

62. A particularly well-controlled observation with a dependent variable, an independent variable, and a control group is a(n) _____.

- - - - - - - - - - - - - - - -

experiment

63. Generally, in an experiment, the experimenter has a <u>hypothesis</u> to be tested. A hypothesis is an educated guess about the relationship being tested. For example, a person studying motor coordination in young children might expect that children with a lot of practice in motor skills would have better coordination than children who have not had such practice. What would be the hypothesis? (In your own words.) _____

_____

- - - - - - - - - - - - - - - - -

Practice in motor skills improves coordination in children.

64. What would be the independent variable in the study in frame 63?

_____

What would be the dependent variable? _____

- - - - - - - - - - - - - - - -

amount of practice; motor coordination

65. In the baby crawler experiment (frames 59, 60), what would the manufacturer's hypothesis be? (In your own words.) _____

_____

- - - - - - - - - - - - - - -

The baby crawler helps babies learn to crawl.

66. An "educated guess" that the experimenter wants to test by means of an experiment is a _____.

- - - - - - - - - - - - - - - - - - -

hypothesis

67. Due to some obvious limitations, the pure experimental method is not always appropriate. For example, to study the effects of maternal deprivation on children's development, the independent variable (manipulated by the experimenter) would be deprivation or absence of the mother.

   (a) In a "pure" experiment, how would the experimenter go about manipulating this variable? _____

   _____

   (b) Do you see any problem in this? _____

   _____

   _____

- - - - - - - - - - - - - - - - - - -

   (a) The experimenter would take a group of children away from their mothers. (b) Breathes there a child psychologist so cold-blooded! There are obvious ethical problems involved when working with children, and such a manipulation would not be possible.

68. One way of getting around this ethical problem would be a <u>natural</u> experiment in which the experimenter selects a group of children who have somehow been deprived of their mothers and compares them with a group of children who have mothers. We could say then that a natural experiment is one in which: (Check one.)

   _____ (a) The experimenter manipulates the dependent variable directly.

   _____ (b) The experimenter manipulates the independent variable directly.

   _____ (c) The experimenter does not manipulate the independent variable directly.

   (Remember: the independent variable is deprivation of mother.)

- - - - - - - - - - - - - - - - - - -

   (c) (The experimenter does not actually deprive the children of their mothers.)

69. Two psychologists want to know whether children who are afraid of dogs will also be afraid of cats. Psychologist A causes one group of children to become afraid of dogs, then observes their reactions to cats, then compares their reactions to those of a group of children who are not afraid of dogs. Psychologist B finds a group of children who are afraid of dogs, studies their reactions to cats, then compares their reactions to those of a group of children who are not afraid of dogs.

Which psychologist ran the natural experiment? _____
Which experiment do you think was the more appropriate under the

circumstances? _____

_____

- - - - - - - - - - - - - - - - - -

Psychologist B ran the natural experiment. In this case, a natural experiment is called for since it would not be ethical to deliberately cause a fear of dogs in children.

Note: The natural experiment has very real limitations; the groups selected for study may differ in many other variables. The experimenter has no control over any of these differences and does not know how they might affect the results.

70. A child psychologist's choice of method of study depends on many things, including physical and practical limitations. But the first factor to consider is whether the psychologist wants to describe or explain a given behavior or behavior change. Of the following methods of child study, which gives descriptive data and which give explanatory data?

_____ (a) longitudinal study

_____ (b) natural experiment

_____ (c) experiment

_____ (d) cross-sectional study

- - - - - - - - - - - - - - - - - -

(a) descriptive; (b) explanatory; (c) explanatory; (d) descriptive

SELF-TEST

This Self-Test is designed to show you whether you have mastered this chapter's objectives. Answer each question to the best of your ability. Correct answers and review instructions are given at the end of the test.

1. Parents sometimes emphasize maturation in talking of their child-ren's development, and sometimes they emphasize experience. Let's look at some of the things parents sometimes say about the develop-mental process. Tell whether each statement emphasizes the role of maturation or experience.

_____ (a) "He's a year older now. That's why he reads so well."

_____ (b) "His parents have always had books around. That's why he reads so well."

_____ (c) "That girl was always tossing a ball around when she was little. No wonder she's such a good baseball player."

_____ (d) "She had more practice riding a bike than her older brother. That's why she's so much better at it."

_____ (e) "He just couldn't get the hang of riding a bike when he was six; now that he's older, his coordination is much better."

2. You are a child psychologist and you want to study how children's drawings differ from age to age.

(a) What method of study would you use? (Check one.)

_____ experiment

_____ cross-sectional study

_____ longitudinal study

_____ natural experiment

(b) Explain your choice. _____

_____

_____

(c) Do you need a control group? Why or why not? _____

_____

(d) Will your data describe or explain the difference? _____

3. Match the following:

_____ (a) personality and   (1) increase in muscular control
           social development   and coordination
                                  (2) integration of sense impressions
_____ (b) perceptual   (3) growth of patterns of interactions
           development   with others
                                  (4) growth of language skills
_____ (c) language   (5) changes in the processes of
           development   thinking, conceptualizing, reasoning

_____ (d) cognitive
           development

_____ (e) motor
           development

4. Imagine you are a research psychologist working for an educational
    development firm. The firm is about to market a program of books
    and records designed to help raise the IQs of six-year-old children.
    You design the following experiment to find out if the program really
    does what it claims to do. You take a group of six-year-old children,
    all with the same IQ score. One-half of the children follow the pro-
    gram; the rest of them do not. Later, all the children are given
    another IQ test. They all score higher on the second test than the
    first, but there is no difference between the scores of those who
    followed the program and those who did not.
    (a) Can the company claim that the program raised the IQs of the

        children who followed it? Explain. _____

        _____

        _____

        _____

    (b) Identify the dependent variable, independent variable, experi-

        mental group, and control group. _____

        _____

        _____

        _____

        _____

5.   Consider the example of a child learning to bat a baseball. Analyze
     this learning situation in terms of stimulus, response, motivation,

     reinforcer, and what connection is learned. _____

     _____

     _____

     _____

     _____

     _____

     _____

6.   Suppose some psychologists want to know how infants of various ages
     react to strangers. They want to study the reactions of three-, six-,
     and nine-month-old babies to the presence of a stranger.

     (a) Which kind of data does this question call for—descriptive or

          explanatory? _____

     (b) Which kind of study would the psychologist do—an experiment or

          an observational study? _____

Answers to Self-Test

Compare your answers to the questions on the Self-Test with the answers
given below. If all of your answers are correct, you are ready to go on
to the next chapter. If you missed any questions, review the frames
indicated in parentheses following the answer. If you missed several
questions, you should probably reread the entire chapter carefully.

1.   (a) maturation; (b) experience; (c) experience; (d) experience
     (e) maturation (Frames 1—8)

2.   (a) You could use either the cross-sectional or the longitudinal
     method; the least time-consuming would be the cross-sectional study.
     (Frames 49—55, 70)
     (b) You are only interested in descriptive data in this case. If you
     wanted to know why children's drawings change from age to age, you
     would try to design an experiment to find this out. (Frames 43, 56)
     (c) No, control groups are used in experiments. (Frame 62)
     (d) The data only describe the difference. (Frames 41—44, 70)

3.   (a) 3; (b) 2; (c) 4; (d) 5; (e) 1 (Frames 13—24)

4.   (a) No, because all the children—even those who did not follow the

program—scored higher on the second test; the program did not make a difference. (Frames 59—60)

(b) dependent variable: IQ score
   independent variable: the program to raise IQ scores
   experimental group: the group that followed the program
   control group: the group that did not follow the program
   (Frames 56—66)

5. The stimulus is the baseball; the response is swinging the bat in a certain way; the motivation might be to win the approval of other children or parents, or the desire to achieve in something, or any number of things (remember: motivation can only be inferred); the reinforcer might be the satisfaction of seeing the ball take off, or the shouts of approval of the other children; what is learned is the connection between the sight of the ball (probably in a certain position in relation to the bat)—the stimulus—and the response of the swinging bat. (Frames 25—40)

6. (a) descriptive (Frames 41—44, 70); (b) observational study (Frames 45—56, 70)

CHAPTER TWO
Perceptual Development

As you read this chapter and the following chapter on cognitive development, you will see that <u>perception</u> and <u>cognition</u> are really part of the same process. That is, we must perceive objects and events before we can react to them or think about them; however, the perceptual process itself is a very complex one and involves aspects of what we commonly call "thinking."

For example, when we perceive a face, what actually registers on our senses is a series of shapes and possibly some movement. Our perceptual system selects out certain aspects to respond to and ignores others. (We may not "see" the background shapes, certain irregularities or defects, hair color, and so on.) Then it organizes the relevant shapes (eyes, nose, mouth) into a whole; it matches this whole against some mental picture (faces that we have seen); and it interprets the collection of shapes as a "face."

So perceptual development is very closely related to cognitive development, and it is difficult to separate the two. In this chapter, however, we will focus specifically on the way in which children and adults register sensory events; we will refer to this initial registering of events as <u>perception</u>.

We will look at some developmental trends in perception and speculate on the reasons for these trends. We will review some of the fascinating research that has been done on infant perception and discuss how this research may help us understand later perceptual development. Finally, we will examine an apparent disturbance in the perceptual development of children—a condition that can have a great effect on children's school performance—"minimal brain dysfunction," or MBD.

OBJECTIVES

After completing this chapter, you will be able to

- list five factors that affect the perceptual process;
- describe the main ways in which people transform stimuli in the act of perceiving them;
- describe the major changes that occur in attention, scanning, organization, and interpretation in the course of perceptual development;
- explain the significance of research results on depth perception in infants;
- describe two types of tests often used by psychologists to study developmental changes in perception and tell what is measured by each;
- summarize what is known about the perceptual disturbance known as MBD.

WHAT IS PERCEPTION?

1. Perception is in a way the very basis of all learning and development. Children learn through interaction with their environment. Thus, the way in which they receive stimuli from the environment has a tremendous influence on what and how they learn. Our five senses are the doors through which stimuli from the environment are received. Through seeing, hearing, smelling, tasting, and feeling we "take in" the world around us. We make use of all these senses to receive stimuli from our environment.

It is often said that our eyes are our "windows upon the world." Describe in your own words what is meant by that phrase.

_____

_____

- - - - - - - - - - - - - - - - - - - -

Our eyes are one means of receiving or taking in stimuli from our environment.

2. Is seeing (vision) the only means by which we receive stimuli from our environment? Explain. _____

_____

- - - - - - - - - - - - - - - - - -

No, we make use of all five senses—seeing, hearing, smelling, tasting, and feeling.

3. The process by which people receive stimuli from the environment is called perception. As we shall see, it is a more complex process than it first appears. Moreover, it is becoming increasingly evident to child psychologists that children of different ages perceive the world differently; that is, the way in which children receive stimuli from the environment changes significantly as they grow.

Which of the following statements are true, and which are false?

_____ (a) Perception is a relatively simple process.

_____ (b) Perception is the process by which people receive stimuli from the environment.

_____ (c) Children of all ages perceive stimuli in the same way.

_____ (d) The way in which people perceive stimuli has a tremendous influence on what and how they learn.

- - - - - - - - - - - - - - - - - -

(a) false; (b) true; (c) false; (d) true

4. Before looking at the developmental changes in perception, we shall look at five of the factors that influence perception—things that determine how well we receive stimuli from the environment. These are factors that influence perception at all ages.

The first factor that influences perception is the state of the receptors themselves—the eyes, ears, nose, taste receptors, and skin receptors. People have varying sensitivities to incoming stimuli. Some people say: "I have absolutely no sense of smell." Others say: "I am extremely sensitive to pain." Still others say they are "blind as a bat" without their glasses. In all cases, they are saying something about the physical condition of their receptors and how this condition affects their perception.

(a) What are the receptors? _____

_____

(b) The physical condition of these receptors influences

_____

- - - - - - - - - - - - - - - - - -

(a) eyes, ears, nose, taste receptors, skin receptors;
(b) perception, or how well we receive stimuli from the environment

5. If you've ever had an eye examination, you probably know that a
    "score" of 20-20 means that you have normal vision; a score of
    20-40, 40-40, or 20-80 means that you have poorer than normal
    vision.

    (a) All other things being equal, which person would have the better
         perception—a person with 20-20 vision or a person with 20-40

         vision? _____

    (b) What are the receptors in this case? _____

- - - - - - - - - - - - - - - - - -

(a) a person with 20-20 vision; (b) the eyes

6. So far, it would appear that perception is a passive process: stimuli
    are simply recorded on the retina, the eardrum, or the taste buds.
    This is not the case, however. There is evidence that we "act on"
    stimuli as we receive them, that we pay attention to some parts more
    than others, construct complete stimuli in our minds on the basis of
    incomplete cues, combine what we see with what we already know,
    and so on. What is "recorded" is almost never an exact replica of
    the stimulus as it is in the environment. Thus, perception can be

    described as a(n) _____ process.
                      active/passive

- - - - - - - - - - - - - - - - - -

active

7. Which statement about perception is true? (Check one.)

    _____ (a) Stimuli are simply recorded on our receptors exactly
                as they appear in the environment.

    _____ (b) Stimuli are transformed in some way as we receive them.

- - - - - - - - - - - - - - - -

(b)

8. So, we need to make a distinction between what is actually "out there"—the <u>stimulus</u>—and what we perceive—the <u>sense impression</u>. As we receive a stimulus, we transform it into a sense impression. These sense impressions are <u>not</u> exact replicas of the stimuli; they are filtered through our senses and as a consequence are changed in the process of perception. They are probably somewhat like caricatures, with some parts of the stimuli emphasized, other parts omitted or distorted.

   (a) Are stimuli and sense impressions the same? Explain. _____

   _____

   _____

   _____

   (b) What we actually perceive is a _____.

                              stimulus/sense impression

- - - - - - - - - - - - - - - - - -

   (a) No, stimuli are filtered through our senses and as a consequence are changed in the process of perception. Sense impressions are probably somewhat like caricatures of the stimuli themselves.
   (b) Sense impression

9. Differences between stimuli and sense impressions are determined both by aspects of the stimulus itself and by the condition of the receptors. Let's consider first the condition of the receptors. As we have seen, a person with 20-20 vision perceives objects better than a person with 20-80 vision. Generally, the better the receptors, the <u>less</u> difference between the stimulus itself and the person's sense impression.

   Two people are listening to the same symphony. One person is slightly deaf in the left ear. Will the two people receive the same sense impression? _____

- - - - - - - - - - - - - - - - - -

   no

10. For which person will the sense impression be most different from the stimulus itself? _____

- - - - - - - - - - - - - - - -

the person who is deaf in one ear

11. Aspects of the stimulus itself can also cause distortions of the sense impression. For many reasons,* it is more difficult to get a complete or clear sense impression of a complex stimulus than a simple one. No matter how perfect our receptors, our sense impression of a rock concert will probably be quite muddled and distorted (actually, by the end of the concert, our receptors may even be impaired!). Our sense impression of a brief flute passage, however, would probably be fairly clear and close to what was actually played.

Explain, in your own words, why there will be less of a difference between the stimulus and the sense impression in the case of a brief

flute passage than in the case of a rock concert. _____

_____

_____

- - - - - - - - - - - - - - - - - -

A rock concert is a more complex stimulus than a brief flute passage.

12. In frame 9, two people were listening to a symphony; one person was slightly deaf in one ear. Differences in the sense impressions of the two people were due to

_____.

aspects of the stimulus itself/the condition of the receptors

- - - - - - - - - - - - - - - - -

the condition of the receptors

13. Some tests of perception demand that children recognize pictures that are incomplete, objects that are poorly lighted, or pictures that are flashed on a screen for only a very brief time.

This type of test attempts to find out how perception is affected by

_____.

aspects of the stimulus itself/the condition of the receptors

- - - - - - - - - - - - - - - - -

aspects of the stimulus itself

_____

*Some of these reasons will be discussed later in this chapter.

14. Differences between stimuli and sense impressions are caused by: (Check one.)

_____ (a) the condition of the receptors

_____ (b) aspects of the stimulus itself

_____ (c) both (a) and (b)

- - - - - - - - - - - - - - - - - -

(c) both (a) and (b)

15. Which of the following statements about perception are true, and which are false?

_____ (a) A blind person who perceives a flower by touching it has the same sense impression of that flower as a person who actually sees it.

_____ (b) Sense impressions are determined by factors both within the environment and within the person.

_____ (c) Two people can always be sure that their sense impressions of an object are the same if they look at the object together.

_____ (d) In the process of perceiving a stimulus, we transform it into a sense impression.

_____ (e) Perception is a passive process.

- - - - - - - - - - - - - - - - - -

(a) false; (b) true; (c) false; (d) true; (e) false

16. To expand our definition, perception is a process whereby stimuli are received from the environment and are changed into _____

_____.

- - - - - - - - - - - - - - - - -

sense impressions

17. Let's look now at some factors that influence sense impressions other than the stimulus itself and the condition of the receptors. Consider a situation that has become well-known through crime novels and courtroom dramas. A crime is committed, and there are several eyewitnesses. Police interrogation reveals, however, that each witness has a different story, that each one "saw"

something different at the time of the crime. One person focused on the get-away car and perceived the criminals only as shadowy, moving figures. Another person received a vivid impression of the criminals' eyes ("dark and frightening"), but did not notice the car at all, except for being aware that it was there. A third person noticed that the criminals' clothes were shabby and torn, but could give no description of their features.

In a complex situation like this, not everyone pays attention to the same things. The witnesses may all have had 20-20 vision and may have looked at the same scene, but what they "saw" depended in part on what they attended to. People select parts of a stimulus situation to attend to, and tend to ignore or "not see" other parts—this is called selective attention.

This bank robbery investigation is an example of how perception is affected by: (Check one.)

_____ (a) good vision

_____ (b) selective attention

_____ (c) the commission of a crime

- - - - - - - - - - - - - - - - - - -

(b)

18. Selective attention appears to be necessary in order to keep the perceptual system from being overloaded. The perceptual system is only able to process so much information at one time and must be protected from receiving more than it can handle. Therefore, it naturally selects only as many parts of the stimulus situation as it can handle at one time and processes those, ignoring the rest.

Which of the following statements is true, and which is false?

_____ (a) Our perceptual system is capable of processing an unlimited amount of information.

_____ (b) Our perceptual system is naturally protected from being overloaded.

- - - - - - - - - - - - - - - - - - -

(a) false; (b) true

19. What is the mechanism that keeps our perceptual system from

becoming overloaded? _____

- - - - - - - - - - - - - - - - - - -

_____

selective attention

20. In the bank robbery situation, perception was very limited—this is the case whenever there is not much time to perceive the stimulus. In some situations we have time to shift our focus rapidly from one thing to another and therefore perceive more. This process of shifting our attention rapidly from one feature of the stimulus to another is called <u>scanning</u>.

When we go to the circus, we do not see everything that is happening, but we do have the impression that we know what's going on in all three rings. Since we cannot actually watch all three rings at the same time, how do we manage to keep track of the action?

_____

_____

- - - - - - - - - - - - - - - - - - -

We scan the three rings, shifting our attention rapidly from one ring to another.

21. The process of shifting our attention rapidly from one feature of the stimulus to another is called _____.

- - - - - - - - - - - - - - - - - -

scanning

22. The reason we must scan very complex stimuli is that our perceptual system is _____.
    limited/unlimited

- - - - - - - - - - - - - - - - - -

limited

23. Our control over attention is sometimes voluntary, sometimes involuntary. We may choose to concentrate on a book and become so absorbed in it that we forget where we are, shutting out all other stimuli around us. On the other hand, we may try to focus our attention on a book, but find that our attention is drawn to a conversation or a television program going on in the same room.

It has been shown that our attention will automatically be drawn to a loud sound or the sound of our own name being spoken. This finding demonstrates that selective attention is _____

always/not always

voluntary.

- - - - - - - - - - - - - - - - -

not always

24. Which of the following situations demonstrate voluntary control over attention, and which demonstrate involuntary control?

_____   (a) While driving under difficult conditions, most people pay careful attention to the road, ignoring small distractions such as noises, scenery, the motion of windshield wipers.

_____   (b) Some psychologists believe that infants will automatically stare longer at complex stimuli than at stimuli with few lines and contours.

_____   (c) Our attention is drawn to new and different stimuli. We have a natural tendency to stare (New Yorkers generally excepted!) at a person whose appearance is unusual in some way.

_____   (d) When mechanics listen to the engines of cars, they are singling out specific sounds for diagnostic purposes; they might focus successively on the sounds of the fuel pump, the carburetor, the valves.

- - - - - - - - - - - - - - - - -

(a) voluntary; (b) involuntary; (c) involuntary; (d) voluntary

25. It has been shown that infants of two and three months are more likely to pay attention to moving objects than to stationary ones. Similarly, they will stare longer at black and white forms than at forms of all one color with no sharp contrasts.

Based on this finding, would you conclude that two- and three-month-old infants are capable of selective attention? _____

- - - - - - - - - - - - - - - - -

yes

26. Since <u>all</u> two- and three-month old infants show these preferences for movement and for black and white contrast, these findings are of particular interest to psychologists. In fact, psychologists have become more and more interested in what types of stimuli attract the attention of very young infants. They feel that knowing these early determinants of attention may lead to a greater understanding of perceptual development.

    They have discovered, for example, that newborn infants will focus their attention on <u>contours</u>, or edges of black lines against white backgrounds. If newborns are shown a black triangle on a white background, they will look longest at the <u>edges</u> of the triangle, particularly the corners.

Which of the following statements about perception do these observations of newborns support? (Check one.)

_____ (a) Perception in newborns involves the passive reception of all incoming stimuli.

_____ (b) Perception in newborns involves a selective screening process of incoming stimuli.

- - - - - - - - - - - - - - - - -

(b) (Recent work on the neurophysiology of cats indicates that there are different areas of the visual cortex that are responsive to various contours or edges in particular spatial orientations. These findings hint that the basis for certain early forms of selective attention may be biological and neurological in nature. In any event, selective attention is a part of the perceptual process from birth.)

27. (a) The factor in the perceptual process that allows us to focus on some stimuli and ignore others is called _____

    _____.

(b) This factor _____ present at a very early age.
              is/is not

- - - - - - - - - - - - - - - - -

(a) selective attention; (b) is

28. Another factor involved in the perceptual process is <u>organization</u>. People have a natural tendency to group stimuli in their environment —to perceive discrete stimuli as fitting together in some way.

For example, look at the following dots:

       . . .   .

Which do you feel is the most accurate description of the dots?

_____ (a)   Four groups of 3 dots each

_____ (b)   a row of dots

- - - - - - - - - - - - - - - - - - -

Most people answer (a)—four groups of 3 dots each.

29. Not only do people <u>describe</u> the dots differently if they are grouped than if they are not grouped, they actually scan them differently. Look at the following two rows of dots.

...   .

....

Could you feel a difference in the way your eyes scanned the two

rows? Explain. _____

_____

_____

_____

- - - - - - - - - - - - - - - - - -

Whether or not you could "feel" it, in the second row the eyes make only one jump; there is a rapid motion from one end of the line to the other: the group of dots is perceived as one line. In the first row the eye motion is jerky, indicating breaks in the scanning; the eyes (and mind) perceive the dots as separate groups.

30. If people are given a long list of numbers to read, they seldom read them off in a steady monotone. Instead, they generally group the numbers in some way, stressing some numbers more than others, frequently establishing a sort of rhythm. [8-5-3-1-<u>9</u> (pause) 6-5-8-2-<u>7</u> (pause), and so on.]

What does this demonstrate about the way we act on stimuli in our

environment? _____

_____

- - - - - - - - - - - - - - - - -

We tend to group or organize stimuli in our environment.

_____

31. As we organize stimuli, we also interpret them. If we see a series of dots like this,

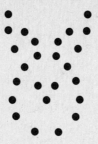

we might perceive them simply as a collection of dots. We are more likely, however, to perceive them as the head of an animal— usually a rabbit. Thus, any time we see shape, even an ambiguous one, we are likely to interpret what we see as something known or familiar.

The Rorschach or ink-blot test is based on this tendency to interpret ambiguous stimuli as something known or familiar. In the Rorschach test, people are presented with meaningless ambiguous figures and asked to tell what they are. A psychologist then analyzes the content of the responses.

The Rorschach test is based on people's tendency to: (Check one.)

_____ (a) interpret any ambiguous shape as something familiar

_____ (b) attend to meaningless shapes

_____ (c) talk about familiar things

- - - - - - - - - - - - - - - - - -

(a)

32. We have seen that our sense impressions are affected first by as- pects of the stimulus itself—size, complexity, and so on—and by the condition of our receptors—whether or not we have normal vision, for example. We also act on incoming stimuli and transform them in some way. What are three ways in which we transform incoming stimuli as we perceive them? (In your own words.)

_____

_____

_____

_____

- - - - - - - - - - - - - - - - -

_____

We selectively attend to some stimuli more than others; we group or organize stimuli; and we interpret ambiguous stimuli as something known or familiar.

33. Developmental changes occur in the three areas of selective attention, organization, and interpretation. At different ages, children focus on different stimulus features; they organize those stimulus features differently; and they put different meanings on what they see.

   Moreover, these developmental changes are partly the result of learning and experience. Partly because of our experiences, we learn to attend to certain stimulus features, to organize information in more effective ways, and to label and interpret stimuli in more adult fashion. For an example of how learning and experience affect perception, consider a child who has never seen a rabbit: the child would not be able to "interpret" any collection of dots as a rabbit.

It has been shown that children's perception gradually improves with age. Which of the following statements best explains why this improvement takes place?

_____ (a) Maturation alone can account for age improvements in perception.

_____ (b) Learning and experience play a large part in perceptual development.

_____ (c) Learning and experience alone can account for age changes in perception.

- - - - - - - - - - - - - - - - -

(b) (Psychologists do not agree on the issue of the role of maturation in perceptual development. Certainly, between the ages of five and seven, there are dramatic changes in several aspects of children's attention that may be associated with the biological changes in the central nervous system that occur around the same time. Most of the research to date, however, seems to indicate that learning is indeed very important to children's perceptual development. We will look at some of that research in the next section.)

STUDYING PERCEPTUAL DEVELOPMENT

34. For children of all ages, perception is a very complex process. As we have seen, almost from the beginning, children selectively attend to stimuli. Similarly, organization and interpretation are integral parts of the perceptual process, even for young children. However,

children of different ages attend to, organize, and interpret their environment in different ways.

There has been no systematic study of perceptual development, and little is known about the processes underlying it. Despite a new surge of interest in early perceptual-motor difficulties,* there is little hard information on what types of experiences aid in perceptual development. Finally, most research in perceptual development has been done in the area of vision, with very little done in other areas.

(a) Are there differences in the way children of different ages perceive their environment? _____

(b) Has there been any systematic study of perceptual development? _____

(c) In what area of perceptual development has most of the research been done? _____

- - - - - - - - - - - - - - - - - -

(a) yes; (b) no; (c) vision

35. In the area of vision, there has been much recent research on <u>form discrimination</u>. Form discrimination is the ability to perceive similarities and differences in the shapes of objects.

One study on form discrimination makes use of a form-board—a board in which blocks of various shapes are to be fitted in the proper holes. Children of 1-1/2 years generally do not place the blocks in the correct holes; they pick up blocks at random and try to make them fit in any hole, regardless of shape. By the age of three, children generally place the blocks correctly on the first trial.

(a) This demonstration shows that form discrimination

_____ with age.
improves/does not improve

(b) Form discrimination is the ability to: (Check one.)

_____ see clearly

_____ perceive similarities and differences in the shapes of objects

_____ play with blocks in an appropriate manner

- - - - - - - - - - - - - - - - - -

_____

*See the last section of this chapter on "Perceptual Development and MBD."

(a) improves; (b) perceives similarities and differences in the shapes of objects

36. Which of the following are true, and which are false?

_____ (a) Form discrimination is an example of a visual skill.

_____ (b) Children of 1-1/2 years and children of 3 years do equally well on the form-board test.

_____ (c) Form discrimination is the ability to perceive similarities and differences in the shapes of objects.

- - - - - - - - - - - - - - - - - -

(a) true; (b) false; (c) true

37. Age changes in form discrimination can also be seen in children's performance on the Embedded Figures Test (EFT). In this test, children are shown a drawing of a certain form; the drawing is then removed, and the children are shown a larger, more complex figure in which the first drawing has been embedded. They are required to pick out the test drawing from the larger figure. In a sense, the test figure is camouflaged by many added lines which confuse the viewer. On the EFT, older children do better than younger children.

An example of a test figure might be the following:

Can you find the figure on the left embedded in the figure on the right? (Actually, it is present in two places.)

- - - - - - - - - - - - - - - - -

38. Which of the following are true, and which are false?

_____ (a) The EFT is another measure of form discrimination.

_____ (b) In the EFT, a person must be able to perceive a figure which has been camouflaged by the addition of other lines and figures.

_____ (c) There are no age changes in the EFT.

- - - - - - - - - - - - - - - - - - -

(a) true; (b) true; (c) false

39. Child psychologists are naturally interested in what causes these developmental changes. The improvement in form discrimination could be due to two things:
      1. changes in the receptors themselves (maturation)
      2. changes in the way a child acts on the visual stimuli (selective attention, organization, interpretation)
    Some recent research by Robert Fantz on infant vision seems to indicate that by six months of age, infants are as capable as adults of detecting very small differences in visual stimuli. That is, their receptors seem to be operating as efficiently as those of an adult.

Given these results on infant vision, which of the two explanations of age changes in form discrimination do you feel is probably more accurate? (Check one.)

_____ (a) Improvement in form discrimination is due to changes in the receptors.

_____ (b) Improvement in form discrimination is due to changes in the way a child acts on the visual stimuli.

- - - - - - - - - - - - - - - - - -

(b)

Note: Fantz' test and equipment do not require that the infants make any response other than "looking"; if they "look" longer at one form than at another, it is assumed that they are able to discriminate between the two forms. In this way, it is a much finer or purer measure of form discrimination than tests which require some extra response such as placing objects in holes. The references at the end of the chapter tell you where to look if you are interested in reading more about these fascinating experiments on early vision.

40. E. J. Gibson, a psychologist interested in perceptual development, believes that improved form discrimination is the result of learning. Very young children have all the physical equipment to make fine

discriminations. They must practice making these discriminations, however, through experience with objects in their environment.

Thus, Gibson would say that the reason 3-year-old children are able to place the blocks correctly in a form-board, while 1-1/2-year-olds cannot, is that 3-year-old children:

_____ (a) are physically more mature

_____ (b) have had more practice in discrimination

- - - - - - - - - - - - - - - - -

(b)

41. According to Gibson, if 1-1/2-year-old children were given a lot of experience playing with blocks and form-boards, would they be able to learn to place the blocks correctly? Explain. _____

_____

_____

- - - - - - - - - - - - - - - - -

Yes, because children are capable of form discrimination at a very early age; only the experience is lacking.

42. Dr. Gibson and her husband demonstrated the effect of learning on form discrimination in the following way: they showed children a standard stimulus, a scribble that looked somewhat like this:

Then they took the standard stimulus away and showed the children a series of pictures, one at a time. The children were to identify each picture as the same as, or different from, the standard. The other pictures all differed in some very slight way from the standard. The procedure was repeated—the standard shown and withdrawn, the pictures presented one at a time—until the children identified all the cards correctly.

Children of all ages were able to learn the necessary discriminations, even though the procedure took longer in the case of younger children. Even four-year-olds, given enough practice, were able to identify all the stimulus items correctly!

This experiment suggests that:

_____

(a) Four-year-old children's receptors _____ capable of mak-
are/are not

ing such fine discriminations.

(b) Form discrimination is acquired gradually through

_____.

maturation/experience

- - - - - - - - - - - - - - - - - -

(a) are; (b) experience

43. Gibson suggests that, as the pictures are presented again and again,
the children are learning what to pay attention to. Improvement in
form perception comes about as the children learn to attend to the
parts or details of the stimulus, rather than to the stimulus as a
whole.

When Gibson says that improvement in form perception is due to
learning, she means: (Check one.)

_____ (a) learning to organize material in a more meaningful way

_____ (b) learning to attend to the details of a stimulus

_____ (c) learning to place blocks in their correct holes on a
form-board

- - - - - - - - - - - - - - - - - -

(b)

44. There does seem to be evidence that as children grow older, they
attend more to parts or details of a stimulus, whereas young children attend more often to the whole stimulus and ignore the parts.
For example, on the Rorschach test, younger children (4 years old)
will report that the inkblot looks like "dirt" or "a rock"; older children, however, will mention specific objects and describe some
details about the objects, such as "a cow with four eyes and no tail."

This finding suggests that there may be age changes in

_____.

the receptors/selective attention

- - - - - - - - - - - - - - - - - -

selective attention

45. Most tests of form discrimination <u>require</u> that a child attend to the
individual parts or details of a stimulus, rather than to the stimulus

as a whole. Sometimes the child is shown a picture and told to find
a picture that matches it. He must pick the matching picture from
a series of pictures all of which, except one, differ in some small
detail from the test picture. This means the child has to notice each
detail of each picture. In other instances, a child is shown a series
of pictures that are all alike except for one, which differs in some
small detail. The task is to pick the one picture that is different
from the others. While not as difficult as the matching task, this
task also demands great attention to detail.

In each of the above form discrimination tests, the child must attend
to: (Check one.)

_____ (a) the stimulus as a whole

_____ (b) details of the stimulus

- - - - - - - - - - - - - - - - - -

(b)

46. Explain why developmental changes in <u>attention</u> probably account for
improvement in most form discrimination tests. (In your own words.)

_____

_____

_____

- - - - - - - - - - - - - - - - -

As children get older, they attend more to the parts or details of a
stimulus; most form discrimination tests require just such attention
to detail.

47. The poor performance of younger children on the EFT is probably
due to the fact that: (Check one.)

_____ (a) they become restless more easily

_____ (b) they do not attend to the details of the stimulus

_____ (c) their receptors have not matured sufficiently

- - - - - - - - - - - - - - - - -

(b) (It is possible that differences in the scanning patterns of older
and younger children account for some of the difference in their
performance. Developmental differences in scanning will be discussed later.)

48. The importance of <u>language</u> in aiding perceptual development must not be underestimated. Language can be used as a tool for directing a child's attention. Say a young child is shown the following figures and asked to pick out the one that is different:

A young child might have difficulty with this discrimination, because it requires looking at a small part or detail. If, however, the child is told "Look at the noses on the faces," the child would probably be able to make the discrimination. Why? (Check one.)

_____ (a) because language encourages a child to organize and interpret stimuli

_____ (b) because the child's attention has been directed to the right detail

_____ (c) because noses are easier to discriminate than eyes or mouths

- - - - - - - - - - - - - - - - - - -

(b)

47. In the above discrimination, what was the additional "tool" that helped direct the child's attention so that the correct discrimination could be made? _____

- - - - - - - - - - - - - - - - -

language

50. The cues for directing attention do not have to be verbal, or language, cues. It has been shown that learned <u>visual</u> cues can also prepare children for attending to the correct stimulus.

In an ingenious experiment on selective auditory perception, Eleanor Maccoby* had children listen to two voices—a male voice and a female voice—both speaking at the same time. The man's voice came from a loudspeaker with the picture of a man on it; the woman's

---

*E. E. Maccoby, Selective auditory attention in children. In L.P. Lipsett and C. C. Spiker, eds., <u>Advances in Child Development and Behavior</u>. (New York: Academic Press, 1967.)

voice came from a loudspeaker with a woman's picture on it. Both loudspeakers were placed at equal distance from the children.

Sometimes the children were instructed to report on what the man said, sometimes on what the woman said. When the children were supposed to report what the woman said, the woman's picture was lighted; when the children had to report the man's words, his picture was lighted. In other words, the children had to selectively attend to either one voice or the other, and their "instruction" was a lighted picture.

The children in the study were drawn from kindergarten and grades 2, 4, and 6. As might be expected, the older children were able to report more of what was said than the younger children. Older children are better at selectively attending to the correct voice. If, however, the children were given the cue (the lighted picture) before the voices spoke rather than after, all of the children reported more of what was said—that is, they were better able to attend to the correct voice.

Which of the following statements best summarizes the results of this study? (Check one.)

_____ (a) Children of all ages can make use of a preparatory cue to help them direct their attention.

_____ (b) Children are better able to direct their attention as they get older.

_____ (c) Both of the statements above are supported by the study.

- - - - - - - - - - - - - - - - - -

(c)

51. In the above experiment, the cue that helped the children attend to the correct voice was a _____ cue.
                                    visual/language

- - - - - - - - - - - - - - - - - -

visual

52. It appears that, as children learn to attend to details of a stimulus, they also become more systematic in their scanning procedure. (Remember that as part of the perceptual process, we all scan complex stimuli; that is, we shift our attention rapidly from one aspect of the stimulus to another.) When looking at a picture or other visual stimulus, the eye movements of younger children are very erratic and show no clear pattern; older children and adults, however, show a marked search pattern.

Let's say a psychologist has an apparatus to trace the eye movements of children as they view a drawing—a scene with a woman reading and two children listening. The <u>scanning patterns</u>, or eye movements, of two children are recorded. One child is 5 years old, the other is 10. The recordings show that one child focuses first on the woman's face, then on the book, the two children, and back to the woman's face. The other child's record shows random shifting of focus from side to side and from one object to another.

Which child is probably the older (10-year-old) child? _____

_____

_____

- - - - - - - - - - - - - - - - - -

the first child—the one who focuses first on the woman's face, then on the book, the two children, and back to the woman's face.

53. As children grow older, their scanning pattern becomes more

_____.

systematic/complex

- - - - - - - - - - - - - - - - -

systematic

54. While it is not known just why this improved scanning comes about with age, it is possible that older children are able to form hypotheses about shapes and objects as they look at them. In the picture of the woman reading to the children, for example, an older child may be constructing a story or situation: "A mother is reading to her children." A younger child, on the other hand, may simply see several unrelated people and objects.

The reason younger children do not scan as effectively as older children might be that: (Check one.)

_____ (a) The vision of younger children is poorer.

_____ (b) Younger children do not form hypotheses about what they see.

_____ (c) Younger children do not look as carefully at shapes and objects.

- - - - - - - - - - - - - - - - -

(b) (This suggestion that a child's ability to analyze stimulus situations and form hypotheses improves with age points out how closely perceptual development is related to the development of thinking. In the next chapter, we will return to this question of how children's hypotheses and concepts change with age.)

55. Choose the correct word or words to complete the following statements.
(a) Developmental improvements in form discrimination are due in part to changes in _____.
          receptors/attention
(b) As children get older, they attend to

_____.
parts of the stimulus/the whole stimulus
(c) Changes in attention are probably the result of

_____.
learning/maturation

(d) Given preparatory cues, children of all ages _____ use
                                                    can/cannot
them to help direct their attention.

- - - - - - - - - - - - - - - - - -

(a) attention; (b) parts of the stimulus; (c) learning; (d) can

56. One reason that children's scanning procedure becomes more systematic with age may be that older children: (Check one.)

_____ (a) form hypotheses about what they are looking at

_____ (b) look more carefully at objects than at shapes

- - - - - - - - - - - - - - - - - -

(a)

57. While we have a natural tendency to organize or group stimuli, the way in which we organize and interpret visual stimuli also depends in large part on learning and experience. As children get older, they become more familiar with various objects in their environment through interacting with them (seeing, handling, touching, and so on.)

Would you expect older children to organize and interpret visual stimuli differently than younger children? Explain.

- - - - - - - - - - - - - - - - - -

Yes, because as children get older, they learn more about their environment through experience with it.

58. One way of looking at how children organize and interpret visual stimuli is by means of a <u>recognition</u> task. Whereas a form discrimination task asks a child to find similarities and differences among the various shapes presented, a recognition task simply demands that a child <u>identify</u> the shape or object presented, that is, to name it.
    Let's look at the following two tasks:

Task A: A child is shown the following series of forms and asked "Which one is not like the others?"

Task B: A child is shown the following form and asked "What is it?"

Which task is a recognition task? _____

Which is a form discrimination task? _____

- - - - - - - - - - - - - - - - - -

Task A is a form discrimination task; Task B is a recognition task.

59. In order to do a recognition task, children must not only attend to the stimulus features but must organize those features into a meaningful whole and go on to interpret what they see. In Task A, the child may or may not have interpreted the series of drawings as boats; it did not matter as long as the child could pick out the differences among the figures. Task A tested only attention to detail.

In task B, what is being tested in addition to the way the child attends to the stimulus features? _____

_____

- - - - - - - - - - - - - - - - - -

the way a child organizes and interprets the stimulus features

60. When psychologists want to study how children of different ages organize and interpret stimuli, they use a

    _____ task.
    form discrimination/recognition

- - - - - - - - - - - - - - - - - -

recognition

61. A recognition test asks a child to: (Check one.)

    _____ (a)   find similarities and differences among objects

    _____ (b)   place blocks in their appropriate places

    _____ (c)   identify shapes and objects

- - - - - - - - - - - - - - - - - -

    (c)

62. A recognition task assumes that the viewer is familiar with the object or shape presented; it studies how much visual <u>information</u> is needed before recognition of that familiar object takes place.

    (a) If a younger child does less well on a recognition task, it means

        that the child requires more _____ than an older
        learning/information
        child before recognition takes place.

    (b) A recognition task: (Check one.)

        _____ assumes nothing about the child's past learning and
        experience
        _____ assumes that the child is familiar with the object or
        shape presented

- - - - - - - - - - - - - - - - - -

    (a) information; (b) assumes that the child is familiar with the object or shape presented

63. On recognition tasks, children take the limited information available to them and essentially construct the whole stimulus in their mind. They fill in the missing parts.

　　The process is similar to what we do in many everyday situations. For instance, as we are driving, we see a sign up ahead; we cannot see it clearly, but we notice its shape and color and the fact that it is at an intersection. We fill in or "imagine" the word STOP, mentally construct a stop sign, and (hopefully!) stop the car.

In this case, in order to recognize or identify the stop sign, we have had to: (Check one.)

_____ (a) simply let the visual stimulus register in our mind.

_____ (b) construct the whole stimulus by filling in the missing parts.

- - - - - - - - - - - - - - - - - -

(b)

64. The information that we cannot get from the stimulus itself (the "blanks," the missing pieces) we must already have available in our mind. It is as if the stimulus is a puzzle with some of the pieces missing. If the stimulus is familiar, however, we have in our mind pieces that we can fit in so that—in our mind—the puzzle is complete.

In a recognition task, then: (Check one.)

_____ (a) We get all the pieces of the puzzle from the stimulus.

_____ (b) We get some puzzle pieces from the stimulus, some from our mind.

_____ (c) All the pieces of the puzzle are in our mind.

- - - - - - - - - - - - - - - - - -

(b) (We do not really know, but probably the stimulus pieces we carry around in our mind do not really fit exactly, but are distorted in some way; therefore, the image we construct may not be accurate. Also, different people may construct slightly different images, based on their past experience with the stimulus they are asked to identify.)

65. People with more experience have more information available in their mind and therefore need less information from the stimulus itself in order to identify it. If children see a certain object often, they will have more "duplicate" pieces available in their mind with which to fill in blanks.

　　Young children usually cannot recognize familiar figures when the shape is merely outlined by dots (as in a follow-the-dot book).

Older children can sometimes identify the figures without actually connecting the dots. Explain, in terms of information, why this is so. _____

_____

_____

- - - - - - - - - - - - - - - - - - -

Older children have more information available in their mind and need less information from the stimulus in order to identify it.

66. In another kind of recognition test, pictures are flashed on a screen for a very brief time (measured in milliseconds), and children are asked to identify them. Older children need less time for recognition than younger children; that is, they can identify the pictures at briefer exposures.

Based on what you know of information and perception, how would you interpret these results? (Check one.)

_____ (a) Older children can get more information from a stimulus than younger children.

_____ (b) Older children need less information than younger children to recognize objects.

- - - - - - - - - - - - - - - - - -

(b)

67. Which of the following statements are true, and which are false?

_____ (a) On a recognition task, a person must construct the whole figure in his or her mind from the pieces available.

_____ (b) Recognition tasks demonstrate differences in selective attention.

_____ (c) There are no differences between older and younger children in performance on recognition tasks.

_____ (d) Experience plays no part in how well we can recognize or identify figures.

_____ (e) The information from which we construct a figure comes both from the stimulus and from our mind.

- - - - - - - - - - - - - - - - - -

(a) true; (b) false; (c) false; (d) false; (e) true

68. Psychologists have commonly used two types of tests to measure developmental changes in perception. What are the two kinds of tests and what does each measure?

_____

_____

_____

- - - - - - - - - - - - - - - - - -

form discrimination test: measures selective attention
recognition test: measures organization and interpretation

69. Another visual phenomenon that has been of interest to developmental psychologists is depth perception. Depth perception is just what its name implies—the ability to perceive, or recognize, depth. Somehow, we all recognize that some things are nearer than others, and we are able to perceive drop-offs.

In which of the following situations is a child demonstrating depth perception?

_____ (a) The child learns to tie shoelaces for the first time.

_____ (b) The child makes a discrimination between a square and a circle.

_____ (c) The child stops at a curb and steps down.

- - - - - - - - - - - - - - - - - -

(c)

70. In perceiving depth, we are responding to certain cues. Exactly what these cues are is not certain, but no doubt we are responding to the fact that things look smaller as they recede into the distance.

When we look down from a very tall building, what are our cues that it is a long way down? (Check one.)

_____ (a) People and cars look very small.

_____ (b) We have to strain our eyes to look down.

- - - - - - - - - - - - - - - - -

(a)

71. When we perceive depth, we are reacting to the fact that things look

    _____ as they recede into the distance.

- - - - - - - - - - - - - - - - - -

    smaller

72. As we have seen, one of the questions developmental psychologists
    generally ask about perception is how much is learned and how much
    is <u>innate</u>, or inborn. An ingenious study by Gibson and Walk* has
    suggested that depth perception, while perhaps not innate, is present
    at a very early age.

        Six-month-old infants were placed on a runway. On either side
    of the runway was a sheet of strong glass. Under the glass on one
    side was a textured pattern of squares, indicating that that side was
    a flat surface. On the other side, the textured pattern was placed
    far below the glass so that an adult would perceive depth, that is,
    the side appeared to drop off at the edge of the runway. The experi-
    menters called this second side a "visual cliff," because it appeared
    to be a drop-off, or cliff. Nearly all six-month-old infants avoided
    the side that appeared to have the drop-off or cliff, even when the
    infants' mothers stood on the "drop-off" side and called to the child-
    ren to cross over.

    This study shows that depth perception is: (Check one.)

    _____ (a) innate (inborn)

    _____ (b) present at a very early age

    _____ (c) definitely a learned response

- - - - - - - - - - - - - - - - - -

    (b)

73. It may be, as in the case of form discrimination, that the <u>capacity</u>
    for depth perception is present at a very early age, but that experience
    with objects at various distances helps to develop it.

        In fact, a related study done later by one of the same researchers
    suggests that this may be the case.** In this study children who

---

*E. J. Gibson and R. D. Walk. The "visual cliff." <u>Scientific
American</u>, 1960, <u>202</u>, 2-9.

    **R. D. Walk, The development of depth perception in animal and
human infants. <u>Monographs of the Society for Research in Child
Development</u>, 1966, 31, <u>5</u>, 82-108.

started crawling late were compared with early crawlers on the visual-cliff apparatus. It was found that infants who are late crawlers are more likely to cross the visual-cliff side than infants who crawled early.

(a) Which babies would be likely to have more experience with objects at various distances—early or late crawlers? _____

(b) From this second study, it would appear that the development of depth perception _____ affected by experience.
        is/is not

- - - - - - - - - - - - - - - - -

(a) early crawlers; (b) is

74. In your own words, explain how the visual-cliff experiment showed that very young infants can perceive depth.

_____

_____

_____

_____

_____

_____

_____

- - - - - - - - - - - - - - - - -

In the visual-cliff experiment, the experimenters wanted to find out if six-month-old infants would crawl across what appeared to be a drop-off or cliff. If they would not crawl across the visual-cliff side, it was assumed that they were demonstrating depth perception. It was found that most babies would not crawl across the drop-off side, even when their mothers called to them. Thus it was concluded that six-month-old infants perceive depth.

75. In what two ways is the development of depth perception similar to the development of form discrimination? (In your own words.)

_____

_____

- - - - - - - - - - - - - - - - -

_____

The <u>capacity</u> for both is present at a very early age, but both are affected by learning and experience.

PERCEPTUAL DEVELOPMENT AND MBD

76. Currently, much attention has been focused on perceptual problems in children. Many schools have set up special programs for children with such problems, and there is much interest in designing diagnostic tests that will allow teachers to pinpoint particular problem areas.

    One pattern of perceptual problems occurs fairly frequently in children; this pattern or syndrome has been labeled <u>minimal brain dysfunction</u>, or <u>MBD</u>. MBD is generally considered a disturbance of the central nervous system, a disturbance that hampers perceptual development. It has been estimated that between 5 percent and 20 percent of school children have some specific symptoms of MBD.

    (a) MBD is generally thought to be a disturbance of: (Check one.)

    _____ the digestive system

    _____ the central nervous system

    _____ the circulatory system

    (b) The term MBD stands for a pattern of _____
    perceptual/emotional
    problems.

- - - - - - - - - - - - - - - - - -

    (a) the central nervous system; (b) perceptual

Note: This disturbance of the central nervous system, with its accompanying symptoms is sometimes called <u>specific learning disability</u> (SLD), or <u>perceptual-motor disability</u> (PMD). These three terms are used almost interchangeably. The main difference seems to be that the term MDB stresses the supposed neurological basis of the disturbance, while the other two terms focus on the perceptual problems themselves.

77. As the name implies, MBD appears to be the result of some brain dysfunction, possibly (but not necessarily) brain damage. It is not a serious or totally incapacitating condition. Its effects are minimal, and in fact, MBD is usually not detected or diagnosed by a neurological exam.

    The term "brain dysfunction" implies problems with the way the brain functions. Why is the term "minimal" included in the term?

_____

_____

- - - - - - - - - - - - - - - - - -

Because the effects of the brain dysfunction are minimal—not serious and not easy to detect.

78. MBD affects mainly <u>motor</u> and <u>perceptual</u> activities.* In terms of their motor behavior, children with MBD are usually <u>hyperactive</u> to some degree (sometimes called hyperkinetic). That is, they are extremely restless, active, excitable, and unable to control their behavior. Because of this lack of control their coordination often is poor; they tend to be clumsy and have frequent accidents.

(a) A first grade teacher has two behavior problems in class: one child is shy, withdrawn, and a very careful worker, yet sits for hours and daydreams; the second child cannot sit still for a minute, sings and talks while working, and frequently falls off the chair. Which child shows symptoms associated with minimal

brain dysfunction? _____

(b) A child who demonstrates restless, active, excitable behavior

is called _____.

- - - - - - - - - - - - - - - - - -

(a) the second child; (b) hyperactive

79. Some children seem to have more than the usual number of accidents; they stumble and fall easily; they have difficulty learning to ride a bike; they cannot get the hang of skipping or jumping rope. We say

that these children have poor _____.
attention/coordination

- - - - - - - - - - - - - - - - - -

coordination

_____

*As a result of problems in these basic areas, children with MBD usually also develop language and learning difficulties, and possibly emotional problems.

80. Poor coordination, along with hyperactivity, may indicate the disorder of _____.

- - - - - - - - - - - - - - - - - - -

MBD, or minimal brain dysfunction

81. Children with MBD also have perceptual problems. In the visual area, they seem to have trouble discriminating forms, words, and letters, presumably because they cannot attend to the details of these forms, words, and letters. For example, an MBD child would probably confuse the words "went," "want," and "wart."

Children who are just learning to read frequently confuse the letters "b" and "d," or "h" and "n." With practice, they soon learn to discriminate them. A teacher might suspect that a child has MBD is the child:

_____ (a) does not soon learn to discriminate among the letters

_____ (b) does not soon learn to discriminate among letters

- - - - - - - - - - - - - - - - - - -

(b)

82. Presumably, the reason that children with MBD have problems discriminating among words and letters is that:

_____ (a) they have trouble attending to details

_____ (b) they have trouble reading

- - - - - - - - - - - - - - - - - - -

(a)

83. Because they have trouble discriminating some basic letters (such as "b" and "d") and words (such as "come" and "came"), children with MBD nearly always have trouble with reading. Dyslexia is the name given to reading problems that result specifically from MBD.

Obviously, all reading problems are not dyslexia. Reading difficulties can result from many things—low intelligence, emotional problems, the special problems of foreign-language-speaking students, MBD, or poor teaching.

If a child's reading problem is diagnosed as dyslexia, we assume that the problem is caused by:

_____ (a) low intelligence

_____ (b) emotional problems

_____ (c) problems of foreign-language-speaking students

_____ (d) MBD

_____ (e) poor teaching

- - - - - - - - - - - - - - - - - - -

(d)

84. In the area of auditory discrimination, MBD children frequently have
trouble perceiving differences in sounds, for example, such words
as "hair" and "hear," "sit" and "sip," "pat" and "bat." As you can
see, the confusions can be between vowel sounds (a and e), or between
sounds of consonants (p and b). Again, making these discriminations
requires attention to detail.

(a) Difficulty in auditory discrimination means:

_____ deafness

_____ difficulty perceiving differences in sounds

_____ hearing loss

_____ difficulty in reading

(b) Auditory discrimination, like visual discrimination, requires

attention to the _____ of the stimulus.
               sounds/details

- - - - - - - - - - - - - - - - - - -

(a) difficulty perceiving differences in sounds; (b) details

85. Because MBD children have difficulty perceiving differences among
sounds, they often have speech problems. If a child hears words
incorrectly, he will be more likely to mispronounce them.

Of course, up until the age of six or so, mispronunciations are
common. By the age of seven or eight, however, children should be
able to discriminate most speech sounds and to articulate them.

Some of the speech substitutions of MBD children are bizarre
and show inaccurate hearing of whole syllables ("pisgetti" for
"spaghetti"); others are less bizarre ("piddow" for "pillow"). Any
consistent mispronunciation in speech, however, may be a sign
that a child has difficulty in auditory discrimination.

Explain how a speech problem might be the result of poor auditory discrimination. (In your own words.) _____

_____

- - - - - - - - - - - - - - - - - - -

If a child hears words incorrectly, he is likely to mispronounce them. (Of course, even in older children there are many different kinds of speech problems; some are due to difficulties with the muscles of speech, with placement of the tongue, and so on. Speech problems should be diagnosed and treated by specialists in the field. MBD often causes speech problems; all speech problems, however, are not due to MBD.)

86. Explain in your own words how children with MBD show problems in motor activities and in visual and auditory discrimination.

_____

_____

_____

_____

_____

- - - - - - - - - - - - - - - - - - -

motor activities: they are hyperactive, tend to have accidents, or tend to be poorly coordinated.
visual discrimination: they have trouble attending to detail, confuse letters such as "b" and "d."
auditory discrimination: they have trouble distinguishing differences between certain similar sounds, such as "p" and "b."

87. Reading problems that are the result of MBD are called _____.

- - - - - - - - - - - - - - - - - - -

dyslexia

88. The motor and perceptual problems of MBD children obviously interact. For example, because of their hyperactivity, these children have trouble concentrating: they cannot keep their attention focused on anything as long as other children. Therefore they will not attend to details as well as normal children.

Three children are asked to describe in detail a picture of a dog. Following are their descriptions.

1st child: "It's a dog—a nice dog. I like dogs. I have a dog at home. And a cat too."

2nd child: "It's a big dog with spots on it; it's got short legs and a long, bushy tail."

3rd child: "A dog. Spotted. Has big teeth—ugh! And a big, waggy tail and teeny, teeny ears."

Let's say that one of the above children has been diagnosed as a hyperactive child. Which child would you suspect is the hyperactive child? Explain your answer. _____

_____

_____

- - - - - - - - - - - - - - - - -

The first child, because his attention wanders and he does not describe any details about the dog.

89. Problems in motor skills can be the result of problems in motor control (such as hyperactivity) or poor perception, or both. Generally, perception and motor activities are impaired. For this reason, skills such as hopping, skipping, and writing are frequently called perceptual-motor skills.

If a child has trouble learning to use scissors, or to write, or to hop and skip (all motor skills), we assume that the difficulties are due to: (Check one.)

_____ (a) problems in motor control

_____ (b) poor perception

_____ (c) neither

_____ (d) both

- - - - - - - - - - - - - - - - -

(d)

90. Because motor skills—particularly those involving fine activity, such as writing—depend in part on perceptual ability, they are often called

_____ skills.

- - - - - - - - - - - - - - - - -

perceptual-motor

91. Which of the following is the most accurate summary of how perceptual and motor difficulties are related in MBD?

_____ (a) The perceptual difficulties of MBD children can affect their motor skills.

_____ (b) The motor disturbances of MBD children can affect their perceptual skills.

_____ (c) Both (a) and (b) are true.

_____ (d) The perceptual and motor disturbances of MBD children are not related in any way.

- - - - - - - - - - - - - - - - -

(c)

92. At this stage of knowledge about MBD, little is known about what actually causes the dysfunction. It is suspected that actual physical injury to the brain is usually involved (prenatal influences, such as drugs; birth complications; head injuries or high fevers during the first few years of life). On the other hand, recent studies have suggested that MBD may be an inherited condition. It has been found that some parents of MBD children show or have shown MBD symptoms themselves.

Suppose a child is suspected of having MBD. A medical history shows no indication of any injury to the brain, either prenatally or postnatally. Can a doctor be sure the child does not have MBD?

Explain. _____

_____

- - - - - - - - - - - - - - - - -

No, because MBD may be inherited.

93. As far as we know, MBD can be the result of:

_____ (a) physical injury to the brain

_____ (b) inheritance from parents

_____ (c) both

- - - - - - - - - - - - - - - - -

(c)

94. While the condition of minimal brain dysfunction is not serious in itself, it can have serious consequences if not recognized early. The

effects are cumulative over time. Without help, MBD children have a harder time learning than other children. Thus they fall further and further behind in school work. At the same time, they are constantly experiencing more failure than non-MBD children, so that their self-concept is damaged. Serious psychological disturbances can result.

Two children are diagnosed as having MBD. One child was 5 when the condition was discovered; the other child was 12. Which child would be more likely to have complications, such as psychological

problems? Explain. _____

_____

_____

- - - - - - - - - - - - - - - - - -

The 12-year-old child, because the effects of MBD are cumulative over time (the child has trouble learning, experiences constant failure, develops a poor self-image, and so on).

95. Obviously, then, children with MBD must be treated as early as possible. Treatment falls into two categories:
   1. special training
   2. drugs
Special training is usually given in school-related activities, to bring the children up to their age or grade level in those areas where they are weakest (auditory discrimination, form discrimination, reading, speech). Drugs are sometimes given to control the hyperactivity. The use of drugs, however, is very controversial at this stage of our knowledge about MBD.

Strangely enough, the type of drug used is a stimulant—amphetamines. Whereas these drugs have a stimulating effect on normal children, they have a calming effect on children with minimal brain dysfunction. It is not yet understood why this is so.

(a) Amphetamines are a _____.
                         stimulant/tranquilizer

(b) Amphetamines have a _____ effect on children
                        stimulating/calming
    with MBD.

- - - - - - - - - - - - - - - - -

(a) stimulant; (b) calming

96. A lot of so-called special training consists of individual tutoring—
    simply providing more of what other children get in the classroom.
    Examples are remedial reading, speech therapy, practice in listen-
    ing. Some special programs for MBD children, however, stress
    the connection between the perceptual and the motor disturbances.
    They give special practice in fine-motor skills (drawing, cutting,
    handling small objects) and in gross-motor activities (jumping,
    hopping, skipping). It is assumed that improvement in these activ-
    ities will lead directly to improvement in school-related activities.
    Two school systems each have special training programs for
    MBD children. In the special class in School A, the teacher spends
    a lot of time teaching the children to jump rope, to balance on a
    balance board, and to tap out rhythms on a drum. School B hired
    extra remedial reading teachers and speech therapists to work
    specifically with the MBD children.

    (a) Which program stresses motor activities as part of its training?

    _____

    (b) What is the rationale for giving special training in motor

    activities? _____

    _____

    _____

- - - - - - - - - - - - - - - - - - -

    (a) School A, which teaches jumping rope, balancing, and so on;
    (b) The rationale is that improvement in motor activities will lead
    directly to improvement in school activities; perceptual and motor
    skills are related.

97. In the area of special training as with drugs, there are disagreements
    as to how best to treat children with MBD. (There are even those
    skeptics who wonder if there really is any such disturbance at all!)
    Obviously, much more must be known about this area—and the
    whole area of learning disabilities—before the controversies will be
    settled. However, the study of learning disabilities in general, and
    research on MBD in particular, emphasizes the importance of child-
    ren's perceptual development to their overall development.

    (a) Is everyone in agreement on what minimal brain dysfunction is

    and how it should be treated? _____

    (b) What are the two kinds of treatment now given (singly or in com-

    bination) for MBD? _____

- - - - - - - - - - - - - - - - - -

    (a) no; (b) special training and drugs

SELF-TEST

This Self-Test is designed to show you whether you have mastered this chapter's objectives. Answer each question to the best of your ability. Correct answers and review instructions are given at the end of the test.

1. What we perceive is never an exact replica of what is "out there" in the environment. Our sense impressions are different from the stimuli themselves. What five factors determine what we will actually perceive? Explain how they work.

_____

_____

_____

_____

_____

2. Perceptual psychologists often speak of the "cocktail party phenomenon." At a cocktail party, you "tune in" or "tune out" different conversations in the room, depending on what you choose to listen to. Why can you not listen simultaneously to all the conversations in the room? What do we call this mechanism by which we tune conversations in or out?

_____

_____

_____

3. Form discrimination tests and recognition tests are often used in studying perceptual development. Describe how each type of test works, and give an example of each.

_____

_____

_____

_____

4. If six-month-old infants can perceive very fine differences in visual stimuli, how would you account for the fact that 1-1/2-year-old children cannot place round blocks in round holes, square blocks in square holes, and triangular blocks in triangular holes on the form-board test?

_____

_____

_____

_____

5. Describe the changes that occur in the course of perceptual development in:

   (a) attention _____

   _____

   (b) scanning _____

   (c) organization _____

   _____

6. Explain how the visual–cliff experiment showed that very young infants can perceive depth.

   _____

   _____

   _____

   _____

   _____

   _____

7. It has been shown that older children can recognize pictures of familiar objects such as chairs and dogs when there are very large gaps in the outline of the figures. Younger children cannot do this. Explain why this might be so in terms of information.

   _____

   _____

   _____

8. If you were a doctor, a psychologist, or a teacher, and you suspected a child had minimal brain dysfunction, what are some of the cues or symptoms you would look for? (Include both behavior and past history.)

   _____

   _____

   _____

9. What kind of special education program might you set up to treat children with MBD?

_____

_____

_____

Answers to Self-Test

Compare your answers to the questions on the Self-Test with the answers given below. If all of your answers are correct, you are ready to go on to the next chapter. If you missed any questions, review the frames indicated in parentheses following the answer. If you missed several questions, you should probably reread the entire chapter carefully.

1. (a) aspects of the stimulus itself (Some objects are more easily perceived than others.)
   (b) the condition of the receptors (Some people hear or see better than others.)
   (c) selective attention (We attend to some aspects of the stimulus and ignore others.)
   (d) organization (We have a natural tendency to group stimuli together.)
   (e) interpretation (We have a natural tendency to interpret stimuli as something known or familiar.) (Frames 1—33)

2. Our perceptual system is limited, and we can take in only so much information at a time; we shift our attention from one thing to another. We call this mechanism by which our attention is focused on one thing at a time selective attention. (Frames 17—19)

3. In a form discrimination test, the child must perceive similarities and differences in the shapes of objects. Examples are the Embedded Figures Test, the form-board test. (Frames 35—37)
   Recognition tasks demand that a child identify the shape or object presented; a recognition test assumes the shape or object is already familiar to the child. Examples are incomplete figures, in which parts or lines are missing (such as follow-the-dots pictures); and a test in which pictures are flashed on a screen for a very short interval of time. (Frames 58—68)

4. It is probably due to attentional factors. Young children attend to the whole stimulus and ignore the parts. Perhaps in the case of the

form-board, the children are focusing on the whole board and ignoring the details—the shapes of the blocks and holes. (Frames 43, 44)

5. (a) Children attend more to parts or details of a stimulus as they get older.
(b) Their scanning pattern is more systematic.
(c) They do better in recognition tasks (are better able to organize and interpret stimuli). (Frames 34—68)

6. In the visual-cliff experiment, the experimenters wanted to find out if six-month-old infants would crawl across what appeared to be a drop-off or cliff. If they would not crawl across the visual-cliff side, it was assumed that they were demonstrating depth perception. It was found that most babies would <u>not</u> crawl across the drop-off side, even when their mothers called to them. Thus it was concluded that they can in fact perceive depth. (Frames 72—74)

7. Because they have had more experience (are more familiar) with the objects, older children have more information available in their mind about them. Therefore, they need less information from the stimulus itself. (Frames 62—66)

8. Behavior: poor coordination; hyperactivity; problems in visual and auditory discrimination; frequent accidents, clumsiness, difficulty hopping and skipping. Also (in older children) reading difficulties, speech problems, emotional problems.
History: possibility of brain damage through prenatal factors, birth complications, head injuries, history of MBD symptoms in the parents. (Frames 78-91)

9. You might include remedial reading and speech therapy, practice in fine-motor and gross-motor activities, and possibly drugs, although their use is still very controversial. (Frames 95-97)

SELECTED BIBLIOGRAPHY

Form Discrimination

Gibson, J. J., and Gibson, E. J. Perceptual learning: Differentiation
or enrichment? Psychological Review, 1955, 62, 32-41.

Infant Vision

Fantz, R. L. Pattern vision in newborn infants. Science, 1963, 140,
296-297.
Fantz, R. L. The origin of form perception. Scientific American, 1961,
204, 66-72.

Depth Perception

Gibson, E. J., and Walk, R. D. The "visual cliff." Scientific American,
1960, 202, 2-9.

Attention, Organization, and Interpretation

Neisser, U. Cognitive Psychology. New York: Appleton-Century-Crofts,
1967. (While this book does not deal specifically with development, it
is a well-written summary of some of the more recent thinking and
research in the area of perception and cognition.)

Information in Perception

Wohlwill, J. F. Developmental studies of perception. Psychological
Bulletin, 1960, 57, 249-288.

MBD

Myers, P. I., and Hammill, D. Methods for Learning Disorders. New
York: Wiley, 1969.
Wender, P. H. Minimal Brain Dysfunction in Children. New York:
Wiley, 1971.

CHAPTER THREE
Intelligence and Cognitive Development

Cognition refers to all those activities that go into thinking, reasoning, and problem-solving. Cognitive development refers to changes in the way children think, reason, and solve problems.

Some of the changes that take place in children's thinking are very dramatic, as you will see in this chapter. The thinking of three-year-olds is qualitatively different from the thinking of ten-year-olds. Young children's capacity for logical thinking, for example, is limited, as any parent who has ever tried to reason with a three-year-old will tell you. Their approach to problem-solving is random and disorganized. Their thinking is concrete, rather than abstract or symbolic (if asked to add 2 and 3, they may ask "two what and three what?").

Child psychologists are interested in the nature of these differences in thinking; they are also increasingly curious as to why such dramatic age changes occur. What role, for instance, does improved memory play in increasing problem-solving ability? Do three-year-olds and ten-year-olds actually picture problems differently in their mind? What is the relation of language to thought? These are some of the questions that will be covered (though not necessarily answered) in this chapter.

Also in this chapter, we will discuss intelligence tests—their makeup, rationale, and scoring. We will look at some of the factors that apparently cause high or low levels of performance on these tests, and what might be done to improve the performance of low-scoring children.

OBJECTIVES

After completing this chapter, you will be able to

- explain the main changes in mental representation of problems and in problem-solving strategies during cognitive development;

- identify the five general steps in problem-solving and describe changes that occur in each step during development;

- explain briefly how Piaget differs from the learning theorists in his ideas about children's intellectual development and "rule-learning";

- summarize briefly Piaget's stages of cognitive development and describe what takes place in each stage;

- describe what an intelligence test measures;

- explain what an IQ score is and how it is obtained;

- describe some of the activities used to increase children's IQ.

PROBLEM-SOLVING AND COGNITIVE DEVELOPMENT

1. Most of our daily activity is <u>goal-directed</u> behavior. We set the alarm, we get up at 7:00 a.m., get dressed, grab a quick breakfast, run for the bus, all in order to get to work or to school on time. The <u>goal</u> is "getting to work or school on time." The goal-directed behaviors are setting the alarm, getting up at 7:00 a.m., eating quickly, and running for the bus.

    Consider the following example. A girl wants to own a dog. She tries to convince her parents, telling them that she will take good care of it, and it would be good to have a watch dog. She also saves up money for a license, and looks up the number of the Animal Rescue League.

    (a) What is the girl's goal? _____

    (b) What are the goal-directed behaviors? _____

    _____

    _____

- - - - - - - - - - - - - - - - -

    (a) owning a dog; (b) convincing her parents, saving money for a license, looking up the number of the Animal Rescue League.

2. For children, as well as for adults, most behavior is directed toward
    a _____.

- - - - - - - - - - - - - - - - -

    goal

3. Sometimes there are obstacles in the way of achieving goals. Then
    we say we have a "problem." Let's say your alarm clock broke and
    for some reason you are unable to buy another one. You must solve
    the problem of "getting to work on time without an alarm clock."

    (a) What is the goal? _____
    (b) What is the obstacle in the way of achieving that goal?

    _____

    (c) What is the problem that must be solved?

    _____

- - - - - - - - - - - - - - - - -

    (a) getting to work on time;
    (b) a broken alarm clock, or the fact that you have no alarm clock;
    (c) getting to work on time without an alarm clock

4. The ability to overcome obstacles in order to achieve a goal is called
    problem-solving ability. As we grow older, our problem-solving
    ability increases. It has been observed, for example, that if you
    take a bottle from a very young infant and place it under a pillow,
    the baby does not know how to retrieve it—does not search for it or
    reach for it, but in effect forgets it. Older infants understand that
    the bottle is simply hidden and will lift up the pillow and retrieve it.
    Older babies can figure out how to retrieve the bottle, while younger
    babies cannot.

    (a) What is problem-solving ability? _____

    _____

    (b) The above example illustrates that: (Check one.)

    _____ Problem-solving ability is not affected by age.

    _____ Problem-solving ability increases with age.

    _____ Problem-solving ability decreases with age.

- - - - - - - - - - - - - - - - -

    (a) the ability to overcome obstacles in order to achieve a goal;
    (b) Problem-solving ability increases with age.

5. This increase in problem-solving ability with age is called <u>cognitive development</u>. A child of four can add one apple to two apples and say that there are three apples; a seven-year-old can do formal addition involving units, tens, and hundreds. By high school age, a child is capable of doing mathematical problems without using actual numbers, that is, algebra.

This increase is problem-solving ability with age is called

_____.

- - - - - - - - - - - - - - - - - -

cognitive development

6. Problem-solving is a process that takes place largely within the mind. It is a special kind of thinking. We can easily describe the <u>behavior</u> that we perform in order to solve a problem; it is quite another thing to describe the process of <u>thinking</u> that occurs in order to arrive at that behavior. Some people have said that the study of thinking is an impossible task because it involves something we cannot see, something within the mind. Students of cognitive development say only that it is difficult—not impossible.

Problem-solving can be described in two ways—in terms of the process of <u>thinking</u> and in terms of <u>behavior</u>. Which is the most difficult to study? Why? _____

_____

- - - - - - - - - - - - - - - - - -

Thinking; because the process of thinking goes on within the mind; it is something we cannot see.

7. In order to solve a problem we must represent it in some general way within our mind. Take the process of doing a jigsaw puzzle. In our search for a missing piece we might focus mainly on the shape (it's shaped sort of like a dog with only three legs) or on the color (it's blue, but darker blue than the sky). Or we might represent it in our mind as a combination of shape and probable colors. In any event we would not simply pick up all the pieces and try them on a trial-and-error basis. In the process of thinking about how to find the missing

piece, what is going on within our mind? _____

_____

- - - - - - - - - - - - - - - - - -

We are representing the missing piece in some way within our mind.

8. Now let's look at some of the ways in which we represent problems. When someone gives you a direction such as "turn right, then right again, then left, then left again," do you find yourself mentally making those turns? Many people do. So one form of mental representation is in terms of actions; we call it an action image.

   Think of a very, very long line stretched out from left to right. You may have pictured it visually; however, you may also have mentally "traveled" the length of the line with your eyes, even to the point of feeling your body turn slightly to allow the eye movement to continue. This latter way of thinking is a form of _____ image.

- - - - - - - - - - - - - - - - -

   action

9. Some psychologists believe that action images are the earliest ones available to a child. They suggest that babies represent objects around them only in terms of their actions in relation to those objects. Thus a baby does not think about an object in the way we usually think about it, by mentally picturing it. A baby thinks a series of connected actions—reaching, grasping, shaking. These action images tend to drop out later in life, but they are present, as we have seen, in some of our thinking.

   Explain how a baby's mental representation of a rattle would be different from an adult's. (In your own words.) _____

   _____

   _____

- - - - - - - - - - - - - - - - -

   A baby is thought to represent a rattle as a series of actions, such as reaching for it, grasping it, shaking it. An adult would probably just "picture" a rattle.

10. An action image is a primitive form of representation. As such, it is not very helpful in problem-solving. A second way of representing problems is in terms of a visual image. Let's see how this works. If a four-year-old is given a form-board and three wooden figures— say, a circle, a square, and a triangle—and told to fit the correct pieces in the correct holes in the form, the child will probably inspect the forms first, then the holes. Only then will the child pick up the pieces and place them correctly. A four-year-old represents the shapes in his or her mind in terms of a visual image; this allows the child to match up the two images and solve the problem.

A two-year-old, on the other hand, will probably start picking up pieces and trying them out until one "feels" right—that is, until it is placed in the right hole. The two-year-old may or may not solve the problem.

Why would you say a two-year-old has more trouble fitting forms in a form-board than a four-year-old? (Answer in terms of how they represent the problem.) _____

_____

_____

- - - - - - - - - - - - - - - - -

Because a two-year-old is probably still representing the problem in terms of action images; the four-year-old is using a visual image.

11. Visual images are generally more helpful in problem-solving situations than action images. However, beyond the simplest problem situations they too are totally inadequate. Let's look at an illustration.

In the following problem, imagine that the two rows of dots are pieces of candy that an examiner has placed in front of a child.

O O O O O O O O O O

O O O O O O O O O O

Are there the same number of candies in each row? How many?

_____

- - - - - - - - - - - - - - - - -

yes, ten

12. Now the examiner rearranges one of the rows, without adding any candies, or taking any away. They now look like this:

O O O O O O O O O

O O O O O O O O O O

Are there still the same number of candies in each row? How do you know this? _____

_____

- - - - - - - - - - - - - - - - -

Yes, no candies were added or taken away; one row of ten was just pushed closer together.

13. Easy, right? Not for a five-year-old child. After one of the rows
    has been rearranged, five-year-olds usually say that there are more
    candies in the top row. When it is pointed out to them that no candies
    have been added or taken away, they will still insist that the top row
    has more candies because it is longer. One reason that five-year-
    olds cannot solve this problem is that they represent the problem in
    terms of the visual image: when one row becomes shorter, it must
    contain fewer candies because it "looks" like less.

    In this example, representing the problem in terms of a visual image

    _____ the child in solving the problem.
    helps/hinders

- - - - - - - - - - - - - - - - - - -

    hinders

14. In order to solve this candy problem, the child must be able to repre-
    sent it in terms of symbols. Once we know there are ten pieces of
    candy in both rows and that none have been added or taken away, we
    can use the mathematical symbol "10" to help us solve the problem.
    We no longer see the problem just in terms of the perceptual image;
    we can think of the symbol "10" and "know" that it stays the same in
    the two situations.
    (a) How does a young child represent the candy problem? (Check
        one.)

        _____ in visual images

        _____ in symbols
    (b) How must this problem be represented in order to be solved?

        _____ in visual images

        _____ in symbols

- - - - - - - - - - - - - - - - - - -

    (a) in visual images; (b) in symbols

15. The numeral "10" is a symbol that is independent of the immediate
    perceptual situation. It can represent 10 pieces of candy, 10 toys,
    or 10 plates of spinach. Once we can think in terms of mathematical
    symbols, we can ignore the specific details of what is in front of us;
    we can reason on a more abstract level.

    We say that symbols are _____ abstract than either action images
                            more/less
    or visual images.

- - - - - - - - - - - - - - - - - - -

more

16. <u>Words</u> are also symbols in that they stand for or represent actual objects or situations. Words, too, can help us to solve more complex problems because they help us to reason on a more abstract level. A child of two or three begins using words and theoretically should be able to represent problems in terms of these symbols. However, children of two or three still appear to use action or visual images for most problems.

Say that small children are asked to match two series of pictures. Each series has a boat, a shoe, a hat, a house, and a dog. However, the dogs, houses, boats, shoes, and hats are totally dissimilar in appearance (for example, a canoe and a liner, or an old-fashioned button shoe and a sandal). It has been found that those children who say the words as they look at the pictures do better (work faster and with fewer errors) in the matching task than those children who do not say the words.

Why do you think this is so? (Check one.)

_____ (a) The words may draw the children's attention to the details of the objects.

_____ (b) The words may help the children ignore the specific details and reason on a more abstract level.

- - - - - - - - - - - - - - - - - -

(b)

17. Being able to represent problem situations <u>symbolically</u> allows people to solve more and more complex problems. We said that cognitive development is an increase in problem-solving ability. We could also say that cognitive development is a result of: (Check one.)

_____ (a) increased perceptual ability

_____ (b) increasing use of symbolic representation

_____ (c) increasing ability to use motor and visual images

- - - - - - - - - - - - - - - - -

(b)

18. (a) In what three ways can problems be represented within the mind?

_____ , _____ ,

_____

(b) Which is the most abstract? _____

— — — — — — — — — — — — — — — — — —

(a) action images, visual images, symbols; (b) symbols

Note: Jerome Bruner, a psychologist, refers to these three kinds of representation as enactive, ikonic, and symbolic.* We will refer to these three types of representation again in the section dealing with Piaget's theory of cognitive development.

19. Much of children's cognitive development can be attributed to their

increasing use of _____ representation.

— — — — — — — — — — — — — — — — — —

symbolic

20. Another thing we must do in order to solve a problem is to organize or work on the material in some way. Let's go back for a moment to the problem of finding a certain piece in a jigsaw puzzle (frame 7). There are two ways a child might work at the problem:
1. Pick up pieces at random and fit them in on a trial-and-error basis.
2. Scan the pieces for a match, or place the remaining pieces in piles based on shape and/or color, thus making the matching process even easier.

We can see that not only are there different ways of representing a problem within the mind, there are different ways of

_____ a problem.
scanning/working at

— — — — — — — — — — — — — — — — — —

working at

21. These different ways of working at a problem we call <u>strategies</u>. In the game of "20 questions," the child is asked to guess what an examiner is thinking about by asking only questions which can be answered by "yes" or "no." Young children usually approach this problem by asking 20 unrelated questions (is it a horse? a tree? a house?).

_____

*Jerome S. Bruner. <u>Studies in Cognitive Growth</u> (New York: Wiley, 1966).

Older children ask questions that will eliminate as many alternatives as possible. They might begin by asking, "Is it animate?" If the answer is "yes," they might then ask, "Is it a person?" From there they would gradually narrow down the possibilities—alive or dead, man or woman, and so on.

We say that the approach of eliminating alternatives is one possible

_____.

strategy/ability

- - - - - - - - - - - - - - - - - -

strategy

22. A strategy is: (Check one.)

_____ (a) a way of representing a problem within the mind

_____ (b) a way of working at a problem

- - - - - - - - - - - - - - - - - -

(b)

23. In the game of 20 questions (frame 21), young children usually ask 20 more or less unrelated questions, while older children eliminate as many alternatives as possible with each question. Which strategy would you say is the most <u>systematic</u>? _____

_____

_____

- - - - - - - - - - - - - - - - - - -

the second strategy, or eliminating as many alternatives as possible with each question

24. As children grow older, their strategies for problem-solving become more systematic. In frame 10, we saw that one child picked up pieces at random and tried them out on a trial-and-error basis; the other child used a systematic strategy. Which child is probably the <u>older</u> of the two? Why? _____

_____

_____

- - - - - - - - - - - - - - - - -

_____

The child who used a systematic strategy, because children's strategies become more systematic as they grow older.

25. As children develop, their strategies for problem-solving become

    more _____.
       systematic/trial-and-error

- - - - - - - - - - - - - - - - -

    systematic

26. Two things that affect people's problem-solving ability are:

    (a) _____

        _____

    (b) _____

        _____

- - - - - - - - - - - - - - - -

    (a) the way in which they represent a problem within their mind
    (b) the way they work at solving the problem (their strategy)

27. In the course of cognitive development, children's problem-solving
    ability improves because their representation of the problem becomes

    more _____, and their strategies become more

    _____.

- - - - - - - - - - - - - - - -

    symbolic; systematic

28. Cognitive development is really an increase in _____
    _____ ability with age.

- - - - - - - - - - - - - - - -

    problem-solving

STEPS IN PROBLEM-SOLVING

29. Let's look a little more closely at the steps involved in solving a
    problem, that is, what goes into problem-solving strategies. Psy-
    chologists generally break the entire problem-solving process into

five phases. In this section, we will focus on these five phases.

Let's say you are given the following six scores and asked to find the average score:

$$10$$
$$8$$
$$11$$
$$19$$
$$9$$
$$12$$

This problem is very simple if you know the right rule to apply. We call this phase of problem-solving, which involves application of the correct rule, the deductive phase. In order to arrive at the correct answer to the above problem, you must apply the following rule: add all the scores and divide the sum by the total number of scores.

In your own words, what does a person do in the deductive phase of problem-solving? _____

- - - - - - - - - - - - - - - - - -

The person applies the correct rule.

30. Obviously as children grow older, they learn more rules that always apply to specific situations. Some rules will be learned from informal experience (fire is hot), some through formal training ($E = mc^2$). Children learn that some rules are logical ($2 + 2 = 4$), some only arbitrary ("ough" is pronounced "oh"—unless it is pronounced "uff" or "ow" or "off"). The main idea is that children's knowledge of rules grows through experience, that is, through interaction with the environment.

We say that the important element in determining how well a child performs in the deductive ("rule-applying") phase of problem-solving depends on _____.

logic/experience

- - - - - - - - - - - - - - - - - -

experience (Some psychologists believe that certain rules cannot be acquired, regardless of experience, until the child has attained a certain stage in cognitive development. We will discuss this hypothesis further when we look at Piaget's theory of cognitive development.)

31. This deductive phase is actually the final step in a process that is more complex than first appears. If you were just given the five numbers, 10, 8, 11, 9, and 12 and told to apply the "correct" rule to

them, you might try adding them, subtracting 5 from each of them, multiplying them all by 3, or any number of other rules, to see if which one seems to fit. We call this process of generating possible rules or hypotheses the <u>inductive</u> phase of problem-solving. The fact is that you know <u>many</u> rules, and before applying one to solve a problem, you must generate whole series of possible rules or hypotheses and then choose the correct rule from among all those possibles.

(a) In your own words, explain what happens in the inductive phase of problem-solving. _____

_____

_____

(b) Which comes first, the <u>inductive</u> or the <u>deductive</u> phase?

_____

- - - - - - - - - - - - - - - - - -

(a) In the inductive phase of problem-solving a person generates a whole series of rules or hypotheses for solving a problem.
(b) the inductive phase (because you must generate the possible rules before choosing the one that fits)

32. This inductive phase is more important in some problems than in others. If instructed to "find an average," you immediately eliminate all rules or hypotheses other than the correct one. Consider this problem, however: you are given the following collections of objects and told to group them into three pairs of objects using some logical rule.

> milk
> water
> box
> cup
> cereal
> pipe

In this problem, you will probably generate and discard many hypotheses before finding a rule that fits.

(a) In which problem would you say the inductive phase is more important: finding an average or grouping objects into logical pairs? _____

(b) Did you come up with a logical rule that fits all three pairs of objects? _____

__ - - - - - - - - - - - - - - - - -

(a) grouping objects into logical pairs;   (b) If you didn't come up with a "rule" that fits, try grouping according to which object goes <u>inside</u> another object. (Milk in a cup, cereal in a box, water in a pipe.)

33. The ability to generate <u>many</u> possible solutions to a problem is called <u>creativity</u>. As we have shown, some types of problems require more creativity than others. Creativity is needed when the answer to a problem is not immediately obvious, or when there is more than one possible answer and the "best" solution must be found.

In which of the following two problem situations would a more creative person have the advantage over a less creative person? Why? (In your own words.)

(a) In response to the energy crisis an auto manufacturer wants to design an engine that uses little or no gas and is economical to build.

(b) A toy manufacturer needs to know which of two toys has sold better in the past year.

_____

_____

_____

_____

_____

- - - - - - - - - - - - - - - - - -

Problem (a), because problem (a) calls for generating many hypotheses in order to find the best solution; the answer to the problem is not immediately obvious and there is more than one possible answer. In problem (b), however, the answer is clear—look at the sales figures for the past year.

34. Creativity, or the ability to generate many hypotheses is most helpful

in the _____ phase of problem-solving.
          inductive/deductive

- - - - - - - - - - - - - - - - -

_____

inductive

Note: Not much is known about the developmental aspects of this inductive phase of problem-solving. It is possible that older children are simply able to generate more hypotheses than younger children. It may be the case, however, that the ability to generate hypotheses is relatively the same for all ages, and that only deductive ability (the ability to select the correct rule) improves with age.

35. You may have noticed in trying to pair up the six objects (frame 32) that you thought of a hypothesis, tried it out or evaluated it, and then either accepted or rejected it on the basis of whether or not it solved the problem. Thus there is a third phase between induction and deduction—an evaluative phase. To review: First, we generate rules and hypotheses; second, we make a choice from among those hypotheses; and third, we apply the correct rule to solve the problem.

Which of the above steps—1, 2, or 3—represents the evaluative phase?

_____

- - - - - - - - - - - - - - - -

2 (making a choice from among the hypotheses generated)

36. Jerome Kagan, a psychologist at Harvard, has shown that there are individual differences in how quickly children make a decision in picking out the correct answer to a problem. He calls this a difference between reflection and impulsiveness. Impulsive children guess at an answer more quickly and thus make more errors than reflective children. On the question: "What is yellow, melts in the sun, and you eat it?" some children might quickly answer "squash" (ignoring the "melts in the sun" specification) or "ice cream" (ignoring the "yellow specification"). Would you say that these children are more reflective or impulsive? Why? _____

_____

- - - - - - - - - - - - - - - -

Impulsive, because they answer quickly without considering all parts of the problem, and thus make errors.

37. While these individual differences persist over time, children tend to become more reflective as they grow older. This is probably due to both maturational and learning factors. Children are urged by teachers and parents alike to "think before you act." They learn tha

they are rewarded for being patient and for controlling their impulses. In addition, ten-year-olds are simply physically capable of concentrating for longer periods of time than five-year-olds.

(a) Which child would be more reflective—a five-year-old or a ten-year-old? _____

(b) What two factors are involved in the development of reflectiveness in children? _____

- - - - - - - - - - - - - - - - -

(a) a ten-year-old; (b) maturation and learning

38. (a) What are the three phases of problem-solving discussed so far? (List in order.) _____, _____, _____

(b) In which phase is creativity the most important?

(c) In which phase is reflectivity the most important?

(d) In which phase is experience the most important?

- - - - - - - - - - - - - - - - -

(a) inductive, evaluative, deductive; (b) inductive; (c) evaluative;
(d) deductive

39. You have already learned that before you even begin to work on a problem to generate possible solutions, you must receive the information and represent it in some way in your mind. Psychologists often call this process <u>encoding</u> because, in a sense, it involves translating the information received into some sort of code within the mind. Remember that you can <u>encode</u> in terms of action images, visual images, or symbols.

If you ask a very young child, "What is a hole?" the child might answer, "A hole is to dig."

(a) Would you say that the child who answers this way is representing the problem in terms of an action image, a visual image, or a symbol? _____

(b) What do psychologists call this process of representing a problem in the mind? _____

- - - - - - - - - - - - - - - -

(a) probably an action image; (b) encoding

40. Encoding is the _____ step in problem-solving.
              first/last

- - - - - - - - - - - - - - - -

first

41. We have learned that encoding (representing a problem in the mind) changes with age and that these changes contribute to increased problem-solving ability. Review the changes that occur in encoding in the course of cognitive development. _____

_____

_____

- - - - - - - - - - - - - - - -

Children encode first only in action images, then in visual images, then also in symbols; the ability to use symbolic representation increases.

42. Encoding is another word for: (Check one.)

_____ (a) generating many hypotheses

_____ (b) representing a problem in the mind

_____ (c) applying the correct rule

_____ (d) making a choice from among hypotheses

- - - - - - - - - - - - - - - -

(b)

Note: What a child "selects out" and "attends to" in a problem is important too. Attention and selective perception were discussed in the last chapter. It is useful to note again that perceptive and cognitive development are very closely related.

43. There is a fifth phase in problem-solving, that of memory. After you have encoded the information in some way, you must remember it in

order to begin acting on it.

Where would you place the <u>memory</u> phase in the diagram below? (Write "memory" on the correct line.)

encoding

_____

induction

_____

evaluation

_____

deduction

_____

- - - - - - - - - - - - - - - - - -

encoding
<u>memory</u>
induction
evaluation
deduction

44. Psychologists today generally agree that memory consists of two kinds of storage—short-term and long-term. Short-term storage lasts for only a few seconds. Once information enters long-term storage, it can be retrieved whenever needed. Therefore, in order for information to be acted upon, it must be transferred to long-term storage.

(a) When a child "remembers" a problem and begins to solve it,

the problem is in _____ storage.
short-term/long-term

(b) From which kind of storage can information be retrieved when-ever needed? _____

- - - - - - - - - - - - - - - - - -

(a) long-term; (b) long-term

45. There appear to be two ways in which information is transferred from short-term to long-term storage:
1. The person "rehearses" the information (repeats it to himself).
2. The person makes a connection between something already known and the new information.

Let's take some examples:

1. A person who wants to remember a telephone number repeats it several times on the way to the phone.
2. Another person remembers a phone number by saying, "It's like my cousin Kathy's number, only the 5 and 2 are reversed."
3. When remembering street directions, a person may repeat to herself while driving, "turn left, then right, then right again."
4. Nonsense syllables (IBS, TIB, SUT), or "words" with no meaning, are more easily remembered if they remind a person of real words. For example, to remember "TIB," a person might think "BIT backwards," or "TUB with an I."

(a) In which of the four examples is the person using <u>rehearsal</u> to remember information? _____

(b) In which example is the person making a <u>connection</u> between the new information and something already known? _____

- - - - - - - - - - - - - - - - -

(a) rehearsal—1 and 3; (b) connection—2 and 4

46. (a) In what two ways does information apparently get transferred from short-term to long-term storage?

_____

_____

(b) When a person must solve a problem, why is it important that the information be transferred into long-term storage? (In your own words.) _____

_____

- - - - - - - - - - - - - - - - -

(a) 1. rehearsal, 2. making a connection between the new information and something already known; (b) because information must be in long-term memory in order to be acted upon, or because in long-term memory information can be retrieved whenever needed.

47. Developmental psychologists have found that young children typically do not rehearse material or instructions to be remembered. Therefore not as much information gets transferred into long-term memory. Experiments have shown that older children, when asked to remember a series of pictures, typically label the pictures and rehearse the labels. Younger children do not apply labels to the pictures, even though they know the names of the objects in the pictures.

(a) What do you suppose would be the result of the younger children's not applying labels to the picture? _____

_____

(b) What do you think would happen if the younger children were told to label the pictures and rehearse the names? _____

_____

- - - - - - - - - - - - - - - - -

(a) The younger children would not rehearse and would remember fewer pictures.
(b) The younger children would remember more pictures if they rehearsed. (In fact, it has been shown that if young children are instructed to rehearse, their "memory" for pictures increases.)

48. Similarly, as a memory strategy, young children do not typically make connections between incoming information and what they already know, whereas older children do. Suppose a group of children is shown a series of geometric figures: some of the figures resemble actual objects—a kite, a bow—and some do not.

(a) Would you expect the older children to remember more of the figures that resemble actual objects than of the "nonsense"

figures? _____

(b) Would you expect the younger children to remember each kind of

figure equally well? Why? _____

_____

_____

- - - - - - - - - - - - - - - - -

(a) yes   (This has been shown to be true.)
(b) Yes, because they would not make any connection between the geometric figures and the objects they resemble.

49. What are two reasons why young children do not remember (transfer information to long-term storage) as well as older children?

_____

_____

_____

- - - - - - - - - - - - - - - - -

They do not rehearse (or label and rehearse).

They do not make connections between information to be remembered and information they already know.

Note: This discussion has left out a third technique for remembering— a device long used by parlor magicians—the mnemonic. Some kinds of information can be placed in long-term storage as it is coming in by using a mnemonic device, or memory trick.

For instance, if you want to remember a list of objects, you might picture a scene such as your street or your house, and visually "place" the objects somewhere in the scene as the names of the objects are read to you. Then when you want to remember them—say two hours later—you simply "take a walk" on the street or in the house, and "retrieve" the objects from where you had placed them. Try this trick with friends, using ten or fifteen objects; only make sure they read the list of objects slowly enough to let you "place" them in a convenient spot.

Other mnemonics include making up a rhyme and picturing words in your mind. For example, to remember someone's name: Mrs. King can be pictured with a robe and a crown, Mr. White, covered with snow.

These mnemonic devices are really just a special case of the strategy of making a connection between the incoming information and something that is already known. Generally, the mnemonic connection made is visual rather than logical and is only helpful with information that has no logical connection.

50. (a) Name in order the five phases of problem-solving.

_____

(b) Explain how each phase develops with age, so that problem-solving ability increases. _____

_____

_____

_____

_____

_____

_____

_____

_____

_____

_____

_____

_____

_____

_____

– – – – – – – – – – – – – – – – – – –

(a) encoding, memory, induction, evaluation, deduction

(b) Encoding: As children grow older, they are able to represent information in more abstract or symbolic ways (from action images to visual images to symbols).

Memory: As children grow older, they are better able to transfer information from short-term to long-term memory (by means of rehearsal and making connections between incoming information and what is already known).

Induction: Some people feel that, as children grow older, they are able to generate more appropriate hypotheses or possible solutions to a problem. However, it is not yet clear how inductive ability actually changes with age.

Evaluation: Children become more reflective with age; that is, they wait longer before deciding on an answer, and make fewer errors.

Deduction: As children grow older, they learn from experience more rules that can be applied in specific situations.

Note: The terms for these five phases vary, but there seems to be general agreement that they are all present in the problem-solving process. Mussen, Conger and Kagan* label the steps in nearly the same way: encoding, memory functions, generation of ideas and hypotheses, evaluation, and implementation of hypotheses. Professor J. P. Guilford, a psychologist at the University of Southern California, calls them recognition, memory, divergent production, evaluation, and convergent production.

PIAGET'S THEORY OF COGNITIVE DEVELOPMENT

51. Until the past few years, it was generally accepted that children learned problem-solving rules by trial and error, following the usual learning model. A rule was thought of as a learned stimulus-response connection:

_____

*P. H. Mussen, J. J. Conger, and J. Kagan. Child Development and Personality (New York: Harper & Row, 1974).

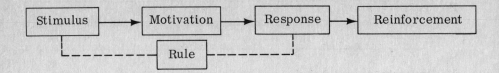

If children made the correct response a certain number of times in a given situation, they were rewarded and thus "learned" the right response.

Learning theorists assumed that a rule is another name for the connection between the _____ and the _____.

- - - - - - - - - - - - - - - - -

stimulus; response

52. According to this model, a child of any age could eventually learn any rule if rewarded for making the correct response. However, a Swiss psychologist, Jean Piaget, has shown that this is simply not the case. There are some problems that very young children cannot solve, regardless of how many times they are "shown", or forced to make, the right responses.

A famous example of this is Piaget's experiment involving conservation of quantity. Piaget shows a five-year-old child two identical glasses with the same amount of water in each. When asked, the child agrees that both glasses have the same amount of water. However, when Piaget pours one of the glasses of water into a taller, thinner container, the child says that the tall container now has more water. When the water is poured back into the original glass, the child says that the two amounts are equal again. No matter how many times Piaget and the child repeat this operation, the child does not grasp the rule—that the quantity of liquid remains the same, regardless of the shape of the glass.

What does Piaget's experiment on conservation of quantity demonstrate about rule-learning in young children? _____

_____

_____

- - - - - - - - - - - - - - - - -

that there are some rules a very young child cannot learn, regardless of how many times the child is shown or makes the right response

53. Piaget believes that in the course of development children progress through several stages. In each stage they view the world differently or encode information in different forms. This difference in encoding accounts in part for differences in problem-solving ability. We will compare Piaget's views on encoding to the outline presented at the beginning of this chapter.

    (a) According to Piaget, a five-year-old cannot solve the conservation of quantity problem, although a ten-year-old can, because of differences in the way in which they _____ the problem.

    (b) Piaget would say that the five-year-old and the ten-year-old are in different _____ of development.

- - - - - - - - - - - - - - - - - -

    (a) encode; (b) stages

54. During most of the earliest stage, the <u>sensori-motor stage</u> (ages 0–2), children encode in terms of <u>actions</u>. When babies move the mobiles above their cribs, what is being represented is not the shape or color of the mobile, but the actions of reaching, touching, and so on.

When babies push against their mothers with their toes as the mothers hold them in the air, are the babies encoding that action in terms of some picture of the mother or in terms of the action of pushing?

_____

- - - - - - - - - - - - - - - - - -

in terms of the action of pushing

55. What is the name of the stage in which this form of mental representation takes place? _____

- - - - - - - - - - - - - - - - - -

sensori-motor stage

56. In the very beginning of this sensori-motor stage, however, the child, according to Piaget, is unable to form <u>any</u> kind of mental representation. Piaget says that until such a mental representation is possible, the child does not have the concept of <u>object permanence</u>. That is, if an object disappears, it ceases to exist.

    As a demonstration of this lack of object permanence, take an object such as a rattle from a three-month-old infant and, while the infant is still watching, hide it from view. The infant will either cry or will appear to forget about it. If the same action is repeated with a ten-month-old infant, the infant will reach for it and attempt to retrieve it in some way.

Piaget would say that the ten-month-old infant has _____

_____, whereas the three-month-old does not.

- - - - - - - - - - - - - - - - - -

object permanence

57. Object permanence is possible only when an infant has: (Check one.)

_____ (a) a view of the object

_____ (b) a mental representation of the object

_____ (c) a desire to retrieve the object

- - - - - - - - - - - - - - - - - -

(b)

58. Gradually, the infant becomes capable of using action images to solve simple problems. This ability might represent the earliest, most primitive form of "thinking."

For example, Piaget tells of observing one of his young children, Lucienne. Piaget has placed a watch chain inside a matchbox, and Lucienne is trying to retrieve it. Piaget has closed the box so that she cannot get the chain out without opening the slit wider, an action she has never done before. She tries several times to retrieve the chain through the small slit:

> "... A pause follows during which Lucienne manifests a very curious reaction.... She looks at the slit with great attention; then several times in succession she opens and shuts her mouth, at first slightly, then wider and wider!

> [Then]... Lucienne unhesitatingly puts her finger in the slit, and instead of trying as before to reach the chain, she pulls so as to enlarge the opening. She succeeds and grasps the chain."*

(a) Explain how Lucienne demonstrated that she was "thinking," using primitive mental images. (In your own words.)

_____

_____

*Jean Piaget. Origins of Intelligence in Children (New York: International University Press, 1952), pp. 337-338.

_____

_____

(b) Was the image of an actual object or of an action? _____

- - - - - - - - - - - - - - - - - -

(a) Lucienne opened and closed her mouth as a way of "thinking"
about how to solve the matchbox problem. The motion of her
mouth represented the solution to the problem—opening the slit
wider.
(b) an action

59. Toward the end of the second year (around 18 months) the child
begins to rely less on action images and more on visual images.
We have already seen that a three-month-old infant has no image
of an object; if it disappears, it no longer exists since the infant
cannot represent it in any way. Later in the sensori-motor stage,
the baby can represent the object in some way. (Piaget says first
in terms of actions then in terms of a visual image.)

We could say that, in the sensori-motor stage, children's repre-

sentations are very primitive, consisting of _____ images

and _____ images.

- - - - - - - - - - - - - - - - -

action; visual

60. (a) According to Piaget, the first stage in a child's cognitive develop-

ment is the _____ stage.
(b) Describe what happens to the child's encoding during this stage.

_____

_____

_____

- - - - - - - - - - - - - - - - -

(a) sensori-motor; (b) At first, the child has no way of encoding
objects or events. Then the child begins to encode in terms of
actions, and eventually, in visual images.

61. Between the ages of two and seven, children begin to be able to encode in terms of symbols. Piaget says that during this period
children have the ability to encode in terms of action, visual, and

symbolic image (for example, an image of a specific cat, perhaps a feeling of holding and fondling a cat, and the word "cat"). Generally, however, children rely on <u>visual</u> encoding, and only gradually increase their ability to use <u>symbols</u> to solve problems. Piaget refers to this second stage (ages 2-7) as the <u>pre-operational</u> stage.

(a) In the pre-operational stage, children begin to be able to make

use of _____ .

(b) In solving problems, however, children tend to rely on

_____ encoding.
action/visual/symbolic

- - - - - - - - - - - - - - - - - -

(a) symbols; (b) visual

62. (a) At what age do children begin to encode in terms of symbols?

_____

(b) What is Piaget's name for this stage of development?

_____

- - - - - - - - - - - - - - - -

(a) about age 2; (b) pre-operational stage

63. Piaget refers to both visual images and symbols as <u>signifiers</u>. That is, both signify or stand for real objects and events. To Piaget, both ways of representing reality can be used to solve problems; it is simply that symbols eventually permit solutions to more abstract or complex problems.

Let's return to the candy problem (frames 11 and 12). A child in the pre-operational stage (ages 2-7) cannot solve this problem, whereas an older child can.

(a) We could say that this is due to the fact that a pre-operational

child encodes the problem in terms of _____ .
symbols/visual images

(b) The use of symbols generally allows a child to solve more

_____ problems than the use of visual images.

- - - - - - - - - - - - - - - -

(a) visual; (b) abstract, or complex

64. (a) The first two of Piaget's stages discussed so far are the

_____ stage (0-2) and the

_____ stage (2-7).

(b) At what stage does a child <u>begin</u> to use symbols?

_____

- - - - - - - - - - - - - - - - -

(a) sensori-motor, pre-operational; (b) the pre-operational stage

65. What prevents a child in the pre-operational stage from solving abstract or complex problems? _____

_____

- - - - - - - - - - - - - - - -

The child still encodes more in visual images than in symbols.

66. In the next stage, the <u>stage of concrete operations</u> (approximately
7-12), Piaget says that children begin to look at more than just one
aspect of a problem at a time. They are capable of representing in
their minds two or more dimensions of a problem at one time and
coordinating the two dimensions. Piaget calls this process
<u>de-centration</u>; by this, he means that children no longer center their
attention (and therefore, their mental representations) on just one
part of the problem.

Thus, in the example of conservation of quantity (frame 52), a
child in this stage can represent both the height and the width of the
containers and thereby can recognize that an increase in one (height)
is compensated for by a decrease in the other (width).

(a) Explain, in your own words, Piaget's explanation of why a ten-
year-old child can solve the conservation of quantity problem
while a five-year-old cannot.

_____

_____

_____

(b) What is Piaget's term for this process? _____

(c) What is the name of the <u>stage</u> in which this change occurs?

_____

- - - - - - - - - - - - - - -

_____

(a) A ten-year-old is capable of representing, or paying attention to, both the height and the width of the containers; a ten-year-old does not center his attention on just one dimension.
(b) de-centration
(c) stage of concrete operations

67. Even though children in this stage can solve more complex problems than those in the pre-operational stage, they still rely more on visual images than on symbols. In fact, the reason Piaget calls this the stage of <u>concrete</u> operations is that children from 7 to 12 are still tied in some way to a concrete image or situation. They have difficulty solving problems in which <u>only</u> symbolic representation is called for, such as algebraic equations.

I once asked a seven-year-old boy to solve the following problem: If it takes a man 5 minutes to walk to the store, how long will it take him to walk back, if he takes the same route and walks at exactly the same speed?

The boy thought for a moment, then asked: "What store is he going to?" When I gave him the name of a specific store, he replied easily, "five minutes."

Why do you suppose it was important for the child to picture a specific store in order to solve this problem? _____

_____

_____

- -

because the child was in the stage of concrete operations: a child in this stage still relies more on visual images than on symbols in solving problems.

68. According to Piaget, the final stage in the process of cognitive development is the <u>stage of formal operations</u> (12 and up). From this point children are not necessarily tied to specific perceptual images in solving problems. They can deal with abstract ideas—symbols and concepts—and the relationships among them <u>without</u> reference to actual objects or situations.

Piaget says that a child can now use <u>higher-order operations</u> in solving a problem—that is, relationships among abstract ideas, symbols and concepts.

(a) When a scientist derives one formula from another, she is using: (Check one.)

_____ specific perceptual images

_____ relationships among abstract symbols

_____ reference to actual objects

(b) What is this final stage of development called? _____

_____

(c) When does it occur? _____

- - - - - - - - - - - - - - - - - -

(a) relationships among abstract symbols;
(b) stage of formal operations; (c) 12 and up

69. Piaget says that this stage is characterized by higher-order operations. By this, he means: (Check one.)

_____ relationships among symbols

_____ relationships among objects

_____ relationships among perceptual images

- - - - - - - - - - - - - - - - - -

relationships among symbols

70. In this stage also, adolescents and adults can fully use their
<u>inductive</u> ability. Think back for a moment to the five phases of
problem-solving we discussed earlier. What happens in the inductive phase? _____

_____

- - - - - - - - - - - - - - - - - -

The person generates hypotheses and possible solutions.

71. Therefore, we could say that the stage of formal operations is also

characterized by increased _____ ability.

- - - - - - - - - - - - - - - - -

inductive

72. Problem solutions do not necessarily have to be things that have ever
been done or thought of before; they can be the result of different or
new combinations of ideas, that is, higher-order operations. Because
persons in this stage are no longer tied to perceptual images, they can

combine and recombine ideas, symbols, and concepts. Thus, <u>invention</u> is now possible.

In order to invent something new, a person has to generate many possible solutions to a problem. Explain why these possible solutions are the result of higher-order operations. _____

_____

- - - - - - - - - - - - - - - - - -

because they are new combinations of ideas (symbols and concepts)

73. Robert Kennedy once said: "Some men look at things that are and ask 'why?' I dream of things that never were, and ask 'why not?'." How does this quotation illustrate the stage of formal operations? (In your own words.) _____

_____

_____

_____

_____

- - - - - - - - - - - - - - - - - -

The quotation illustrates that new solutions to problems can come from different or new combinations of ideas; that a person in the stage of formal operations is capable of <u>invention</u>, or new relationships between abstract ideas.

74. Name the four stages of cognitive development as proposed by Piaget.

1. _____ (0-2)

2. _____ (2-7)

3. _____ (7-12)

4. _____ (12 and up)

- - - - - - - - - - - - - - - - -

1. sensori-motor stage
2. pre-operational
3. stage of concrete operations
4. stage of formal operations

75. Which stage is characterized by:

(a) de-centration and ability to solve the conservation of quantity

   problem? _____

(b) the ability to generate hypotheses and new solutions to old

   problems? _____

(c) encoding problems in terms of action and visual images only?

   _____

(d) inability to solve the conservation of quantity problem?

   _____

- - - - - - - - - - - - - - - - - -

(a) stage of concrete operations; (b) stage of formal operations;
(c) sensori-motor stage; (d) pre-operational stage (also, sensori-
motor stage)

76. Piaget has not been completely clear about how children progress
from one stage to another. It may be that children simply mature
neurologically so that new perceptions and connections are now
available to them. Psychologists have noted that changes in many
areas of thinking occur around age seven (when children leave the
pre-operational stage). These changes suggest that some sort of
reorganization within the brain itself may occur around this time.
It is exciting to imagine that psychologists will someday be able to
tie these changes in thinking to actual neurological changes, but at
this point, it is only speculation.

Note: This has been an extremely simplified and abbreviated account of
a very complex theory. Piaget and his coworkers have been observing
and working with children for over forty-five years and have gathered a
wealth of information and hypotheses about how and why children develop
intellectually. In addition, many American psychologists have taken
Piaget's observations, subjected them to experimental controls, and
added new ideas and insights. If you are interested in reading about
these ideas in more depth, refer to any of the three books listed at the
end of the chapter under "Piaget and Cognitive Development."

WHAT DOES AN INTELLIGENCE TEST MEASURE?

77. Until now, we have been looking at cognitive development—systematic changes in a child's intellectual (or problem-solving) ability. In this section we want to see how this intellectual ability can be measured. However, intelligence tests are not designed to reflect age changes in intelligence; rather, they are designed to measure differences in intelligence among individuals within a given age group.

    Psychologists use intelligence tests when they want to know: (Check one.)

    _____ (a) how a child's problem-solving ability changes with age

    _____ (b) how a child compares with others in the same age group

- - - - - - - - - - - - - - - - - -

    (b)

78. The general lack of concern for the developmental or age-change aspects of intelligence is probably due to the origin of intelligence tests. In the early 1900's, Alfred Binet, a French psychologist, was asked to construct a test that would identify children who would not be able to profit from the regular school experience, namely, mentally retarded children. These children would then be removed from the public school system in order to eliminate overcrowding in the classroom.

    In other words, the original intelligence test was designed to measure: (Check one.)

    _____ (a) individual differences among children of various ages

    _____ (b) the developmental aspects of intelligence

- - - - - - - - - - - - - - - - - -

    (a)

79. Intelligence tests really measure individual differences on two points: problem-solving ability, and past learning and experience. While it would be ideal to have a test that measured only problem-solving ability, most tests also include many items such as word definitions and information questions, which rely heavily on information a child must pick up from the environment.

    Look at the following questions from intelligence tests. Which questions would you say measure past learning and experience more than problem-solving ability? Explain.

_____ (a) Which line shows the shortest way to get from A to B?

_____ (b) Who discovered America?

_____ (c) How many pounds in a ton?

_____ (d) What's foolish about this statement: "The mother fish
left the baby fish in the nest and flew away to get food."

_____

_____

- - - - - - - - - - - - - - - - - - -

(b) and (c) Of course, practically all questions are dependent in some
way on past experience. For example, in (d), a child must have had
some experience with fish and birds (seeing or hearing about them) in
order to answer correctly. Some questions, however, are more obviously dependent on past learning and experience than others.

80. Intelligence tests measure individual differences in: (Check one.)

_____ (a) problem-solving ability

_____ (b) past learning and experience

_____ (c) both

- - - - - - - - - - - - - - - - - - -

(c)

81. Most intelligence tests measure a wide variety of skills and abilities.
In some tests (for example, the Stanford-Binet), children of different
ages do not even answer the same types of questions. Four-year-olds
might be asked to copy geometric figures, complete an unfinished
figure, name simple everyday objects, or follow a series of directions. Twelve-year-olds might be asked to solve complex verbal
problems or try to repeat as many ideas as possible from an abstract
passage that has been read to them.

In other tests (for example, the Wechsler Intelligence Scale for
Children, or WISC), children of all ages are presented with the same
type of questions, but the actual questions become more difficult with
age. For example, on the WISC both five-year-olds and ten-year-olds

answer similarity items (for example, "In what way are _____ and _____ alike?"), but the similarities become increasingly difficult. Five-year-olds might be asked how <u>plums</u> and <u>peaches</u> are alike, but the examiner would stop before reaching the question of how <u>liberty</u> and <u>justice</u> are alike. Ten-year-olds would be asked all the items.

(a) Name one way in which the Stanford-Binet and the WISC differ in the questions they present to children. _____

_____

_____

(b) Do most intelligence tests measure just one skill or a variety of skills? _____

- - - - - - - - - - - - - - - - - -

(a) The Stanford-Binet does not present the same type of questions to children of all ages, whereas the WISC does. (b) variety of skills

82. Remember that in the course of cognitive development children begin to represent problems symbolically; thus their <u>abstract reasoning ability</u> increases. This increasing ability to use abstract reasoning is reflected in intelligence test items. Items at the upper age levels demand that the child use abstract reasoning; at the lower age levels the questions are concrete, not abstract.

One of the items on the Stanford-Binet is called "absurdities." The child is presented with a situation and asked "What's silly about that?" In order to perceive the absurdity in the situation the child must be able to analyze it and reason about it on an abstract level.

Would you say this "absurdity" item probably appears at the 5-year-old or the 12-year-old level of the test? Explain. _____

_____

_____

- - - - - - - - - - - - - - - - - -

At the 12-year level, because it is an item that calls for abstract reasoning; at the lower levels, the questions are concrete, not abstract.

83. In addition, tests at higher age levels rely more heavily on <u>language ability</u> than tests at lower age levels. This tendency, too, reflects actual age changes in children's abilities; ten-year-olds have a larger

vocabulary than five-year-olds and are better able to use words to help in problem-solving.

Which text would rely more heavily on language ability—a test for a 6-year-old or a test for a 12-year-old? _____

- - - - - - - - - - - - - - - - - - -

a test for a 12-year-old

Note: In practice, it is very difficult to test for abstract reasoning ability without using language. Remember that words are symbols and as such are closely related to using abstract reasoning. Chapter Five, "Language Development," will discuss at more length the relationship between language and thought.

84. If two children have similar scores on an intelligence test, it does not mean that they have correctly answered the same items. Intelligence tests contain many different types of items. Two children can obtain the same overall score but have different patterns of abilities. As we know from experience, some children are good in reading and have trouble with math, and vice versa. Yet they may both have answered the same number of items correctly on an intelligence test for their age level.

Let's say two children of the same age take the Stanford-Binet Intelligence Test. One child does particularly well in tests of abstract reasoning, but poorly in the memory tests; the other does well in vocabulary and memory tests, but poorly in abstract reasoning. Their overall scores are the same.

(a) Are the two children equally intelligent? _____

(b) Do they have the same pattern of abilities? _____

- - - - - - - - - - - - - - - - - - -

(a) yes; (b) no

85. An intelligence test score shows differences in: (Check one.)

_____ (a) overall intelligence

_____ (b) patterns of abilities

_____ (c) both of these

_____ (d) neither of these

- - - - - - - - - - - - - - - - - - -

(a)

86. Intelligence tests are frequently used as part of an overall evaluation of a child's learning ability. If a child is not doing well in school, a school psychologist may administer an intelligence test, along with some other diagnostic tests, to try to find out why. Test results are used to find any specific problem areas which the child and teacher can work on.

    If an intelligence test is being used in this way, do you think it would be important to look at the child's pattern of abilities as well as his

    total score? Explain. _____

    _____

    _____

    _____

- - - - - - - - - - - - - - - - - - - -

    Yes, because the purpose of the evaluation is to find specific problem areas; by looking at a child's patterns of abilities a psychologist can get an idea about where the child's strengths and weaknesses lie.
    (In fact, most school psychologists today are more interested in what the test shows about a child's area of strengths and weaknesses than they are in the overall score. It is this author's contention that as psychologists learn more and more about the factors that make up intelligence, the idea of a single score on intelligence will appear more and more absurd.)

87. Which of the following statements are true of intelligence tests, and which are false:

    _____ (a) Intelligence tests measure only problem-solving ability.

    _____ (b) Intelligence tests measure individual differences in intelligence among children of the same age.

    _____ (c) Intelligence tests measure a wide variety of skills.

    _____ (d) Items on an intelligence test are more abstract for older than for younger children.

    _____ (e) The original intelligence test was designed to show systematic age changes in children's intellectual development.

    _____ (f) Intelligence test scores show individual differences in overall intelligence and in patterns of abilities.

_____ (g) There is no difference between upper and lower age
             levels on how much language ability the items require of
             a child.

- - - - - - - - - - - - - - - - - -

(a) false; (b) true; (c) true; (d) true; (e) false; (f) false;
(g) false

WHAT IS AN IQ?

88. The concept of the intelligence test score itself is straightforward.
     Children are presented with many different kinds of items and attempt
     to pass them. A score is obtained based on the number of items
     passed. If two children of the same age obtain the same score, they
     are considered to have equal intelligence.

     Let's say two seven-year-olds are given the Stanford-Binet Intelli-
     gence Test; one obtains a score of 89 and the other a score of 110.

     (a) Which child is more intelligent? _____

     (b) What is the score based on? _____

- - - - - - - - - - - - - - - - - -

(a) the child who scored 110; (b) the number of items passed

89. Now, it would be expected that a ten-year-old would be able to pass
     more items than a nine-year-old; children know more as they grow
     older. However, remember that intelligence tests are designed to
     reflect individual differences at any given age level, not develop-
     mental changes in intelligence.
         Therefore, the intelligence test score must reflect not only how
     many items a child passes, but also how well the child's performance
     compares with other children the same age. An intelligence test
     score must show how well a child does, taking chronological age into
     account.

     If a six-year-old and a five-year-old pass exactly the same items on
     an intelligence test, which child should be given more credit for his

     or her performance? Why? _____

     _____

- - - - - - - - - - - - - - - - - -

The five-year-old, because he or she is younger, or because a five-
year-old would not be expected to know as much as a six-year-old.

90. Therefore, <u>intelligence</u> as it is expressed in an <u>IQ</u> (intelligence quotient) <u>score</u> means <u>intelligence compared with others of the same age group</u>. If seven-year-old Sally does better than another seven-year-old, she has a higher IQ than the other child. If, however, she does better than five-year-old Jimmy, she does <u>not</u> necessarily have a higher IQ than Jimmy. Jimmy is not expected to do as well as Sally because he is not as old and the IQ takes this age difference into account.

(a) The IQ expresses: (Check one.)

_____ intelligence compared with all other children who take the test

_____ intelligence compared with others of the same age group

(b) If a ten-year-old passes more items than a nine-year-old, does that mean the ten-year-old has a higher IQ? Explain.

_____

_____

_____

- - - - - - - - - - - - - - - - - -

(a) intelligence compared with others of the same age group;
(b) No, because the nine-year-old is not expected to do as well as the ten-year-old, or because the IQ takes the age difference into account.

91. The intelligence test score is assumed to represent the child's <u>mental age</u>—the age level at which his or her mind is operating. This mental age is not necessarily the same as actual, or <u>chronological</u>, age. If a child passes all the items that a six-year-old is expected to pass, the child's mental age is considered to be six, regardless of the child's actual age.

Say that a ten-year-old child passes all the items that a twelve-year-old normally passes.

(a) What is the ten-year-old's mental age? _____

(b) Are the child's mental age and chronological age the same?

_____

_____

- - - - - - - - - - - - - - - - - -

(a) twelve years; (b) No, the child's mental age is higher than his or her chronological age.

92. On the Stanford-Binet Intelligence Test, the items are arranged according to age level, and children are given a certain number of years and months of <u>credit</u> for the particular items they pass.

If a child receives credit on the Stanford-Binet for ten years and three months, does this score represent the child's mental or chronological age? _____

- - - - - - - - - - - - - - - - - -

mental age

93. If a child's mental age is higher than his chronological age, the child is considered to be more intelligent than a child whose mental age is the same as his chronological age.

Let's say that two children both get scores indicating a mental age of six. One of the children is five and the other is six. Which one would be considered more intelligent? _____

- - - - - - - - - - - - - - - - - -

the five-year-old

94. An intelligence test score is always expressed in terms of an IQ, or <u>intelligence quotient</u>. The IQ represents the child's mental age divided by his actual, or chronological, age. The formula for computing the IQ is:

$$\frac{\text{Mental Age}}{\text{Chronological Age}} \times 100$$

or

$$IQ = \frac{MA}{CA} \times 100$$

If a child is ten years old and gets a score of twelve years on the Stanford-Binet, the child's IQ would be: (Fill in the blanks.)

$$\underline{\hspace{1cm}} \times 100 = \underline{\hspace{1cm}}$$

- - - - - - - - - - - - - - - - - -

$\dfrac{12}{10} \times 100 = 120$

95. What is the formula for computing an IQ?

_____

- - - - - - - - - - - - - - - - - -
_____

$$IQ = \frac{\text{Mental Age}}{\text{Chronological Age}} \times 100$$

96. If a child has a mental age of eleven and a chronological age of eleven, what is the child's IQ? _____

- - - - - - - - - - - - - - - - - -

$\dfrac{11}{11} \times 100 = 100$

97. Notice that if a child's mental age and chronological age are the same, the child's IQ is exactly 100.

    (a) If a child's mental age is higher than his or her chronological age, his or her IQ is _____ than 100.
        higher/lower

    (b) If a child's mental age is lower than his or her chronological age, his or her IQ is _____ than 100.
        higher/lower

- - - - - - - - - - - - - - - - - -

    (a) higher; (b) lower

98. An IQ between 90 and 110 represents <u>average</u> intelligence for a given age; that is, most children of that age score between 90 and 110.

    (a) If a child's IQ is 123, the child is considered to be

        _____ in intelligence.
        average/above average/below average

    (b) If a child's IQ is 94, the child is considered to be

        _____ in intelligence.
        average/above average/below average

    (c) If a child's IQ is 89, the child is considered to be

        _____ in intelligence.
        average/above average/below average

    (d) If a child's IQ is 107, the child is considered to be

        _____ in intelligence.
        average/above average/below average

- - - - - - - - - - - - - - - - - -

    (a) above average; (b) average; (c) below average; (d) average

99. (a) If a child has an IQ of 100, what is the relationship between the child's chronological age and mental age? _____

_____

(b) How does the child's intelligence compare with others of the same age? _____

- - - - - - - - - - - - - - - - -

(a) The child's chronological age and mental age are the same.
(b) The child has <u>average</u> intelligence.

100. The Wechsler Intelligence Scale for Children (WISC) arrives at its scores somewhat differently. A raw numerical score is obtained based on the total number of items passed. Then that score is compared directly with the <u>average</u> score for children that age and converted to an IQ score. The interpretation of the WISC IQ is the same as for the Stanford-Binet:
   1. It is <u>as if</u> the score represents mental age over chronological age (although no mental age is actually figured).
   2. The score shows how well the child did <u>compared with others the same age</u>.

(a) Is the WISC IQ computed in the same way as the Stanford-Binet IQ?

_____

(b) Can IQ's from the two tests be interpreted in the same way? Explain. _____

_____

_____

- - - - - - - - - - - - - - - - -

(a) no; (b) Yes, the scores can both be interpreted as MA over CA, or the scores both show how well the child did compared with others the same age.

101. Explain, in your own words, why children's IQ scores remain the same although children know more as they grow older.

_____

_____

_____

- - - - - - - - - - - - - - - - -

_____

The IQ score takes a child's chronological age into account; it expresses a child's intelligence in terms of mental age divided by chronological age.

Note: Theoretically, a child's IQ score should remain constant as the child grows older (that is, both chronological age and mental age should increase at an equal rate). As we will see in the next section, however, this is not always the case, due to influences within the child's environment.

INFLUENCES ON IQ AND COGNITIVE FUNCTIONING

102. Because people generally think of the IQ as representing a pure measure of innate ability, they generally attach more importance to an IQ score than is warranted. As we have seen, some of the tests do measure various aspects of problem-solving ability; however, many items reflect past learning and experience, and thus are influenced by the environment in which the child grows up. If a child has never seen a thimble, a zebra, or a compass, and there are questions on the intelligence test about these objects, the child will score: (Check one.)

_____ (a) higher than a child who has seen these objects

_____ (b) lower than a child who has seen these objects

_____ (c) the same as a child who has seen these objects

- - - - - - - - - - - - - - - - -

(b)

103. Considering the tasks that are included on a test of intelligence, which would you say an IQ measures?

_____ (a) problem-solving ability

_____ (b) past learning and experience

_____ (c) both problem-solving ability and past learning and experience

- - - - - - - - - - - - - - - - -

(c)

104. Nearly all IQ tests are geared to the experiences of middle-class children; they assume that the children taking the tests have "typical"

middle-class backgrounds and have had similar experiences. Children who have not had these typical middle-class experiences will be at a disadvantage on any test of this kind. The terms educationally disadvantaged or socially disadvantaged have been coined to refer to children who are lacking in these typical middle-class experiences.

Suppose, for example, that the following were a question on an intelligence test:

"A Siamese and a tabby are both _____."

If a child has never seen or read about Siamese cats or does not know that some cats are referred to as tabbies, the child would have no way of answering the question.

(a) Most IQ tests require learning and experiences that

_____ children have had.
all/middle-class

(b) The term "educationally disadvantaged" refers to children who: (Check one.)

_____ have not had typical middle-class experiences

_____ have not been to school

- - - - - - - - - - - - - - - - - -

(a) middle-class; (b) have not had typical middle-class experiences

105. Activities that attempt to provide disadvantaged children with appropriate learning and experiences are called enrichment activities. Enrichment activities attempt, through class trips, classroom demonstrations, and projects, to expose the children to objects, ideas, and situations with which most middle-class children are already familiar.

A Head Start class is taken on a trip to the fire station; later in the classroom, the children look at pictures of firefighting equipment and talk about their trip. This type of experience would be part of

an _____ program.

- - - - - - - - - - - - - - - - - -

enrichment

106. Compensatory education programs such as the Head Start program generally include enrichment activities in their curriculum. Based on your knowledge of the effect of learning and experience on IQ scores, what would you expect might be one result of providing

enrichment activities in education programs for the culturally disadvantaged? _____

- - - - - - - - - - - - - - - - - - -

The children's IQ scores would improve.

107. We saw earlier that intelligence test scores are affected specifically by language ability, particularly at the upper age levels. Thus, another way to increase children's IQ scores is to increase their

_____   _____.

- - - - - - - - - - - - - - - - - - -

language ability

108. Another goal of compensatory education programs (such as Head Start) is to increase children's IQs by increasing their language ability. This task is approached in a variety of ways—individual tutoring on speech and language, encouraging the children to talk and express their ideas, reading them poems and stories, and so on. Studies of such training programs have produced conflicting results as to whether the programs have any lasting effect on IQ level. Any compensatory education program does, however, seem to produce at least temporary IQ gains, and this result is very encouraging, considering the wide variety of techniques used.

What have been the effects of compensatory education? (Check one.)

_____ (a) IQ level has been permanently affected by the programs.

_____ (b) There are conflicting results, but IQ levels appear to be at least temporarily affected.

_____ (c) There have been no permanent or temporary effects on IQ level as a result of these programs.

- - - - - - - - - - - - - - - - - - -

(b)

109. Describe two ways in which compensatory education programs attempt to increase IQ levels of disadvantaged children. _____

_____

_____

_____

- - - - - - - - - - - - - - - - - -

1. by providing experiences that most middle-class children have
    had by the time they enter school;

2. by attempting to increase language ability

110. Some specific language enrichment programs will be described in
     Chapter Five on "Language Development." One program, however,
     is particularly relevant to <u>cognitive</u> development. A study by Blank
     and Solomon reports on a program that taught preschool children to
     use language as an aid in organizing thoughts and being better able to
     deal with abstract material.*

     The children were given daily individual tutoring sessions with
     various training tasks. All the tasks, however, required the child-
     ren to understand and use language in order to deal with abstract
     problems (that is, the children had to organize and structure their
     ideas, discuss hypothetical situations, and choose among alternative
     solutions).

     What would you say was the chief focus of this program? (Check one.)

     _____ (a) getting children to talk more

     _____ (b) getting children to use language in order to deal with ab-
                  stract material

     _____ (c) providing enrichment in the form of relevant experiences

- - - - - - - - - - - - - - - - - -

     (b)

111. This program was very successful in increasing the IQ scores of the
     tutored group. Since disadvantaged children appear to be deficient
     both in language ability and in <u>abstract reasoning</u> (at least as reflected
     in school-related activities), it appears that this type of program is
     particularly well suited to their needs. Studies have shown that dis-
     advantaged children not only use <u>less</u> language, but use it less
     effectively for organizing their thinking in such a way that abstract
     reasoning is possible.

     (a) The type of program described in the Blank and Solomon study

          _____ effective in raising the IQ level of disadvantaged
          was/was not
          children.

---

*M. Blank, and F. Solomon. A tutorial language program to develop
abstract thinking in socially disadvantaged preschool children. <u>Child
Development</u>, 1968, <u>39</u>, no. 2, 379-389.

(b) What was special about the way Blank and Solomon sought to increase language ability? _____

_____

_____

- - - - - - - - - - - - - - - - - -

(a) was; (b) They focused on increasing children's language ability so that they could better deal with abstract reasoning.

112. Another program that attempts to increase children's ability to use language is Sesame Street. One of the language areas that Sesame Street attempts to teach is relational terms—"up and down," "in and out," "here and there." Use of these relational terms helps children to structure and organize material so as to understand more complex problems and relationships—in short, to use abstract reasoning.
(a) Give some examples of what is meant by relational terms.

_____

(b) How does this aspect of language increase children's abstract reasoning ability? _____

_____

_____

- - - - - - - - - - - - - - - - - -

(a) "up and down," "in and out," "here and there"
(b) It helps them to structure and organize material, or it helps them understand more complex problems and relationships.

113. The ability to use abstract reasoning is directly related to the ability to use _____.

- - - - - - - - - - - - - - - -

language

114. A third important factor influencing IQ is motivation. Most middle-class children are motivated to do well on an intelligence test. If children enter the testing situation, however, with an "I don't care" or a "Let's get this over" attitude, they will not do as well as they would have if they had a real desire to succeed on the test. For a variety of reasons, disadvantaged children generally "turn off" to school and school-related activities. They have lower aspirations

and do not see a testing situation as a chance to test their own abilities, but rather as one more excercise they are forced to go through.

(a) Compare this attitude with that of middle-class children.

_____

_____

(b) Does motivation have an effect on a child's IQ score? _____

- - - - - - - - - - - - - - - - - - -

(a) Middle-class children are usually motivated to do well on an intelligence test. (b) yes

115. Parents' attitudes and early child-rearing practices directly affect childrens' motivation. Some of these parental attitudes and practices will be discussed in Chapter Four on "Personality and Social Development." We will just note here that if parents encourage children in their earliest attempts at mastery (such as walking and talking), the children later in life will show a strong desire to "achieve" in most situations, including test situations.

Which of the following statements is true, and which is false?

_____ (a) Early child-rearing practices have little effect on ·
children's motivation.

_____ (b) Parents who want their children to have a strong desire
to achieve should encourage them in their early attempts
at mastery.

- - - - - - - - - - - - - - - - - -

(a) false; (b) true

116. While early child-rearing practices are very important in establishing a desire to achieve, it is encouraging to note that most compensatory education programs report increased motivation as an indirect result of the training. The Blank and Solomon study, for example, reports that "the most striking gains in the program were the apparent joy in learning and the feeling of mastery which the children displayed as the tutoring progressed. Both mastery and enthusiasm for learning will come only when the child can be shown how to become actively involved in the learning process."

(a) Do compensatory education programs show increased motivation

in children? _____

(b) What do Blank and Solomon believe is the way in which increased

motivation comes about? _____

_____

_____

- - - - - - - - - - - - - - - - - -

(a) yes; (b) through showing the child how to become actively involved in the learning process

117. One program, the Early Training Project at Peabody College, * in
order to strengthen its attempts to promote achievement motivation
in the children, also held weekly meetings with the mothers. At
these meetings, the mothers were encouraged to reward their children's attempts to achieve and generally to be more aware of children's
motives. Again, there were significant gains in IQ for the children
who (along with their mothers) participated. It was felt that the emphasis on promoting achievement and the involvement of the mothers
were both important factors in causing the improved IQ score.

Why were the mothers included in this program? What were they en-

couraged to do? _____

_____

_____

_____

- - - - - - - - - - - - - - - - - -

They were included in order to strengthen the program's attempts to
promote achievement motivation in the children. The mothers were
encouraged to reward their children's attempts to achieve and to be
more aware of children's motives.

118. List three important influences on children's IQ scores.

_____ ,

_____ , _____ .

- - - - - - - - - - - - - - - - - -
_____

*S. W. Gray, and R. A. Klaus. An experimental preschool program
for culturally deprived children. Child Development 1965, 36, no. 4,
887-898.

past learning and experience; language ability; motivation, or desire to achieve

119. (a) Which of the above influences is most likely to have an effect on a child's <u>abstract reasoning</u> ability? _____

(b) Which is most affected by early encouragement of attempts at mastery? _____

(c) Which is most likely to affect a child's score on information items? _____

- - - - - - - - - - - - - - - - -

(a) language ability; (b) motivation; (c) past learning and experience

SELF-TEST

This Self-Test is designed to show you whether you have mastered the chapter's objectives. Answer each question to the best of your ability. Correct answers and review instructions are given at the end of the test.

1.   How does problem-solving ability change during cognitive development? Include in your discussion the changes in mental representation and in problem-solving strategies.

_____

_____

_____

_____

_____

_____

2.   Describe the five steps generally recognized to be parts of the problem-solving process. What changes occur at each step in the course of cognitive development?

_____

_____

_____

_____

_____

_____

_____

_____

_____

_____

3.   (a) How does Piaget differ from the learning theorists in his ideas about children's intellectual development and rule-learning?

_____

_____

_____

_____

_____

(b) What are the four stages Piaget believes a child goes through in the course of cognitive development?

_____

_____

_____

_____

4. In Piaget's theory:

(a) at what stage is invention possible? _____

(b) at what stage does decentration occur? _____

(c) at what stage does a child encode mostly in terms of actions?

_____

5. What was the purpose of the original (Binet) intelligence test?

_____

_____

_____

6. Explain why a child's IQ often remains the same over the years, despite the fact that the child knows more from year to year.

_____

_____

_____

_____

7. Does an IQ represent innate problem-solving ability, or is it affected by environmental factors?   Explain.

_____

_____

_____

_____

_____

_____

8. Suppose you were designing a program for disadvantaged children—a program designed to "raise their level of cognitive functioning" (increase their IQ). What sorts of things would you include in your program? (Think in terms of the three major influences on IQ presented in the chapter.)

_____

_____

_____

_____

_____

_____

Answers to Self-Test

Compare your answers to the questions on the Self-Test with the answers given below. If all of your answers are correct, you are ready to go on to the next chapter. If you missed any questions, review the frames indicated in parentheses following the answer. If you missed several questions, you should probably reread the chapter carefully.

1. During cognitive development, children's problem-solving ability increases; they become capable of solving more abstract and complex problems. One reason for this increased problem-solving ability is that children's mental representations of the problem become more symbolic, and their strategies for solving problems become more systematic. (You may have also included a discussion how the mental representations actually change—from action images to visual images to symbols.) (Frames 7—28)

2. Encoding, memory, induction, evaluation, deduction.
Encoding: As children grow older, they are able to represent information in more abstract or symbolic ways (from action images to visual images to symbols).
Memory: Children are better able to transfer information from short-term to long-term memory.
Induction: Some people feel that, as children grow older, they are able to generate more appropriate hypotheses or possible solutions to a problem. However, it is not yet clear how inductive ability actually changes with age.
Evaluation: Children become more reflective with age; that is, they wait longer before deciding on an answer and make fewer errors.
Deduction: As children grow older, they learn from experience more rules that can always be applied in specific situations. (Frame 5(

3.   (a) learning theorists believe that children learn rules simply by
being rewarded for the right response; the rule is the learned
stimulus-response connection. Piaget believes that children's
rule-learning ability is affected by the way in which they encode
problems. (Frame 51-53)
(b) 1.   sensori-motor stage (0-2)
2.   pre-operational stage (2-7)
3.   stage of concrete operations (7-12)
4.   stage of formal operations (12 and up)
(Frame 74)

4.   (a) stage of formal operations; (b) stage of concrete operations;
(c) sensori-motor stage (Frames 53—75)

5.   To predict which children would not be able to profit from the regular
school program; to determine which children were mentally retarded;
or to show individual differences. (All are acceptable to answer 5.)
(Frames 77—78)

6.   The IQ is a way of expressing a child's intelligence in relation to
others the same age. It takes into account the chronological age of
the child, as expressed in the formula for IQ:

$$\frac{\text{Chronological Age}}{\text{Mental Age}} \times 100,$$

or, $$\frac{CA}{MA} \times 100$$

Therefore, even though the child knows more each year, the IQ will
remain more or less the same. (Frames 88—95, 101)

7.   IQ scores are affected by environmental factors. Some of the items
on the test actually measure past learning and experience. Language
ability (which is learned) is a factor in abstract reasoning, and the
test, especially at higher levels, measures abstract reasoning. IQ
is also affected by children's motivation or desire to succeed; motivation is affected by child-rearing practices. (Frames 83, 102—104)

8.   The program should include enrichment activities—providing
experiences which middle-class children have had by the time they
enter school. It should stress language learning, especially language
as applied to organizing thoughts and ideas (this helps in abstract
reasoning). Also, it could include activities involving the parents—
encouraging them to reward achievement and attempts at mastery.
(Frames 105—119)

SELECTED BIBLIOGRAPHY

Piaget and Cognitive Development

Bruner, Jerome S. et al. Studies in Cognitive Growth. New York:
    Wiley, 1967.
Elkind, David, and Flavell, John H., eds. Studies in Cognitive
    Development. New York: Oxford University Press, 1969.
Ginsburg, Herbert, and Opper, Sylvia. Piaget's Theory of Intellectual
    Development: An Introduction. Englewood Cliffs, N.J.: Prentice-
    Hall, 1969.

Steps in Problem-Solving

Guilford, J. P. The Structure of the Intellect. Psychological Bulletin,
    1956, 53, 267-293.
Kagan, J. Individual differences in the resolution of response uncertainty.
    Journal of Personality and Social Development, 1965, 2, 154-160.

IQ and Intelligence Tests

Terman, L. M., and Merrill, M. A. Measuring intelligence: A guide
    to the administration of the new revised Stanford-Binet tests of
    intelligence.
Wechsler, D. Wechsler Intelligence Scale for Children. New York:
    The Psychological Corporation, 1952.

Training Programs for Disadvantaged Children

Blank, M., and Solomon, F. A tutorial language program to develop
    abstract thinking in socially disadvantaged preschool children.
    Child Development, 1968, 39, no. 2, 379-389.
Bogatz, G. A., and Ball, S. The second year of Sesame Street: A con-
    tinuing evaluation. Vol. 1 and 2. Princeton: Educational Testing
    Service, 1971.
Gray, S. W., and Klaus, R. A. An experimental preschool program for
    culturally deprived children. Child Development, 1965, 36, no. 4,
    887-898.

CHAPTER FOUR
Personality and Social Development

This chapter focuses on how children develop a <u>social self</u>—how they learn to interact with others and to define themselves in terms of their interactions. For study purposes, the chapter is divided into two main sections. The section on <u>social development</u> deals with general developmental trends. All children, in the course of growing up, must resolve certain issues regarding their relationships with others, and there appear to be certain principles that govern when and how they resolve these issues.

The section on <u>personality development</u> focuses on some specific personality traits on which children (and adults) have been found to differ. We will review some of the data on the development of these traits in children.

OBJECTIVES

When you complete this chapter, you will be able to

- trace how a child develops a healthy personality through interaction with others;
- demonstrate the importance of the early mother–child interaction on later social and emotional development;
- describe personality in terms of traits or motives;
- show how four of these personality traits probably develop in children;
- explain the frustration-aggression hypothesis;
- describe how behavior modification works;
- summarize some things parents can do to help their children become competent and well adjusted

SOCIAL DEVELOPMENT

1. Humans are extremely social animals. What we are like as adults—
    our likes, dislikes, personality, mannerisms—are determined in
    large part by the relationships we have as we grow up. Psycholo-
    gists generally agree that in the process of social development
    children develop three qualities that are necessary in order to
    function effectively as social beings. These three elements of a
    healthy personality are:
    1. The ability to love: the capacity to form close relationships
    2. Self-esteem: a positive feeling about oneself
    3. A sense of identity: an awareness of one's own abilities,
        limits, goals, and aspirations

    Below are some generalizations that have been made about social
    development. Decide whether each statement refers to the develop-
    ment of the ability to love, self-esteem, or a sense of identity.

    _____ (a) A strong mother-infant bond assures that
                                a child will be able to establish close re-
                                lationships with others later in life.

    _____ (b) A question repeatedly asked by adolescents
                                is "Who am I?"

    _____ (c) If children are made to feel consistently
                                stupid, bad, or ugly, they will not have
                                very high opinions of themselves as they
                                grow older.

    _____ (d) The function of teen-age gangs is to help
                                give adolescents a feeling of belonging, of
                                being a certain kind of person.

    _____ (e) Without the ability to form close attach-
                                ments to other people, a person becomes
                                withdrawn, isolated, and eventually men-
                                tally ill.

    _____ (f) When parents say to a child "I like you but
                                I don't like what you did," they are allow-
                                ing the child to feel good about himself
                                while learning what is acceptable behavior.

    _____ (g) It is through our relationships with others
                                that our personality develops. If we can-
                                not relate to others, our growth as a
                                person is stunted.

- - - - - - - - - - - - - - - - - - - -

(a) the ability to love; (b) a sense of identity; (c) self-esteem;
(d) a sense of identity; (e) the ability to love; (f) self-esteem;
(g) the ability to love

2.   In your own words, describe the three elements of a healthy personality. _____

_____

_____

_____

_____

- - - - - - - - - - - - - - - - - -

1. The ability to love: the capacity to form close relationships
2. Self-esteem: a positive feeling about oneself
3. A sense of identity: an awareness of one's abilities, limitations,
goals and aspirations (what one wants out of life and is capable of
achieving)

3.   In a sense both self-esteem and a sense of identity are established
through our relationships with others. If someone we feel close to
tells us we are important, we feel important; if we find we relate
better to quiet, introverted people than exuberant, extroverted people, we have discovered something about what we are like. Given
this fact—the importance of our relationship with others—which of
the three aspects of social development would you say is probably

the most important? Why? _____

_____

_____

- - - - - - - - - - - - - - - - - -

I'd say the ability to love, because the ability to form close relationships is the basis of our developing self-esteem and a sense of
identity.

4.   Whether or not a child can form close relationships is probably the
first issue in social development which the child must deal with. In
broad terms, the developmental sequence is as follows: a child must
first learn to form close relationships with others; this must occur
in infancy if it is to occur at all. Next, a child must deal with the
issue of his or her self-esteem—whether or not a positive self-image

is developed. This process takes place during the years of early and middle childhood. Finally, in adolescence, a child concentrates on figuring out what he or she as a person wants out of life, and what realistically he or she can accomplish.

Below are the three issues in social development we have been discussing. Beside each, write in the <u>stage</u> at which each issue must be resolved (that is, infancy, early and middle childhood, or adolescence).

<u>Issue</u>   <u>Stage</u>

(a) the development of self-esteem   _____

(b) the development of the ability
      to love   _____

(c) the development of a sense of
      identity   _____

- - - - - - - - - - - - - - - - -

(a) early and middle childhood; (b) infancy; (c) adolescence

The Ability to Love

5.   The ability to love is established very early in life. It stems from the very first relationships the baby has with its mother or caretaker. From these early interactions, the child learns that the world is a warm, safe place, filled with people who care for him or her. Only if the child learns this, can the child give love to others—form close relationships—in later life.

What would you expect to be the consequences if a child were deprived of its mother or some other close caretaker at a very early age?

_____

_____

- - - - - - - - - - - - - - - - -

The child probably would not develop the ability to love, or the ability to form close relationships.

<u>Note</u>: Erik Erikson, a noted psychologist, refers to this basic ability to form close relationships as a "sense of trust." Erikson feels that if infants cannot "trust" their earliest environment to make them feel safe and secure, they will not be able to form close, trusting relationships with others in later life.

6. In the 1940's there were many studies of children who were reared in
    large institutions, or orphanages. The institutions were generally
    large and impersonal, the staff overworked, and the babies left alone
    in their cribs for long periods of time.

    Studies of infants raised in these institutions from birth have gen-
    erally shown that by the second half of the first year, these infants
    lose interest in their environment. They do not demonstrate the
    usual babbling, cooing, and crying, and they become passive, unre-
    sponsive, and indifferent to others in their environment. Moreover,
    follow-up studies of such institution-reared children showed that they
    remained emotionally isolated throughout their lives and were able to
    form only superficial relationships with others.

    (a) What do you think was lacking in these institutions that caused the
         babies to stop babbling, cooing, and crying by the sixth month or

         so? _____

         _____

    (b) If you were the director of such an institution, what would you do

         to remedy the situation? _____

         _____

         _____

         _____

- - - - - - - - - - - - - - - -

    (a) a close caretaker; someone to spend time with the infants, to
    hold them, play with them, and so on
    (b) One possibility would be to provide such caretakers—people
    hired specifically to spend time holding, playing with, and talking
    to the babies. You may have suggested others. (Fortunately, the
    trend in recent years has been away from large, impersonal in-
    stitutions and toward more personalized care.)

7. It has been show   increased "mothering" of institutionalized
    babies causes th   o become more socially responsive, not just to
    the caretakers,   to other people as well.

    Would you conclude from this that babies learn to relate only to the
    persons who care for them, or that this learning generalizes to

    other situations? _____

    _____

- - - - - - - - - - - - - - - -

    _____

This learning generalizes to other situations.

Note: Throughout this discussion on infants and how they form relationships, the term "mother" will be used most of the time for the person who is the "primary caretaker" of the child. Obviously, this primary caretaker could be a father, grandmother, nurse, governess, and so on. The term "mothering" refers to the type of care involved, not to the actual biological relationship.

8.   What is learned from the mother-child relationship generalizes to all other social relationships. Psychologists have asked: exactly what is it that a mother does in these first few months that is so important to an infant's later development?

     What is the first thing you think of that a mother does for her baby?

     _____

     _____

     _____

- - - - - - - - - - - - - - - -

If you are like most people, you probabl_____ __ ___ _ a _____r f__ding the baby, or possibly changing the baby_____ _____ the ___eta functions. If you answered "rocking," "c____ ___ "playing __ __" or the like, read on!

9.   Child psychologists once thought that the important factor in e____ __ lishing the mother-baby relationship was that the mother fed the ' when the baby was hungry. In terms of the learning model you learned in Chapter One, the baby learns to approach the mother (l for her, cry, babble, reach out) whenever the baby is hungry. In this model the stimulus is the mother, the baby's motivation is hunger, the response is approaching the mother, the reinforcement is food or milk, and what is learned is the sti___ s-response connection.

     (a) Fill in the blanks in the following le___n___ ____lel:

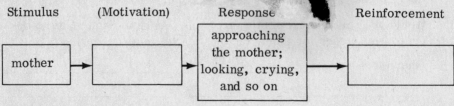

Stimulus   (Motivation)   Response   Reinforcement

| mother | | approaching the mother; looking, crying, and so on | |

(b) What is learned? _____

_____

- - - - - - - - - - - - - - - - -

(a)

Stimulus	(Motivation)	Response	Reinforcement
mother	hunger	approaching the mother	food or milk

(b) the connection between the stimulus (mother) and the response (approaching the mother)

10. From this initial experience it was theorized, the infant learned to search out the mother for all its needs, and "mother" became a source of pleasure and gratification. This response of searching out the mother generalized to searching out other people, and thus the child developed the ability to form emotional relationships.

Pro___ ___ __arry Harlow at the University of Wisconsin was not con___ ___eding was the important aspect of the mother-child relat___ ___periment he raised infant monkeys with two _ nd___ ___tes. One was a wire-mesh mother substitute ___ its "chest," which "fed" the baby monkeys ___ a terrycloth mother substitute that did not give ___w used baby monkeys because of the similarity of their ___those of human infants.

___ __eeding is the most important thing in the mother-child relation-ship, which mother substitute should the baby monkey spend the most time with? _____

- - - - - - - - - - - - - - - -

the wire-mesh substitute

n tha

11. In Harlow's ex__ em t___ t__ reverse was true. The baby monkeys spent more tin but __ he terrycloth monkey—lying on it, clinging to it, and so on. ___ __en frightened, they ran to the terrycloth figure more often than to the wire-mesh figure. In short, the soft terrycloth monkey seemed to be a source of comfort to the baby monkeys.

What does this suggest that baby monkeys need in addition to food?

_____

_____

_____

- - - - - - - - - - - - - - - - -

warmth, softness, comfort—whatever was provided by the terrycloth figure

12. Thus research has confirmed what grandparents have known since the beginning of time: that the comforting responses a mother makes— cuddling, soothing, rocking (rocking is a particularly comforting motion to both human and monkey infants)—are as necessary for a child's emotional development as food is to a child's physical development. How does the expression: "Man does not live by bread alone" reflect this fact? (In your own words.)

_____

_____

_____

- - - - - - - - - - - - - - - - -

It points out that human beings need comfort from and relationships with other people (love) in addition to food. Emotional needs are as important as physical needs.

13. While such stimulation and comfort from the mother are important in themselves, they also provide the infant with a chance to show off <u>his</u> repertoire of responses—babbling, cooing, smiling, clinging, cuddling, grasping, scanning the mother's face. Harlow and others are now speculating that babies of all species have certain responses that they must be able to exercise in order for development to occur normally. The mother or primary caretaker provides the stimulus that evokes these responses.

    The institution-reared children in frame 6 in their first few months cried continually and showed great agitation; after several months, however, they stopped this behavior and became very passive. In fact, they showed none of the usual infant behavior of cooing, crying, looking around (scanning), and moving around.

(a) From this, what responses would you guess are part of the usual repertoire of newborn infants? _____

_____

(b) Why did the institution-reared infants not demonstrate those responses? _____

- - - - - - - - - - - - - - - - - -

(a) babbling, cooing, crying, scanning, moving around, and so on;
(b) presumably because they did not have a chance to exercise those
responses (there was no caretaker-stimulus to elicit those responses)

14. It is obvious that a mother must perform the necessary caretaking
functions (feeding, bathing, and so on) in order for her infant to develop physically. She also, however, must provide for the social
development of the child. Name two ways in which a mother contrib-
utes to the social development of her infant. _____

_____

_____

- - - - - - - - - - - - - - - - -

She provides warmth, softness, comfort; she allows the infant to
exercise certain responses—babbling crying, cooing, and so on.

15. There is as yet little information on what happens when infants get
adequate care from not one but several caretakers. In the studies of
institutionalized infants, there were many caretakers (nurses); in all
cases, however, the institutions were understaffed and care was
minimal. Nurses propped bottles, changed diapers, and otherwise
interacted little if at all with their charges.

What kind of situation would be needed in order to discover the effects
of several caretakers on an infant's social development?

_____

_____

- - - - - - - - - - - - - - - - -

a situation in which the infants received adequate care from several
caretakers

16. One such situation is the Israeli kibbutz, or collective farm settlement. In the kibbutz the mothers work, and their children spend the
day in a child care center. Arrangements vary depending on the
structure of the kibbutz, but the care is generally excellent and provides much warmth and stimulation. Overall, the research on these
communal child-rearing attempts shows no damaging effects on social

development, mental health, or intelligence. Some observers have noted a tendency for the children to be more superficial in their relations with others, but there is no real agreement on this point.

Based on these results, which of the following statements would you say are probably true, and which are false?

_____ (a) The effects of having more than one caretaker (multiple mothering) are always detrimental to physical, mental, and intellectual development.

_____ (b) If infants receive adequate care, warmth, and stimulation, they are not harmed by being reared by many caretakers instead of one.

_____ (c) Given otherwise adequate care, there is little or no difference between children raised from infancy by one caretaker or many caretakers.

_____ (d) Relating to more than one caretaker in infancy <u>may</u> cause the child later in life to be less close in his relationships with others.

- - - - - - - - - - - - - - - - - -

(b), (c), and (d) are probably true, (a) is false

Note: With rapid changes in our society, the increased role of fathers in caretaking, the rise of infant child care centers, and various attempts at communal living, there is a need for research on the effects of multiple mothering. Hopefully such research will be forthcoming.

17. We have seen some ways in which the <u>mother</u> affects the mother-child relationship. However, the <u>child's</u> behavior also has an effect on this relationship.

Suppose a mother has twins. One of the twins is a quiet, contented infant; the other is colicky for the first three months. The mother spends an equal amount of time with each of them, holding, rocking, and feeding them. By the time they are three, she is upset to find that she has a closer relationship with the quiet contented twin than with the one who had been colicky.

In this case, which of the following statements is probably true? (Check one.)

_____ (a) The mother's behavior toward the two babies was the only thing which affected the relationship.

_____ (b) The difference in the babies' behavior had an effect on
the relationship.

- - - - - - - - - - - - - - - - - -

(b) is probably true

18. Exactly <u>how</u> the baby's behavior affects the mother–child relationship
is not clear. Learning theorists tend to explain it in terms of reinforcement. From the mother's point of view, caring for a colicky
baby is not a rewarding job. She gets little or no positive reinforcement from the responses of holding, feeding, and rocking. One
effect of this situation might be that gradually she would do less
<u>mothering</u> of the colicky baby, even though she still spends the same
amount of time with each baby.

In your own words, explain why the mother might do less mothering
of a colicky baby than one who is easy to handle.

_____

_____

- - - - - - - - - - - - - - - - - -

If a behavior (in this case, the mother's) is not reinforced, it tends
to decrease or stop.

19. A clinician might express it differently, saying that the mother feels
"rejected" by the infant and, in turn, shows or feels less warmth
toward the infant. But the effect would be the same.

Whether mothering is measured by some quality of "warmth" or by
"amount of mothering behavior," it can be affected by: (Check one.)

_____ (a) the mother's behavior

_____ (b) the baby's behavior

_____ (c) both mother's and baby's behavior

- - - - - - - - - - - - - - - - - -

(c)

20. All other things being equal, which type of child would you expect to
have more difficulties in later social adjustment—a colicky baby or a
noncolicky baby? Explain your answer using the idea of generalization. _____

_____

- - - - - - - - - - - - - - - - -

A colicky baby. The difficulties in the mother-child relationship might generalize to other relationships later in life. (Obviously all other things are <u>not</u> equal. Many other factors are involved in children's social development. A colicky child is not doomed to lifelong social problems!)

21. Two babies differ in their initial <u>responsiveness</u> to their environment. One baby is alert, scans the mother's face constantly while feeding, coos and babbles in response to the mother's singing and talking, and smiles easily and at an early age. The other baby seems less aware of his surroundings, is less verbal, doesn't smile as often, and is late in developing the smiling response. The mothers, however, start out as equally warm and loving toward their babies.

    (a) Would you expect the same degree of interaction between mother and baby in the two cases? _____

    (b) In which case would you expect the closest mother-child relationship? Explain, in terms of amount of mothering.

    _____

    _____

    _____

- - - - - - - - - - - - - - - - -

(a) probably not; (b) The responsive baby would probably elicit more mothering responses, and therefore we would expect the mother-child relationship to be closer.

22. In summary, it appears that the ability to love is formed

    _____ in life, _____ all other social
    early/late   interferes with/generalizes to

    relationships, is based on a _____ relationship, _____
                                  feeding/warmth   is/is not

negatively affected by multiple mothering, _____ affected by the
is/is not
behavior of the baby.

- - - - - - - - - - - - - - - - - -

early; generalizes to; warm; is not; is

23. Based on what you have just learned about the effect of the early
mother-child relationship on social development, describe an ideal
situation in which a child is likely to develop the ability to love. (In

your own words.) _____

_____

_____

_____

_____

_____

_____

- - - - - - - - - - - - - - - -

There should be an early, close relationship with one or more caretakers. There should be an opportunity for cuddling, holding, and
rocking the baby. The baby should be encouraged to respond—to
exercise his repertoire of responses. Hopefully, the baby would
by nature be an "easy" responsive child who would elicit many
mothering responses from the caretaker(s).

Self-Esteem

24. From the moment children are born they begin to develop positive
and negative feelings about themselves. Developmentally, however,
the most important ages for the development of self-esteem are early
and middle childhood—ages 3-10. These are the years during which
children concentrate on dealing with their feelings about themselves
and their self-worth.

We say that children who feel "good" about themselves and see
themselves as valued persons have high self-esteem. Children who
consistently have negative or "bad" feelings about themselves are
said to have low self-esteem.

Which of the following children would you say probably have low self-
esteem? Which have high self-esteem? (Write "high" or "low"

beside each description.)

_____ (a) Jeffrey doesn't like to try out new activities in school because he is always afraid that he won't be able to do them right.

_____ (b) Alison often provokes fights with other children; when they refuse to play with her on the playground, however, she complains that "nobody likes me because I'm ugly."

_____ (c) Charles seems to have a good idea of what his strengths and weaknesses are. Because he knows math is his difficult subject, he is not upset when he gets a "C" on a math test.

_____ (d) When David was learning to play baseball, he often threw down his bat and ran off the field crying "I'll never be able to learn, I'm just stupid."

_____ (e) Elaine has been called a born leader because she always seems so confident in whatever she is doing that she convinces others to do it too.

- - - - - - - - - - - - - - - - -

(a) low; (b) low; (c) high; (d) low; (e) high

25. Children receive feedback from their environment which tells them whether they are good and worthwhile, or bad and worthless. Obviously parents have a large effect on the child's development of self-esteem. It is from our parents that we get our earliest feedback as to what kind of a person we are. If parents act in a loving and accepting way toward us, they give us the message that we are somehow lovable.

What message would you suspect a child would receive from punishing or rejecting parents? _____

_____

- - - - - - - - - - - - - - - - -

that he or she is bad and worthless

26. Generally, it has been found that parents of low self-esteem children are either openly hostile or indifferent and inattentive in their relationships with their children. They pay little attention to their children's interests, ideas, and wishes. On the other hand, parents of high-esteem children are (as you might expect) warm and accepting toward their children. They show this by expressions of affection

and by showing an interest in the children's activities, opinions, and views.

Read the following statements about children and child-rearing practices. Label "high" those that you would expect parents of high self-esteem children to agree with. Label "low" those you would expect parents of low self-esteem children to agree with.

_____   (a) Children should not annoy their parents with their unimportant problems. Parents have more important things to worry about.

_____   (b) Children have a right to their own points of view and should be allowed to express their opinions.

_____   (c) Children are happier and better behaved if parents show an interest in their affairs.

_____   (d) The trouble with paying attention to children's problems is that they usually just make up a lot of stories to keep you interested.

_____   (e) Children should have a say in the making of family plans.

- - - - - - - - - - - - - - - - - -

(a) low; (b) high; (c) high; (d) low; (e) high (These statements were part of an actual questionnaire administered to parents in a study on self-esteem. The study is referenced at the end of the chapter.)

27. Two more factors which differentiate parents of high and low self-esteem children are the <u>amount</u> and <u>type</u> of punishment used. Parents of low self-esteem children are more likely to use punishment than reward. The punishment is harsh and frequently involves the threat of loss of love.

   Parents of high self-esteem children use rewards more often than punishment. When punishment is used, however, it is appropriate to the situation. That is, it is not unduly harsh, and it is directly related to the bad behavior. For example, if a child throws food on the floor in anger, the child might be made to clean up the mess.

Read the following statements made by parents about child-rearing and parental control.
   1. "When my child misbehaves, I say 'Some day I'm just going to leave and never come back.' "
   2. "I always say 'You can catch more flies with honey than with vinegar.' So I try to praise my child when she's doing something right rather than criticize her when something's wrong."

3. "I hit him harder and harder every time after he runs away, but it just doesn't seem to help."

4. "I say 'The punishment should fit the crime.' If a child steals something, he should take it back and apologize. That's punishment enough."

5. "Once my daughter broke a window when she got mad. I made her clean up the pieces and give us ten cents out of her allowance every week for two months to help pay for it."

6. "I got so tired of Billy not hanging up his clothes that I gave him a beating and sent him to bed."

7. "Whenever Jeremy hangs up his coat, he gets a gold star on his chart; at the end of the week, he gets a special treat if he has at least five gold stars."

8. "Giving kids rewards all the time is like bribing them to be good. The only way they'll be good is if they get punished for being bad."

9. "I tell her Daddy's just not going to love her anymore if she doesn't stop picking on her little brother."

(a) Decide whether each statement would be made by parents of low self-esteem children, or high self-esteem children. Write "high" or "low" self-esteem in the left-hand column.

(b) In the right-hand column explain the reason for your answer. These reasons are what the parent seems to believe in: punishment over reward, reward over punishment, appropriate punishment, harsh punishment, threat of loss of love.

Low or High Self-Esteem   Reason

1. _____

2. _____

3. _____

4. _____

5. _____

6. _____

7. _____

8. _____

9. _____

Low or High Self-Esteem	Reason
1. low self-esteem	threat of loss of love
2. high self-esteem	reward over punishment
3. low self-esteem	harsh punishment
4. high self-esteem	appropriate punishment
5. high self-esteem	appropriate punishment
6. low self-esteem	harsh punishment
7. high self-esteem	reward over punishment
8. low self-esteem	punishment over reward
9. low self-esteem	threat of loss of love

28. Finally, it has been found that parents of high self-esteem children are more likely to enforce rules and guidelines of behavior than parents of low self-esteem children. If children are sure ahead of time that expected standards of behavior will be enforced they are less likely to get in trouble and require punishment.

Another reason that high self-esteem children are rewarded more than punished is that they can expect their parents to

_____ established rules and guidelines.
overlook/enforce

- - - - - - - - - - - - - - - - - -

enforce

29. In each of the following pairs of parent descriptions, check the one that describes parents of high self-esteem children:

(a) _____   are hostile or indifferent

_____   are warm and accepting

(b) _____   use punishment more than reward

_____   use reward more than punishment

(c) _____   use punishment that is harsh or threatens loss of love

_____   use punishment that is appropriate to the situation

(d) _____   are consistent in enforcing rules of behavior

_____   are inconsistent in enforcing rules of behavior

- - - - - - - - - - - - - - - - -

(a) are warm and accepting; (b) use reward more than punishment;
(c) use punishment that is appropriate to the situation; (d) are consistent in enforcing rules of behavior

Note: The above discussion on parental behavior and self-esteem necessarily oversimplifies the situation somewhat. It may appear from this
discussion that either you have self-esteem or you do not have it—that
you think either positively or negatively yourself. Obviously, most of us
are somewhere in the middle; we may be fairly confident at most times,
yet go through periods of self-doubt or negative feelings. Similarly,
most parents are not wholly warm or cold, harsh or loving, accepting or
rejecting. Most of us try, with varying degrees of success to be "good"
parents and do what we think is right for our children.

30. Parents are not the only influence on children's self-esteem, although they are very important. Part of the positive and negative
feedback about a child's worth comes from that part of the environment that we call society. If society values strength above
intelligence, which child would be more likely to get positive feedback from those around him or her—a strong child or an intelligent

child? _____

- - - - - - - - - - - - - - - - - -

a strong child

31. The values of society then are also important in determining a child's
self-esteem. If a child is "different" in some way from what society
considers acceptable, the resulting feedback will probably have a
negative effect on the child's self-esteem. One of the most obvious
examples of this is the effect of prejudice on the self-esteem of
black children. Studies have shown that white and black children
both prefer white dolls over black dolls or pictures of white children
over pictures of black children. Black people are labeled with "bad"
attributes more often than white people—again, by white and black
children both.

Do these studies show that our society has a positive or a negative

effect on the black child's self-esteem? _____

- - - - - - - - - - - - - - - - - -

negative

32. It has been shown that those children who are labeled "attractive" by
our society do better in school, have fewer problems growing up,
and are generally given more positive personality attributes than
those children who are not labeled "attractive." If blacks were rated
as more attractive by society, how do you think that would affect their

self-esteem?   _____

_____

- - - - - - - - - - - - - - - - - -

It should increase their self-esteem. (Hopefully this is already happening. The emphasis on black pride, black heritage, the "black is beautiful" slogan—all these appear to be changing society's attitude on black "attractiveness." This new attitude cannot help but increase the self-esteem of black children.)

33. Another trait that affects how "attractive" a child is judged by our society is rate of maturing. It has been found that for boys, being an early maturer has a more positive effect on self-esteem than being a late maturer. It may be that an early maturer is bigger, stronger, and "tougher" than his peers, and that these traits are greatly admired by them. Or he may be better at sports and other competitive situations.

    At any rate, late-maturing boys tend to be more anxious, restless, and poorly adjusted than early maturers. In one study, late maturers revealed deep feelings of inadequacy as measured by a projective test (projective tests will be discussed further in frame 49).

All other things being equal, which would tend to have the higher self-esteem—boys who mature early or those who mature late?

_____

- - - - - - - - - - - - - - - - -

boys who mature early (Interestingly enough, this finding does not hold for girls. In fact, the reverse may be true; that is, that late-maturing girls are better adjusted than early-maturing girls.)

34. Two very clear influences on the development of a child's self-esteem are:
    1. parents
    2. _____

- - - - - - - - - - - - - - - - -

society, or the values of society, or what society considers attractive or acceptable

Sense of Identity

35. By adolescence, children have learned to relate to others in a variety
of situations. They have established certain feelings about themselves, hopefully more positive than negative. Now they must learn
who they are in relation to all the others in their environment. They
need to know what makes them unique individuals.

   We often say that adolescents go through an <u>identity crisis</u>. That
is, they are trying to sort out what <u>they</u> really think and believe and
are capable of; in doing so, they must question all that they have
read or been told.

   Often, when teen-agers talk among themselves, they ask, "Who am
I?" "What will I become?" "What will I do with my life?" By asking these questions, they are searching for: (Check one.)

_____   (a) a sense of identity

_____   (b) the ability to love

- - - - - - - - - - - - - - - - -

(a)

36. This search for identity comes at what period in a child's life?

   _____

- - - - - - - - - - - - - - - - -

   adolescence

37. A sense of identity involves knowing at least two things about yourself:
   1. your abilities: what you are and are not capable of
   2. your values: what is important and unimportant to you

Consider the following three observations about adolescents:
(a) During adolescence, young people often compare feelings about
   people and ideas with their friends.
(b) Teen-agers often go from one hobby or project to another, sometimes at a dizzying rate.
(c) Teen-agers often associate in gangs or cliques. In the safety of
   these groups, they try out many new ideas, behaviors, and beliefs.

In which of the above situations are they learning about their <u>abilities</u>?
In which are they learning about their <u>values</u>?

   _____

- - - - - - - - - - - - - - - - -

(a) values; (b) abilities; (c) values

38. In adolescence young people are learning about what is important and unimportant to them (their _____) and what they are and are not capable of (their _____).

- - - - - - - - - - - - - - - - - -

values; abilities

39. Once young people know their values and abilities, they can set realistic goals for themselves. If they do not really know their capabilities, they may for instance make unrealistic career plans which would lead to frustrations and difficulties in later life. If they adopt values which are not really what they believe, they may make many unhappy choices in their personal and emotional lives.

Why is it important for adolescents to establish a sense of identity?

_____

_____

_____

_____

- - - - - - - - - - - - - - - - - -

So that they can set realistic goals for themselves; so that they can make appropriate choices in career plans and in their personal lives

40. At this stage of development peer groups are very important. In the early years children look to their parents for approval (reinforcement) of their behavior. In adolescence approval of their peer group (gang) is more important than rewards from their parents.

Consider the following situation: A 12-year-old boy is buying his "back to school" wardrobe. His parents want him to buy shirts, crew neck sweaters, ties, and corduroy trousers. His peer group wears nothing but faded jeans and T-shirts. If allowed to choose for himself, what clothes would the boy buy? Why? _____

_____

_____

_____

- - - - - - - - - - - - - - - - - -

Jeans (prefaded, if possible!) and T-shirts, because the approval of his gang or peer group is more important to him than the approval of his parents.

41. Parents differ as to how much leeway they will allow their adolescent children, depending on their temperaments, their relationships with the child, and the seriousness of the possible consequences of the child's rebellion. (Most parents would not knowingly allow their child to "try out" robbing a bank.)

   Parents can help at this difficult stage in a child's life by clarifying (whenever possible) their own basic values, so the child will have them as a yardstick for measuring other ideas and values. Adolescence is a particularly confusing time and the values of the peer group are very attractive. If parents are themselves not clear about their own values, or if they cannot communicate these values to their child, that child as an adolescent will have a hard time resisting group pressure and sorting out his or her own values from theirs.

   Given that adolescents are often confused and likely to be strongly influenced by the views and values of their peer group, what is the most important thing that parents can do to help adolescents in their search

   for identity? _____

   _____

- - - - - - - - - - - - - - - - -

   clarify their own basic values (to themselves and to the child)

42. This section on social development has covered only the broad principles of how children learn to relate to others. One area which has not been touched on here is the area of behavioral control—how children learn certain rules for relating to one another. These controls include conscience, moral judgment, the ability to share, and so on. To learn more about how some of these behavioral controls are developed, see Chapters 5 and 6 in Social Development and Personality edited by G. C. Thompson, F. J. DiVesta, and J. E. Horrocks (New York: Wiley, 1971).

PERSONALITY DEVELOPMENT

43. In Chapter One, we said that personality development dealt with habitual ways of behaving with others. This definition is a simplified one; it is based on observations of children's behavior, making no

assumptions about what is going on inside a child. That is, it deals only with what we can _____ of a child's behavior.

                 observe/guess

- - - - - - - - - - - - - - - - -

observe

44. Generally, however, when we speak of personality, we are referring to more than just a person's behavior. We are usually also making inferences about what is going on inside the person that causes the person to behave in a certain way. Think back for a moment to the learning model in Chapter One:

| Stimulus | → | Motivation | → | Response | → | Reinforcement |

(a) Which box represents the person's observable behavior?

_____

(b) In this model, which box represents what is going on inside the person? _____

- - - - - - - - - - - - - - - - - -

(a)

| Response |

(b)

| Motivation |

45. So personality, as most people conceive of it, is similar to motivation. Remember that there are many kinds of motives that cause people to act in certain ways. When we are speaking of personality, we often use the terms traits or characteristics, with much the same meaning as motives.

Check the terms that could be used in referring to an aspect of a person's personality.

_____ (a) reinforcement   _____ (b) response

_____ (c) motive   _____ (d) trait

_____ (e) stimulus   _____ (f) characteristic

_____ (g) motivation

- - - - - - - - - - - - - - - - -

(c), (d), (f), and (g)

46. In what way are the terms <u>trait</u> and <u>motive</u> similar?

_____

_____

- - - - - - - - - - - - - - - - - - - -

They refer to inferences about what is going on inside a person or what causes a person to act in a certain way.

47. Children's behavior in relation to others includes a wide variety of responses and response tendencies. Similarly, a person's personality is composed of a large number of traits or characteristics.

Four aspects of children's social behavior that have been of great interest to psychologists are:
1. Dependent behavior: clinging, seeking attention and nurturance from others
2. Mastery and achievement: enjoyment of overcoming obstacles or mastering tasks
3. Aggressive behavior: forcefulness; imposing one's will or ideas on others, often by the use of force
4. Fear reaction: attempting to avoid or run away from situations that are perceived as dangerous or frightening

In which of the following situations is a child showing aggressive behavior? dependent behavior? mastery and achievement? fear reaction?

(a) Billy always cries and runs into the house whenever the neighbor's dog comes into the yard. _____

(b) Donna, aged 5, will not play by herself, but wants her mother to be with her and pay attention to her the whole day long.

_____

(c) Sarah picks fights with other children in school by knocking down their block structures or grabbing their toys away from them.

_____

(d) John enjoys building model planes, and always tries to make each one he does just a little better than the one he did before.

_____

- - - - - - - - - - - - - - - - - - -

_____

(a) fear reaction; (b) dependent reaction; (c) aggressive behavior;
(d) mastery and achievement

48. The four traits or motives that are related to these social behaviors
    are:
    1. dependency
    2. need for achievement or mastery
    3. aggression
    4. anxiety

    What has always made the study of personality so interesting, as well
    as so difficult, is that there is not a simple one-to-one relationship
    between a child's observable behavior and the motivation behind it.
    For various reasons, people often learn to mask their underlying
    traits or motives. For instance, clinical insight has made us aware
    that a child who is passive and withdrawn may be filled with anger
    and hostility; or that a child who strives to excel in sports may not be
    seeking mastery and achievement, but parental recognition (dependency
    motive). Traits or motives can show themselves in many different
    ways, and it is not always obvious what motive is causing a particular
    behavior.

    Regarding the relationship between traits and behaviors: if a child
    does not show obvious aggressive behavior (fighting or rough and tum-
    ble play), can we be sure that he or she is low in the trait or motive

    of aggression? Explain your answer. _____

    _____

    _____

    _____

    _____

- - - - - - - - - - - - - - - - - -

    No, because motives and behaviors do not always match; traits and
    motives can show themselves in many different ways; the child may
    be masking the aggression in some way.

49. Thus it is not always possible to infer a personality trait from ob-
    served behavior. To put it another way, it is difficult to devise
    measures that will tap underlying traits or motives. Psychologists
    sometimes use standardized behavioral measures to tap these traits;
    sometimes they rely on self-report—how aggressive or dependent the
    child says he or she is; often, projective measures are used—that is,
    traits or motives are inferred from the way a child answers certain
    questions or responds in a doll-play situation. Self-report measures

assume that a child knows his or her underlying motives and will tell the examiner the truth. Projective measures assume that the psychologist's clinical insights are sound—that certain answers or responses really do reflect anxiety or dependency, or whatever.

We have already seen how difficult it is to measure a personality trait by observing behavior. Can you see any difficulty with the other two types of measures described (self-report and projective measures)? _____

_____

_____

_____

_____

_____

_____

- - - - - - - - - - - - - - - - - -

For self-report measures: children are not always aware of how aggressive or dependent or anxious they are, or they might not want to admit it. For projective measures: psychologists' insight and therefore their inferences may not always be correct. (Actually, many projective tests are standardized; that is, psychologists give the test to many people and gather norms on how people who are judged "high" and "low" on a certain trait respond on the test. The topic of test standardization is a complex one and will not be covered here.)

50. We have seen that a personality trait can be expressed in many different ways; its expression may vary from situation to situation. However, psychologists assume that the underlying trait or motive is stable across situations. For example, a child might show aggression at home by yelling, swearing, or hitting a little brother; in school, the child might simply refuse to work and might sit sullenly at the desk. The school behavior might not even be seen as aggressive behavior. If we were able to measure the child's underlying aggression, it would be the same in both situations. Which would we say is more stable, the inferred aggression or the

aggressive behavior? _____

- - - - - - - - - - - - - - - - -

the inferred aggression

51. It is difficult to characterize behavior as aggressive or shy or dependent, because it can change from situation to situation. We assume, however, that the underlying personality trait remains

stable across _____.

- - - - - - - - - - - - - - - - - -

situations

52. Another characteristic of personality traits is that they are <u>stable over time</u>. That is, if a child is shy and withdrawn at age five, the child will tend to be a shy, withdrawn adolescent. The way in which the child expresses this trait, however, will be different at different ages. The shy five-year-old may hide behind the door when strangers come and may prefer to play alone, rather than with other children. As an adolescent the child might spend much time reading or listening to records and might avoid going to parties and meeting new people. Which would you say remains stable over time? (Check one.)

_____ (a) the trait of shyness

_____ (b) the shy behavior

- - - - - - - - - - - - - - - - - -

(a)

53. Name two ways in which personality traits or motives are <u>stable</u>.

_____, _____

- - - - - - - - - - - - - - - - - -

stable over time; stable across situations

54. Now let's look at the following research results:
   (a) Kagan and Moss (1960) found that dependency ratings of girls aged 6-10 correlated with later dependency ratings made on them as adults. (Girls rated dependent as children were also found to be dependent as adults.)
   (b) Preschoolers who show a strong desire for mastering intellectual skills tend to show this same motivation throughout their lives.
   (c) Fears of strange objects, settings, or people decline with age during the preschool years.
   (d) In one longitudinal study it was found that preschool boys who showed rage and tantrum behavior became men who angered easily and expressed verbal aggression freely.

(e) Anxiety measured by responses to a questionnaire appears to remain relatively the same over time.

Which of the above results probably demonstrate a <u>stable</u> personality trait or motive? Name the trait or motive.

_____

_____

- - - - - - - - - - - - - - - - - -

(a) dependency, (b) need for achievement and mastery, (d) aggression, (e) anxiety
The fears described in (c) do not represent a personality trait because they are not stable over time.

55. We will examine what is known about how four personality traits or motives develop—dependency, the need for achievement or mastery, aggression, and anxiety. Parental influences will be stressed, since parents are a crucial factor in determining a child's personality. However, in an age when parents tend to be extremely anxious and self-conscious about parental roles, attitudes, and child-rearing practices, it is important to emphasize that many <u>other</u> factors also influence a child's personality development.

Which of the following factors do you think might possibly have an influence on how a child "turns out"? (Check them.)

_____ (a) the family's socioeconomic status

_____ (b) the culture in which the child lives

_____ (c) heredity

_____ (d) physical appearance

_____ (e) rate of maturing

_____ (f) birth order (oldest, youngest, only child, and so on)

_____ (g) age and sex of siblings

_____ (h) friends and playmates

_____ (i) nursery school attendance

- - - - - - - - - - - - - - - - - -

<u>All</u> of the factors listed have been shown to affect various aspects of a child's personality development! It is a formidable list and merely indicates that no one factor alone accounts for a child's personality—a fact that should provide some consolation for parents who often wring their hands and say, "Where did I go wrong?"

Dependency

56. While dependency as a personality trait is not clearly defined (even in psychological literature), it implies a need for and a reliance on other people. Obviously, we are all dependent on others to some extent, more so as an infant and less so as our own abilities mature and develop. We might say that to be <u>dependent</u> is to rely on others <u>excessively</u>. Children are of necessity dependent on adults because they cannot provide for all of their own needs. When a five-year-old child asks a grown-up for help in crossing a busy street, that dependent behavior is very appropriate to the situation. A ten-year-old child, however, who demands constant attention and approval from adults is behaving inappropriately. In the second case, the dependent behavior is inappropriate or excessive, and therefore would be seen as a <u>personality trait.</u>

    Which of the following situations illustrates excessive dependency, or dependency as a personality trait? (Check one.)

    _____ (a) an infant crying for a two o'clock feeding

    _____ (b) a six-year-old clinging to mother and refusing to go to school

- - - - - - - - - - - - - - - - - -

(b)

57. Why doesn't the <u>infant's</u> dependency on mother for feeding represent a personality trait? _____

    _____

    _____

- - - - - - - - - - - - - - - - -

Because the dependency is not excessive; an infant must depend on the mother for feeding and comfort since a baby cannot take care of those things.

58. As children get older, they show their dependency in different ways. Instead of clinging or crying (as a two-year-old might do), a five-year-old is more likely to seek <u>attention</u> or <u>approval</u>. In seeking attention or approval excessively, however, the child would still be demonstrating a high degree of dependency.

    In which of the following first grade situations would you say the child is showing a high degree of dependency? (Check them.)

_____ (a) Susie primps in front of the mirror for a long time every morning. She always points out her new shoes, dress, or haircut to her teacher and classmates, and cries if they do not express approval.

_____ (b) Paul plays the class clown and is always thinking up new stunts to make the other children laugh.

_____ (c) Russ asks the teacher for help when a problem is difficult and he doesn't understand it.

_____ (d) Sara likes to sit next to the teacher, hold the teacher's hand at recess, and stay after school to help clean the erasers and blackboard.

- - - - - - - - - - - - - - - - - -

(a), (b), and (d); all three are seeking special attention and approval. (c) Does not really represent excessive dependency; it is appropriate to ask a teacher for help when needed. If the child asked for help repeatedly, on easy as well as difficult problems, it would indicate excessive dependency.

59. Let's examine how a child develops excessive dependency. If parents consistently reward a child for coming to them for help, attention, or approval, would you expect dependent behavior to increase? Why?

_____

_____

- - - - - - - - - - - - - - - - -

Yes, because reward (reinforcement) increases the probability that a response will occur.

60. Rewarding a child for dependency will increase dependent behavior. It has been shown, however, that a combination of reward and punishment for dependent behavior produces the most dependent children. Sears, Maccoby and Levin, in a study on patterns of child-rearing, found that mothers who sometimes lost their tempers and punished their children for dependency and other times responded "sweetly and nurturantly" had the most dependent children. Similarly, high dependency is produced if mothers show irritation but nevertheless give their children the attention they want.

(a) In the second example (the mother who shows irritation but gives attention), what is the reward and what is the punishment?

(b) In this situation what is it that produces high dependency

- - - - - - - - - - - - - - - - -

(a) The reward is attention, the punishment is the mother's irritation or displeasure.
(b) the combination of reward and punishment for the dependent
behavior

61. If parents were trying to make their child highly dependent, how
would they go about it? _____

- - - - - - - - - - - - - - - - -

both punish and reward the child for dependent behavior

Need for achievement and mastery

62. The need for achievement and mastery is effectively the opposite of
dependency, at least as children develop the ability to do more
things by themselves. Mastery and achievement motivation represent children's desire to deal effectively with their environment. By
age four or five, achievement motivation is negatively correlated
with dependency; that is, if a child is rated high on dependency, the
child is rated low on achievement motivation. Can you explain why
this is so? _____

- - - - - - - - - - - - - - - - -

because a child who wants to deal effectively with the environment
does not want to depend on others excessively

63. As children develop the ability to do things by themselves they must
be both encouraged to do them and rewarded for doing them. Winterbottom studied two groups of children. In one group the mothers

rewarded and encouraged their children in their early attempts to master the skills of walking and talking. In the other group, the mothers did not give the same kind of encouragement for these early attempts at mastery.

Winterbottom later tested both groups of children at 8-10 years of age. She found significant differences between the two groups on:
1. grades in school
2. achievement motivation scores on a projective test

The group that was encouraged and rewarded for mastering the skills of walking and talking scored higher in both cases.

The projective test was designed to measure the amount of motivation within the children to achieve; the school grades measured their actual achievement.

In this study, would you conclude that reinforcement of early attempts at mastery affects only <u>behavior</u>, or both achievement behavior and

achievement motivation? _____

_____

- - - - - - - - - - - - - - - - - -

Reinforcement seems to affect both achievement behavior and achievement motivation. (A later study by Rosen and D'Andrade supports this conclusion—early encouragement of achievement leads to high achievement motivation.)

64. In a lengthy and complex study, Diana Baumrind studied three different groups of children, each group representing a different personality structure. She compared the child-rearing practices of the parents of the three groups of children. One of the many questions she asked in this study was, "What are some of the child-rearing practices that appear to produce mastery and achievement motivation in children?"

One group of children in the study was rated as mature, content, independent, and self-reliant. The parents of these children encouraged and rewarded maturity as the mothers in Winterbottom's study did. In addition, the parents scored high on measures of <u>firmness of control</u> and <u>warmth</u>. In other words, they had specific guidelines and expectations for behavior and enforced them firmly, but were also warm and nurturant toward their children.

Look back to frames 24 through 29.

(a) Do the parents in the Baumrind study appear to be similar to the

parents of the high self-esteem children? _____

(b) Would you expect children high in achievement mot

be high in self-esteem? _____

- - - - - - - - - - - - - - - - -

(a) yes; (b) I would. Even though no studies have been done to show that this is the case, it is a good hypothesis.

65. Summarize the ways in which parents can increase mastery and achievement motivation in their children. _____

_____

_____

_____

_____

- - - - - - - - - - - - - - - - -

Reward and encourage early attempts at mastery.
Give specific guidelines and expectations for behavior and enforce them.
Be warm and nurturant.

Aggression

66. One of the main concerns of parents seems to be the suppression of aggressive or violent behavior. In order to control aggressive behavior, we must understand what causes it.

   Psychologists have noted that if a person is <u>blocked</u> or <u>prevented</u> from achieving a <u>goal</u>, that person often reacts with aggressive behavior. In which of the following situations would you expect the child to react aggressively? Why?

_____ (a) A child accidentally goes too near a stove and gets burned.

_____ (b) A child reaches for a toy and someone snatches it away.

_____

- - - - - - - - - - - - - - - - -

(b), because the child was blocked from achieving a goal (the toy)

67. A child sneaks into the kitchen when no one is looking and takes a handful of cookies. Just as the child is about to eat them, mother discovers the child and takes away the cookies. The child reacts by

stamping his feet, crying, and hitting his mother.

(a) What was the <u>goal</u> in this case? _____

(b) What prevented the child from achieving that goal? _____

_____

(c) What kind of behavior resulted? _____

- - - - - - - - - - - - - - - - - -

(a) eating the cookies; (b) mother taking away the cookies;
(c) aggressive behavior

68. Often what is blocking the child from achieving a goal is simply that the goal or expectation is too high. A child of average intelligence who expects—or is expected—to get all A's in school may not be able to achieve that goal. What would you expect might be one result of

such a situation? _____

- - - - - - - - - - - - - - - - - -

The child might show aggressive behavior.

69. Sometimes parents find it difficult not to intervene when children try to do things for themselves. For instance, a father might take the spoon away from an infant who is attempting to feed herself (although perhaps making a mess in the process!) and begin to feed the child himself. If parents did this repeatedly, would you expect the child to

develop a lot of aggression? Explain. _____

_____

_____

- - - - - - - - - - - - - - - - - -

Yes, because the child would be repeatedly prevented from achieving a goal—in this case, feeding herself.

70. Thus, a child can be blocked from achieving a goal either by parents who <u>expect</u> too much or by parents who <u>protect</u> too much, and aggression can result. Consider the following cases.
1. Chris is not a very well-coordinated child, but he got on the Little League team because his father is the coach. He leads the league in strikeouts.
2. Chris's sister, Ginny, wants to play hockey; she tries to sneak off with the hockey stick when she goes skating, but her mother

always takes it away from her. Her mother feels that hockey is too dangerous.

3. Henry's mother will not let him play outside in the winter because he might catch a cold. He got a new sled for Christmas from his grandparents and wants to try it out.

4. John, 15, is a mediocre student, but his father, a Harvard alumnus, is going to try to get John into Harvard. John's rebelliousness is beginning to be a concern to his parents.

5. Harvey is continually bringing home stray dogs and cats to keep, but his parents say he cannot keep any of them. Animals carry germs and it is "unhealthy" to have them around children.

(a) In which of the cases would you say the parent is too protective?

_____

(b) In which cases would you say the expectations are too high?

_____

- - - - - - - - - - - - - - - - - -

(a) In cases 2, 3, and 5, the parents are probably being too protective. (b) In cases 1 and 4, the parents' expectations are probably too high.

71. Some psychologists maintain that being blocked from achieving a goal always leads to increased aggression, whether the aggression is expressed or not. If the little girl in frame 69 reacted by pounding the tray with her fists, these psychologists would say she reacted to the situation with aggression. Suppose, however, she reacted by putting her fingers in her mouth or crying. Would these psychologists still say the situation increased her aggression? Why?

_____

_____

_____

- - - - - - - - - - - - - - - - -

Yes, they maintain that being blocked from achieving a goal always leads to aggression, even if the aggression is not expressed openly.

72. These psychologists say that being prevented from achieving a goal leads to frustration and this, in turn, always leads to aggression. They refer to this process as the frustration-aggression hypothesis.

From what you know so far, complete the following diagram of the frustration-aggression hypothesis.

Being blocked from a goal	leads to →		leads to →	

- - - - - - - - - - - - - - - -

Being blocked from a goal	leads to →	Frustration	leads to →	Aggression, or aggressive behavior

73. The generalization that being prevented from achieving a desired goal always leads to aggression, whether or not expressed, is called the

_____ hypothesis.

- - - - - - - - - - - - - - - -

frustration-aggression

74. In your own words, summarize the frustration-aggression hypothesis.

_____

_____

_____

_____

- - - - - - - - - - - - - - - -

The hypothesis states that frustration, or being blocked from a goal, <u>always</u> leads to aggression (aggressive motivation), whether or not that aggression is openly expressed.

75. Let's look at what influences aggressive <u>behavior</u> and then relate this information to what is known about the trait or motive of aggression. We know that once an aggressive act occurs, it is more likely to be repeated if it is rewarded. We say then that aggressive behavior is, at least in part, a <u>learned</u> response.

Let's say Harry is told he cannot go to the baseball game after school. He reacts by slamming his bat on the floor, yelling, and crying. His mother says, "Oh all right, go ahead."

(a) What was the cause of the aggressive behavior? _____

_____

(b) Was the aggressive behavior rewarded? _____

(c) Is the aggressive behavior more or less likely to occur again?

_____

- - - - - - - - - - - - - - - - - -

(a) being blocked from achieving a goal (going to the baseball game);
(b) yes; (c) more

76. When parents "give in" to temper tantrums they are rewarding the child for aggressive behavior. The child "learns" to react aggressively whenever he cannot have his way. If, in the previous example, the mother had simply ignored the child's behavior or sent him to his room, would the aggressive behavior be more or less likely to occur? Explain. _____

- - - - - - - - - - - - - - - - - -

Less, because she did not reward it.

77. Because children's aggressive behavior increases if it is reinforced and decreases if it is not reinforced, we say that aggressive behavior is, at least to some extent, _____.

- - - - - - - - - - - - - - - - - -

learned

78. Parents have long noticed that their children become more aggressive upon entering nursery school. Why is this so? From observation and study, it appears that, in group situations, children reinforce each other's aggressive behavior. Children who are passive in the nursery school group get their toys taken away from them, and find themselves last to be served at snack time. Aggressive behavior "pays off" in group situations.

From studies of children in nursery school, it appears that in group situations aggressive behavior tends to be _____.

                                                    ignored/reinforced

- - - - - - - - - - - - - - - - - -

reinforced

79. In a nursery school setting, it is also more likely that passive children will be subject to more frustrating situations than at home.
Their toys will be taken away, they will be prevented from eating
until after all the other children have eaten, and so on. Thus, when
teachers force aggressive children to act more cooperatively, they

might also be minimizing _____.

- - - - - - - - - - - - - - - - - -

frustration

80. There are really two ways then, in which parents and teachers can
intervene to decrease aggressive behavior in children. Given that
frustration can lead to aggressive behavior and that reinforcement
increases aggressive behavior, what are two ways in which parents

and teachers can intervene? _____

_____

_____

- - - - - - - - - - - - - - - - - - -

Minimize frustrations or frustrating situations; do not reward or
reinforce aggressive behavior.

81. Are frustration and reinforcement the only factors that increase
aggressive behavior in children? No, according to Albert Bandura,
a psychologist at Stanford University. He has shown that children
will also <u>imitate</u> aggressive models. He observed two groups of
children in a play situation. One group had previously seen a film
showing other children behaving aggressively in that same situation
(pummeling, punching, and throwing a punching clown); the other
group had not seen the film. Bandura found that those children who
had seen the film behaved more aggressively in the play situation
than those who had not seen the film. He concluded that aggressive

behavior can be increased through _____ of aggressive models.

- - - - - - - - - - - - - - - - -

imitation

82. There is a continuing debate over the effect of television violence on
children's behavior. Some people say it has no effect; others such
as the Newton, Massachusetts-based group, "Action for Children's

Television," believe that it does cause children to behave more aggressively.

Which argument is supported by the results of Bandura's study?

_____

_____

- - - - - - - - - - - - - - - - - -

the argument that television violence does cause children to behave more aggressively

83. Bandura's results showed that: (Check one.)

_____ (a) Children's aggressive behavior can be increased through reinforcement.

_____ (b) Children only show aggression when they are frustrated.

_____ (c) Children's aggressive behavior can be increased if they are shown aggressive models.

- - - - - - - - - - - - - - - - - -

(c)

84. Three factors that have been shown to cause aggressive behavior in children are:

1. _____

2. _____

3. _____

- - - - - - - - - - - - - - - - - -

1. frustration (or being prevented from achieving a goal)
2. reinforcement
3. imitation of aggressive models

85. Of the three factors listed above, it is hypothesized that one of them increases the <u>motive</u> of aggression, even if no aggressive behavior

is shown. Which one? _____

- - - - - - - - - - - - - - - - - -

frustration

_____

86. Based on the previous information, what are three actions parents and teachers can take to minimize aggressive behavior in children?

_____

_____

_____

- - - - - - - - - - - - - - - - -

Minimize frustration; do not reward or reinforce aggressive behavior; try to prevent children from seeing examples of aggressive models (either on television or from adult behavior).

87. What are two ways to minimize children's frustration?

_____

_____

- - - - - - - - - - - - - - - - -

Set realistic goals and expectations; don't be too protective of the child.

88. As we all know, it is impossible to provide a totally frustration- and aggression-free environment for a child. Can you imagine a child learning to walk without falling down a few times? Or a mother who is not going to "frustrate" her child's attempts to eat a box of cookies just before dinner? Frustrations are a part of normal growth and development and group living. Similarly, we cannot totally isolate our children from the world and its violence. The nightly news alone provides its share of aggressive models.

All parents have to deal with aggressive acts on the part of their children. Jennifer cannot be allowed to hit her younger brother with a truck no matter how "frustrating" he may be.

Parents generally use some form of punishment for aggressive behavior. As we know from experience it generally works; the punishment generally prevents the child from repeating the aggressive act. According to the frustration-aggression hypothesis though, the punishment would also cause frustration in the child.

(a) Explain why punishment would also cause frustration.

_____

_____

(b) Would the frustration-aggression hypothesis predict a resulting

_____

increase or decrease in aggression within the child?

_____

- - - - - - - - - - - - - - - - - -

(a) Punishment prevents the child from achieving a goal (hitting her brother, pulling the cat's tail); therefore, it causes frustration.
(b) The frustration-aggression hypothesis would predict an increase in aggression.

89. Thus, we would expect punishment to decrease aggressive behavior, but to increase aggressive motivation. Indeed, that effect was neatly demonstrated by Robert R. Sears in 1951. He divided a group of preschool children into three groups: 1. Those whose parents punished very little for aggression; 2. those whose parents were moderately punitive; 3. those whose parents were highly punitive. He then observed the three groups in a school setting. The moderately punished group showed the most aggression; the mild and severe punishment groups both showed significantly less aggression than the moderately punished group. We can represent the results this way:

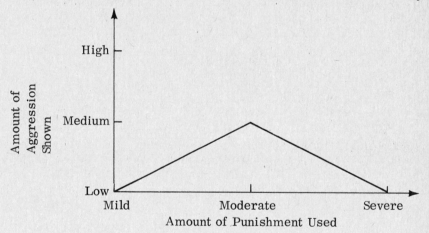

Amount of Punishment

(a) According to these results, can you say that severe punishment does decrease aggressive behavior in children? _____

(b) Does severe punishment decrease aggressive behavior more than moderate punishment? _____

(c) Does severe punishment decrease aggressive behavior more than mild punishment? _____

- - - - - - - - - - - - - - - -

(a) yes; (b) yes; (c) no—they work equally well

90. In a later doll–play situation, however, the severely punished group showed significantly <u>more</u> aggression than either of the other two groups. Graphically, the results could be represented this way:

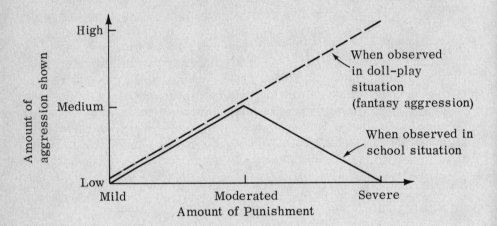

(a) In the doll–play situation the severely punished group showed

    _____ aggression.
    high/medium/low
(b) In the school situation, the severely punished group showed

    _____ aggression.
    high/medium/low

- - - - - - - - - - - - - - - -

(a) high; (b) low

91. Sears called the aggression shown in the school situation <u>overt</u> <u>aggression</u>; he called the aggression shown in the doll–play situation, <u>fantasy aggression</u>. Thus, he concluded that severe punishment for

aggression decreases _____ aggression but increases

_____ aggression.

- - - - - - - - - - - - - - - -

overt; fantasy

92. Fantasy aggression is believed to be a measure of aggressive motiva-
    tion, or the amount of aggression within the child. Does severe
    punishment decrease the amount of aggression within the child or just

    the aggressive behavior? _____

- - - - - - - - - - - - - - - - -

    just the aggressive behavior

93. In fact, severe punishment actually increases the amount of fantasy
    aggression, while mild punishment decreases both overt and fantasy
    aggression. Given that mild and severe punishment both work equally
    well in controlling children's aggressive behavior, which do you think
    is the preferable method of control? Explain.

    _____

    _____

    _____

    _____

- - - - - - - - - - - - - - - - -

    Mild punishment, because mild punishment decreases both overt and
    fantasy aggression, while severe punishment actually increases the
    amount of fantasy aggression (or aggressive motivation).

Note: The debate will continue to rage over whether punishment is
necessary at all—even mild punishment. This is the gray area in which
psychology can really give no answers. The answers depend on the individuals involved, their temperaments, relationships, attitudes, and
so on. It should be noted, however, that aggressive behavior is frequently rewarding in itself. A child feels "good" about punching her
brother who just broke her truck. Perhaps some mild form of punishment is necessary to counteract this "good" feeling on the part of the
child.

94. Summarize the Sears experiment. Explain in your own words exactly
    what it demonstrated about the relationship of punishment and aggres-
    sion. Be sure to discuss both overt and fantasy aggression.

    _____

    _____

_____

_____

_____

_____

_____

_____

_____

_____

_____

_____

- - - - - - - - - - - - - - - - -

Sears studied three groups of children—one group whose parents punished very little for aggression, a group whose parents were
moderately punitive, and a group whose parents were highly punitive.
The highly punished group and the group that received little punishment for aggression were <u>both</u> low on overt aggression (as shown in a
school setting). The moderately punished group showed the most
aggression in this setting. However, when fantasy aggression was
studied (that is, aggression shown in a doll-play situation), the mildly-
punished group continued to show the least aggression, while the
severely punished group showed <u>more</u> aggression than either of the
other two groups. Sears concluded that severe punishment decreases
the amount of aggressive behavior but <u>increases</u> the amount of fantasy
aggression (aggressive motivation).

95. Summarize four ways in which parents and teachers can minimize
aggression and aggressive behavior in children.

_____

_____

_____

_____

- - - - - - - - - - - - - - - - -

Minimize frustration; minimize children's exposure to aggressive
models; do not reward aggressive behavior; use mild rather than
severe punishment (if any) for aggressive behavior.

_____

Anxiety

96. While fears and fear reactions change with age and are quite unpre-
dictable, anxiety as a personality trait tends to be fairly stable over
time and across situations. While there have been some studies
showing broad developmental changes in children's fears and fear
reactions, more research has been done on children's anxiety. Why
do you suppose this is so? (If you're not sure, refer to frames 50

through 53.) _____

_____

_____

- - - - - - - - - - - - - - - - - -

Because anxiety is stable over time and across situations;
psychologists are interested in traits that are stable.

97. The trait of <u>anxiety</u> is very close in meaning to the term <u>worry</u>. An
anxious child worries about getting bad marks, being hurt, or being
punished. We know from experience that some people worry more
than others. We assume that people who worry a lot have high

_____.

- - - - - - - - - - - - - - - - - -

anxiety

98. When we worry, we <u>anticipate</u> that something bad will happen to us,
even if it has never happened before. An anxious child may never
have been bitten by a dog, but anticipates that it might happen; the
child may never have had a poor report card, but anticipates that it
might happen in the next marking period.

Read each of the following statements about worry or anxiety. Label
each one "true" or "false."

_____ (a) When we worry, we remember bad things that have
             happened to us.

_____ (b) When we worry, we anticipate that something bad will
             happen to us.

_____ (c) We can worry about something that has never happened
             to us.

- - - - - - - - - - - - - - - - - -

(a) false; (b) true; (c) true

99. Even though the "bad" things have not actually happened, the worry
may not be unrealistic. A vicious dog could suddenly appear on the
block and bite the child. In the next marking period, the child may
have trouble understanding some new math concepts and receive a
bad mark in math.

Label each of the following statements "true" or "false."

_____ (a) Worries are always unrealistic.

_____ (b) Worries are always realistic.

_____ (c) Worries can be either realistic or unrealistic.

- - - - - - - - - - - - - - - - -

(a) false; (b) false; (c) true

100. There is evidence, however, that many worries of children are
unrealistic. In 1933, Jersild, Markey, and Jersild did a study in
which they asked 400 children, aged 5 to 12, what they were afraid
of. About 20 per cent of the answers dealt with fear of the dark,
fear of being alone, and fear of imaginary creatures. Many of
their fears represented remote dangers, such as wolves, tigers,
criminals, and so on.

(a) Is it more realistic for an urban American child to worry about

being bitten by a dog or by a tiger? _____

(b) Since urban American children worry a lot about tigers and
imaginary creatures, we say that many of their worries are

_____.

realistic/unrealistic

- - - - - - - - - - - - - - - - -

(a) being bitten by a dog; (b) unrealistic

101. Psychologists generally agree that what anxious children actually
fear is not the tiger or the imaginary creatures, but their own
feelings. We have seen that anxious children <u>anticipate</u> many difficulties in their everyday lives, as if they feel they will not be
able to cope with situations that come up, and that somehow they
will fail. Possibly, then, anxiety stems from the child's anticipa-

tion of _____.

worries/failure

- - - - - - - - - - - - - - - - -

failure

102. Which of the following would probably lead a child to anticipate failure?

_____ (a) parents who are warm and nurturant

_____ (b) parents who have high expectations

_____ (c) parents who are permissive

- - - - - - - - - - - - - - - - - -

(b) parents who have high expectations

103. Thus, children's fear of failure may actually be a fear of not being able to live up to their parents' expectations. Parents' standards of moral behavior, of school achievement, or of athletic powers may be too high to meet. Refer for a moment to frame 68. When parental expectations are too high, what does the frustration–aggression hy-

pothesis predict will always result? _____

- - - - - - - - - - - - - - - - -

aggression

104. So we would expect the child who is high in anxiety to also be high in aggression. Seymour Sarason, a psychologist who has studied anxiety extensively, believes that anxiety is the result of a complex interaction between high expectation of parents, aggression, and dependency. The child with high expectations builds up aggression against his parents but cannot express it because of high dependency. Thus, anxiety develops.

According to Sarason a child with very high parental expectations should be high in which of the following traits?

_____ (a) dependency

_____ (b) aggression

_____ (c) anxiety

- - - - - - - - - - - - - - - - -

all three of them

105. It has been shown that parents have higher expectations for their oldest child than for those born later. Given this fact, which children

would you expect to be higher in anxiety—first-borns or later-borns?

_____

- - - - - - - - - - - - - - - - - -

first-borns

106. First-born children (particularly boys) have been shown to be more
anxious, have more "nervous symptoms," and are overrepresented
among patients at child guidance clinics. Would you also expect
these children to be higher in aggression and dependency? Explain,

according to Sarason's explanations. _____

_____

_____

_____

- - - - - - - - - - - - - - - - - -

Yes, because anxiety probably is the result of a complex interaction
of high parental expectations, aggression, and dependency. (First-
born children have been found to be high in anxiety and dependency.
They are low in aggressive behavior but probably high in aggression,
or anger.)

107. Anxiety is usually measured by means of self-reports of behavior and
attitudes. These are questionnaires that present a wide variety of
situations and ask children if they ever worry about them. Generally,
the more "yes" answers, the higher the anxiety.

Let's say that an anxiety scale for children contains 30 items. If one
child answers "yes" to 10 items, and another child answers "yes" to
20 items, which child has the higher anxiety?

_____

- - - - - - - - - - - - - - - - - -

the child who answers "yes" to 20 items

108. Anxiety scores on these tests have been correlated with many other
variables. One such variable is learning. In contrast to low-anxiety
children, high-anxiety children do better on simple learning tasks
but worse on complex learning tasks.
     In a typical study, the experimenter might take two groups of
children, a high-anxiety group and a low-anxiety group. Assume the

groups are comparable in all other respects. The experimenter
gives each group two learning tasks:

Task A: The children must learn to press a buzzer whenever a
green light comes on.

Task B: The children must learn a code in which each letter of the
alphabet is represented by a different symbol.

(a) On which task(s) would the high-anxiety children probably do

better? Why? _____

_____

(b) On which task(s) would the low-anxiety group probably do better?

Why? _____

_____

- - - - - - - - - - - - - - - - - - -

(a) The high-anxiety group would probably do better on the first
task, because it is a simple learning task.

(b) The low-anxiety group would probably do better on the second
task because it is a complex learning task.

109. In school situations, most learning is fairly complex, involving
ideas, concepts, and abstract thinking. It would be expected, then,
that the trait of anxiety would hinder children's performance in
school.

Actually, it appears that children with a <u>moderate</u> amount of
anxiety do best overall in school. Apparently, there must be some
"push" to achieve, or children will not really make an effort. However, too much anxiety interferes with learning.

To summarize:

(a) Children with _____ anxiety do better on simple
              high/medium/low
     learning tasks.

(b) Children with _____ anxiety do better on complex
              high/medium/low
     learning tasks.

(c) Children with _____ anxiety do best in school.
              high/medium/low

- - - - - - - - - - - - - - - - - -

(a) high; (b) low; (c) medium

110. If anxiety becomes too strong, people have great difficulty dealing with any task at all. People with severe anxiety are often afraid even to leave the house. Often, however, people with a great deal of anxiety learn to lessen this anxiety, at least temporarily, so that they can continue to function in the frightening or anxiety-producing situation. These techniques for lessening anxiety are called <u>defense mechanisms</u>.

   There are many kinds of defense mechanisms. Let's look at one example: a child has a frightening experience one summer at the lake and nearly drowns. His parents expect that he will always remember the lake and be afraid of it (or of water). Next summer, they return to the lake; the child insists he has never been there before. He has forgotten it entirely.

   (a) Why did the child "block out" or forget the frightening

   experience? _____

   _____

   (b) What do psychologists call such techniques for lessening anxiety?

   _____

- - - - - - - - - - - - - - - - - -

   (a) Because the child had to return to the lake; the child had to deal with the frightening situation; (b) defense mechanisms

111. Why do highly anxious people revert to the use of defense mechanisms?

   _____

   _____

- - - - - - - - - - - - - - - - -

   in order to lessen their anxiety so that they can function in the anxiety-producing situations

112. All children use defense mechanisms to some extent. For example, most children at one time or another try to explain their "bad" behavior by saying "someone else" made them do it:

   "Susie pushed me and that's why I knocked over the blocks."
   "But Joe made me take the quarter that was on the table."

   This blaming of others is not always a lie; very often, the child actually feels or believes that he or she is not to blame for what happened. A highly anxious child might use this defense mechanism frequently, thus relieving his or her anxiety over not living up to expectations.

Explain how this defense mechanism—putting the blame on someone else—helps relieve a child's anxiety. _____

_____

- - - - - - - - - - - - - - - - - - -

If the child is not responsible for the "bad" behavior, he or she need not feel anxious about it.

113. In the above situation, what do you think the child is really afraid of? (Check one.)

_____ (a) being bitten by dogs

_____ (b) not living up to parents' expectations

_____ (c) the "bad" behavior

- - - - - - - - - - - - - - - - - -

(b)

114. (a) What is a defense mechanism? _____

_____

(b) Do only highly anxious people use defense mechanisms?

_____

- - - - - - - - - - - - - - - - -

(a) a technique for lessening anxiety; (b) No, we all use them from time to time.

115. As a parent, what can you do to help prevent your child from developing a lot of anxiety? _____

_____

_____

- - - - - - - - - - - - - - - -

Set realistic goals and expectations; do not set standards of behavior that are too high.

Behavior Modification

116. Behavior modification is a technique for modifying certain behaviors by applying knowledge of reinforcement principles. Teachers or others who work with children can use this technique to help eliminate disruptive or maladaptive behavior (for example, aggressive behavior) and to promote adaptive behavior, such as cooperation or creativity.

     In theory, the technique is very simple (though perhaps not always so easy in practice!). Recall that if a response is reinforced, it tends to be repeated; if there is no reinforcement, the response tends to drop out.

     Let's take the case of children's attention-getting behavior in the classroom. If teachers want to keep children from acting this way, what should they do whenever an attention-getting response is made?

     _____

     - - - - - - - - - - - - - - - - -

     not reinforce it, or stop rewarding the dependent response

117. Take the case of Paul, the class clown (example (b), frame 58).
     (a) What is rewarding or reinforcing to Paul in this situation?

     _____

     (b) What would decrease Paul's attention-getting behavior in this

     situation? _____

     _____

     - - - - - - - - - - - - - - - - -

     (a) the laughter of the other children; (b) if the other children didn't laugh or pay attention to his clowning

118. Let's say Paul's teacher takes the other children aside and explains to them that she does not want Paul's clowning to continue because it is disruptive to the class. By using a great deal of skill, she is able to convince the other children not to reinforce Paul's disruptive behavior. After a week of this, Paul stops clowning; however, he begins a series of other behaviors to attract the children's attention. He raises his hand repeatedly to ask trivial questions; he breaks his pencil frequently so that he must get up to sharpen it; he pulls the erasers off his pencils so that he must ask to borrow an eraser from

one of his neighbors. What would you say about Paul's attention-getting behavior? (Check one.)

_____ (a) His attention-getting behavior has disappeared.

_____ (b) He has substituted a different attention-getting behavior for the old, nonreinforced one.

- - - - - - - - - - - - - - - -

(b)

119. So, when Paul's teacher stops reinforcing his old, undesired behavior, she must begin to reward him for the specific behavior that she wants to take its place. For example, she might want him to sit quietly at his seat and work by himself. What might she do to get him to increase this particular behavior? (In your own words.)

_____

_____

_____

_____

- - - - - - - - - - - - - - - -

The teacher would reward or reinforce it. She might stop by his seat when he is working quietly by himself and say, "That's good work, Paul" or "I like the way you're working so quietly by yourself."

120. It has been found that attention of any kind is generally rewarding to children. In Paul's case, it is particularly rewarding because of his high level of dependency. If Paul modifies his behavior in this situation, he is still behaving in a certain way in order to get attention; he is simply behaving in a more acceptable way.

(a) Which would you say has changed in this situation—the response or the reinforcement? _____

(b) Can the teacher assume she has decreased Paul's underlying dependency? _____

- - - - - - - - - - - - - - - -

(a) the response; (b) no

121. In other words, Paul's motive probably remains unchanged. He is still doing things for the same reward (attention), which means that his motive is probably still _____.

- - - - - - - - - - - - - - - -

dependency

122. The technique of behavior modification makes no assumptions about the child's personality or motivation. It is simply a way of applying the principles of reinforcement to modify_____.
                                                      behavior/personality traits

- - - - - - - - - - - - - - - -

behavior

123. In order to increase acceptable behavior using behavior modification, you reward the _____ behavior and do not reward
                        acceptable/unacceptable

the _____ behavior.
        acceptable/unacceptable

- - - - - - - - - - - - - - - - -

acceptable; unacceptable

Note: Notice that there has been no mention of punishment in this discussion. The effectiveness of punishment, even a mild one such as criticism from the teacher or staying after school, is still open to question. Generally, it seems that behavior modification works best using only positive reinforcement. (Teachers, however, continue to use negative reinforcement, probably more to satisfy their own needs than because it works to control or modify children's behavior.)

124. (a) How would a person set about changing someone's behavior by means of behavior modification? _____

_____

_____

(b) Does behavior modification also attempt to change a person's motives? _____

- - - - - - - - - - - - - - -

(a) Reinforce the desired or acceptable behavior and do not reinforce the unacceptable behavior; (b) no

A Note on Child-Rearing Studies

125. This chapter has presented some data from large-scale studies on the effects of various child-rearing practices. Some of these studies are listed at the end of this chapter. One of the major difficulties in trying to pin down exactly what parental behaviors, characteristics, and attitudes cause what personality traits and behaviors in children is that parent-child interactions are extremely complex. Parents may be warm but at the same time rigid in their methods of control. We might expect that a permissive parent is warm and accepting, but sometimes permissiveness is the result of neglect and rejection, where the parents just don't care what the child does.

The studies do seem to show, however, that children with overall "good" adjustment—children who do not have difficulties in their social development—have parents who are warm and accepting, who care about their children and let them know it.

For example, in some of the earlier studies, various specific child-rearing practices, such as age and severity of weaning, bottle-feeding versus breast-feeding, and age and severity of toilet training were thought to cause certain difficulties in later adjustment. In all of these studies, however, it appears that the factor of parental <u>warmth</u> or <u>coldness</u> may be the crucial one in determining whether or not children will have difficulties in their social adjustment.

Say two mothers both wean their babies at an early age. One mother does so because she feels the baby is ready for it. She continues to hold the baby often, cuddling and rocking the infant. The other mother feels no great warmth toward the infant. The reason she weans early is because she is anxious to be rid of the added burden of breast-feeding.

(a) Which would you expect to be the more important factor in determining how the two babies develop—age of weaning or parental

warmth? _____

(b) All other things being equal, which child would you expect to be

the more well-adjusted of the two? _____

_____

- - - - - - - - - - - - - - - - -

(a) parental warmth; (b) the child whose mother continued to hold, cuddle, and rock the baby. (In later life, this parental warmth may be shown by signs of approval or other indications that a child is loved and accepted for himself.)

126. As children grow older, it is also very important to encourage them to act independently, to make decisions on their own, based on their age and ability. Studies show that, in order for children to become competent and mature, they must not be <u>overprotected</u>; that is, they must be allowed the freedom to make decisions and even to make mistakes.

When parents are cautioned not to be overprotective, they are advised to: (Check one.)

_____   (a) allow their children to make all their own decisions

_____   (b) allow their children to make as many decisions as possible, based on their age and ability

- - - - - - - - - - - - - - - - - -

(b)

127. Finally, all the child-rearing studies seem to indicate that parents must be <u>consistent</u> in applying and enforcing rules. Parents of competent, well-adjusted children set very clear rules and are consistent in enforcing those rules. Thus, children know the limits within which they are free to move around. If parents are not consistent, children are never sure whether any new behavior is acceptable or unacceptable; therefore, they are afraid to try new things even if encouraged.

Even when children have parents who are warm and encourage independence, these children may not feel free to try new things. What is it that the parents may be failing to provide for these children?

_____

- - - - - - - - - - - - - - - - -

consistency in applying and enforcing rules

128. Explain how inconsistency in applying and enforcing rules may prevent children from being free to try new things. (In your own words.)

_____

_____

_____

- - - - - - - - - - - - - - - - -

_____

The children may not be sure whether any new behavior is acceptable or unacceptable, so they may be afraid to try new things.

129. From various child-rearing studies, it appears that there are three things parents can provide for their children in order to encourage healthy personal and social adjustment. These three factors are:

   1. _____

   2. _____

   3. _____

- - - - - - - - - - - - - - - - - -

1. warmth and nurturance
2. encouragement of independence
3. consistency in applying and enforcing rules

Note: At the end of the chapter are references for some of the significant large-scale studies on the effects of various child-rearing practices. If you should decide to read any of these for more depth in the area of personality and social development, keep the above three factors in mind in interpreting the results.

SELF-TEST

This Self-Test is designed to show you whether or not you have mastered this chapter's objectives. Answer each question to the best of your ability. Correct answers and review instructions are given at the end of the test.

1. Fill in the chart below with the element of personality that is formed at each age, and the parental behavior that is more important at each age from the lists below.

    <u>Elements of personality</u>

    self-esteem
    ability to love
    a sense of identity

    <u>Important parental behaviors</u>

    clarifying basic values
    mothering
    using reward more than punishment

Age	Element of personality formed	Important parental behavior
Infancy		
Early and Middle Childhood		
Adolescence		

2. Explain why the early mother-child interaction is so important to later social and emotional development. What is most important in this early mother-child relationship?

    _____

    _____

    _____

    _____

    _____

    _____

3. On the basis of the sketchy evidence available, does it appear that there are any detrimental effects on a child's social development from

having multiple caretakers if the care is adequate? Where has such multiple caretaking been studied?

_____

_____

4. How did Harry Harlow demonstrate that feeding is not the most important function that the mother provides for her infant?

_____

_____

_____

_____

5. In addition to parental influences, are there any other influences on a child's self-esteem? Explain, in terms of positive and negative feedback and attractiveness.

_____

_____

_____

6. Why are personality traits or motives of more interest to psychologists than personality defined in behavioral terms?

_____

_____

7. How is excessive dependency developed in a child? _____

_____

8. Describe the frustration–aggression hypothesis.

_____

_____

_____

9. Describe the Sears experiment in which the effects of mild, moderate, and severe punishment were studied.

_____

_____

_____

_____

_____

10. Suppose you are a member of ACT (Action for Children's Television); you are trying to convince a local TV station that the violence in the Saturday morning cartoons has a detrimental effect on children. How would you back up your argument?

_____

_____

_____

11. Explain why first-born children are generally more anxious than later-born children. What are anxious children really afraid of?

_____

_____

_____

12. What is a defense mechanism? _____

_____

13. Suppose you are a nursery school teacher and you want to get your children to go from immature play (such as water play) to more mature play (form-boards and puzzles). How would you go about this, using behavior modification techniques?

_____

_____

_____

_____

14. Based on data from several child-rearing studies, what aspects of child-rearing appear to be important to help children become competent and well adjusted?

_____

_____

Answers to Self-Test

Compare your answers to the questions on the Self-Test with the answers given below. If all of your answers are correct, you are ready to go on to the next chapter. If you missed any questions, review the frames indicated in parentheses following the answer. If you miss several questions, you should probably reread the entire chapter carefully.

1.

Age	Element of personality formed	Important parental behavior
Infancy	ability to love	mothering
Early and Middle Childhood	self-esteem	using reward more than punishment
Adolescence	sense of identity	clarifying basic values

(Frames 4, 6—14, 24—29, 41)

2. Through the early mother-child interaction, the child develops the ability to love or to form close relationships. The ability to form close relationships is at the basis of all other social development. Physical contact between mother and child seems to be very important; it may help the baby to feel safe and protected. Also, just by her presence and attention, the mother (or the caretaker) probably acts as a stimulus to elicit the usual infant behaviors of cooing, smiling, scanning. If there is no close caretaker in the first few months of a baby's life, these responses do not develop. (Frames 5—14)

3. There do not appear to be any detrimental effects. (You may have added that children raised with multiple caretakers are possibly more superficial in their later relationships with others, but the evidence is not conclusive.) Multiple caretaking has been studied in the Israeli kibbutz or farm settlement. (Frame 16)

4. (Refer to frames 10 through 13 if necessary.) Harlow demonstrated that, when given a choice between terrycloth and wire-mesh mother substitutes, baby monkeys preferred the soft terrycloth figures, even when the wire-mesh figures gave milk. The monkeys ran to the terrycloth figure when frightened, and spent much time clinging to it. (Frames 10—13)

5. Yes, <u>society</u> also gives positive or negative feedback to a child; this feedback has a direct effect on a child's self-esteem. Society rewards the things it labels "attractive." (Frames 30—34)

6. Because personality traits (motives) are more stable across time and situations than personality defined in terms of behavior. (Frames 50—52)

7. When parents both reward and punish the child's attention-getting behavior. (Frame 59)

8. The frustration-aggression hypothesis states that aggression <u>always</u> results from frustration (or from being blocked from achieving a goal), even if aggressive <u>behavior</u> does not result. (Frames 71—74)

9. (Refer to frames 89 through 93 if necessary.) The Sears experiment showed that both severe and mild punishment decreases the amount of aggressive behavior in children. However, if punishment is severe, fantasy aggression (as observed in a doll-play situation) increases. This appears to demonstrate that severe punishment only decreases the aggressive <u>behavior</u>, not the aggression itself. (Frame 94)

10. Point out Bandura's study, which showed that viewing aggressive models caused children to act more aggressively in a similar situation. Point out that children learn by <u>imitation</u>. (Frames 81—83)

11. Parents have higher expectations for first-born children than for later-borns. Anxious children are really afraid of failing to live up to their parents' high expectations. (Frames 98—106)

12. A defense mechanism is a technique for lessening anxiety. (Frame 114)

13. Your answer should include the following points:
    (a) Do not reward (praise or pay attention to) children when they engage in water play.
    (b) Reward them when they use the form-boards or puzzles.
    (Frames 116—124)

14. Your answer should include these three ideas: Parents should be warm and nurturant, encourage independence, and be consistent in controls. (Frame 129)

SELECTED BIBLIOGRAPHY

The ability to love

Erikson, Erik H. Childhood and Society, 2nd ed. New York: Norton, 1963.
Harlow, H. F. The nature of love. American Psychologist, 1958, 13,
   673-685.
Harlow, H. F., and Harlow, M. H. Learning to love. American Scientist,
   1966, 54, 3, 244-272.
Harlow, H. F., and Suomi, S. J. Nature of love—simplified. American
   Psychologist, 1970, 25, 161-168.

Self-esteem

Coopersmith, Stanley. The Antecedents of Self-Esteem. San Francisco:
   W. H. Freeman, 1967.

Sense of identity

Erikson, Erik H. Identity and the life cycle. Psychological Issues,
   1959, 1.
Erikson, Erik H. Identity, Youth, and Crisis. New York: Norton, 1968.

Kibbutz

Rabin, A. I. Behavior research in collective settlements in Israel:
   Infants and children under conditions of "intermittent" mothering in
   the kibbutz. American Journal of Orthopsychiatry, 1958, 28,
   577-586.
Spiro, Medford E. Kibbutz: Venture in Utopia. New York: Schocken,
   1963.   General background.

Maternal deprivation

Goldfarb, W. Psychological privation in infancy and subsequent adjust-
   ment. American Journal of Orthopsychiatry, 1945, 15, 247-255.
Harlow, H. F., and Harlow, M. H. Social deprivation in monkeys.
   Scientific American, 1962, 207, 136-146.

Behavior modification

Look through recent volumes of the Journal of Applied Behavior Analysis.

Child-rearing practices

Baumrind, Diana. Child care practices anteceding three patterns of pre-
   school behavior. Genetic Psychology Monographs, 1967, 75, 43-88.
Kagan, J., and Moss, H. A. Birth to Maturity: The Fels Study of
   Psychological Development. New York: Wiley, 1962.

Sears, R. R., Maccoby, E. E., and Levin, H.   Patterns of Child-Rearing.
   New York: Harper & Row, 1957.
Whiting, J. W. M., and Child, I. L.   Child Training and Personality.
   New Haven: Yale University Press, 1953.

Aggression and dependency

Sears, R. R., Whiting, J. W. M., Nowlis, U., and Sears, P.S.   Some
   child-rearing antecedents of aggression and dependency in young
   children.   Genetic Psychology Monographs, 1953, 47, 135-234.

Anxiety

Sarason, S. B. et al.   Anxiety in Elementary School Children.   New York:
   Wiley, 1960.

Need for achievement and mastery

Rosen, Bernard C., and D'Andrade, Roy G.   The psychosocial origins of
   achievement motivation.   In Thompson, George C., DiVesta, Francis
   J., & Horrocks, John E., eds.   Social Development and Personality.
   New York: Wiley, 1971.
Winterbottom, M. R.   The relation of need for achievement to learning
   experiences in independence and mastery.   In J. W. Atkinson, ed.
   Motives in Fantasy, Action, and Society.   Princeton, N. J.: Van
   Nostrand, 1958, pp. 453-478.

Social development and personality

Thompson, George C., DiVesta, Francis J., and Horrocks, John E.,
   eds.   Social Development and Personality.   New York: Wiley, 1971.

CHAPTER FIVE
Language Development

In this chapter we will discuss how children learn the basic elements of language—sounds, meaning, and grammar. We will examine the uses of language and the ways in which children use language more effectively as they grow older. Finally, we will present and critically examine some of the research that has been done on language and social class.

OBJECTIVES

After completing this chapter, you will be able to

- distinguish between language comprehension and language production;

- show how imitation, reinforcement, and expansion help children learn how to speak;

- explain how children demonstrate knowledge and use of grammatical rules;

- discuss the issue of whether or not children have an innate language processing system;

- describe some of the uses of language and show ways in which children use language more effectively as they get older;

- explain how verbal mediation works to help children regulate their behavior and solve problems;

- describe the differences in language ability between middle- and lower-class children;

- discuss and critique the various types of programs for improving the language ability of disadvantaged children.

THE ACQUISITION OF LANGUAGE

1. One of the most remarkable aspects of children's development is the growth in their ability to use and understand language. In the space of three or four years (by about age four) they master the complexities of speech and grammar, to say nothing of a vocabulary of over 2000 words. They can combine and recombine these 2000 words into phrases and sentences they have never heard before, nearly all of them grammatically correct. And they can understand words and sentences they have never heard before, based on the grammatical context in which the words are used. There are of course many more words and irregular grammatical usages still left to learn, but it can be said that the child of four has mastered the basic elements of grammatical speech.

What do psychologists mean when they say that children of four have mastered the basic elements of grammatical speech? (Check those statements that apply.)

_____ (a) They can understand new words when these words are used in grammatical context.

_____ (b) With the words they know, they can create new sentences they have never heard before.

_____ (c) They have mastered all the irregular grammatical usages.

_____ (d) They have learned all the words they will ever use.

- - - - - - - - - - - - - - - - - -

(a) and (b)

2. When speaking of language acquisition, however, it is important to distinguish between <u>comprehension</u> and <u>production</u>. <u>Comprehension</u> of the language refers to how much a child actually understands of what is spoken. <u>Production</u> is that part of language that the child actually uses in speech.

Therefore, if psychologists say a child's comprehension of words is greater than the child's production, they mean that: (Check one.)

_____ (a) The child uses more words than he or she actually understands.

_____ (b) The child understands more words than he or she actually uses.

- - - - - - - - - - - - - - - - - -

(b)

3. If a child understands 560 words but has only been recorded as using
    296 words in speech, which is greater: the child's comprehension or

    production? _____

- - - - - - - - - - - - - - - - - -

    comprehension

4. In fact, this is usually the case; children usually comprehend much
    more than they actually produce. An observational study of two-
    year-old children showed that the number of words the children
    actually used in everyday speech varied from 6 to 126. That is,
    some children in the study used as few as 6 and others as many as
    126. Data collected in a different study indicates that two-year-old
    children can <u>understand</u> an average of 272 words, far more than
    were actually used by any two-year-old in the observational study.

    (a) The observational study on children's production described

         above suggests that there is _____ variation among child-
                                      much/little
         ren in number of words used.
    (b) Overall, however, which is higher, comprehension or production?

         _____

- - - - - - - - - - - - - - - - - -

    (a) much; (b) comprehension

5. This difference between comprehension and production is understand-
    able from what we know about memory. Studies of memory have
    shown that it is easier to recognize a word that we have seen before
    than it is to <u>recall</u> it—that is, to name it.
        In <u>recognition</u>, the word is already provided; the person only needs
    to pick it out from a whole series of words. In <u>recall</u>, however, the
    person has no <u>clues</u>, nothing to jog the memory; the word is not pro-
    vided.

    Which of the following are recognition tests and which are tests of
    recall?

    _____   (a) Children are shown the word "dog" and
                                      later asked to remember the word, by
                                      picking it from among a series of animal
                                      names.

_____ (b) Children are shown a list of ten words and later asked to remember as many of them as they can by naming them.

_____ (c) Children are shown a list of ten words. Later they are shown a list of forty words and asked to pick out the ten they have seen before.

- - - - - - - - - - - - - - - -

(a) recognition; (b) recall; (c) recognition

6. Which is more difficult, recognition or recall? Why?

_____

- - - - - - - - - - - - - - - -

Recall, because there is nothing to jog the memory. (The name is not provided.)

7. When we are trying to comprehend what someone is saying, we are simply looking for words, phrases, or grammatical structures that we have heard before. The words and grammar are provided for us and all we must do is recognize them (or even a part of them) in order to understand what is being said.

In order to produce a word, phrase, or grammatical structure, we must actually dredge up the words and rules of grammar from our memory without any external clues to jog our memory.

Therefore, it could be said that language comprehension requires

_____ and language production requires
recognition/recall

_____.
recognition/recall

- - - - - - - - - - - - - - - -

language comprehension: recognition; language production: recall

8. Consider your own experience in learning a foreign language. You have probably had occasion to say at one time or another: "I can understand French (or Spanish or whatever), but I cannot speak it very well."

Understanding a foreign language is generally easier (at first anyway) than speaking the language, because speaking requires

_____.

recall/recognition

- - - - - - - - - - - - - - - - - -

recall

9. To produce correct words and sentences in a foreign language requires a lot of practice. There is evidence that young children, on
their own, practice their language usage, just as adults do when
learning a foreign language. In a charming and well-written book,*
Ruth Weir, a child psychologist, describes her study on the language
development of her own child. She collected tape recordings of her
2-1/2-year-old son's nighttime monologues—the sounds he made
just before falling asleep. She found that, in the course of his
monologues, he would play with words, practice using them in
different ways, drill himself on sounds, and work on correcting
errors of pronunciation.

The recordings of these monologues seem to demonstrate that:
(Check one.)

_____ (a) Children who are learning a language practice in much
the same way as adults do.

_____ (b) Children's language practice differs from the language
practice of adults.

- - - - - - - - - - - - - - - - - -

(a)

10. In the course of these monologues, the 2-1/2-year-old child was
frequently able to correct himself on errors that he generally made
in everyday speech. This fact suggests that: (Check one.)

_____ (a) His comprehension was greater than his production.

_____ (b) His production was greater than his comprehension.

- - - - - - - - - - - - - - - - -

(a)

11. In the very earliest stages of language comprehension, children are
primarily trying to sort out the blur of sound around them into

_____

*Ruth Weir. Language in the Crib (The Hague: Mouton, 1962).

discrete sounds or groups of sounds. Infants must first <u>discriminate</u> among the sounds swirling around them and pick out those that seem to recur.

It can be said that for infants, language comprehension is primarily a task of: (Check one.)

_____ (a) discrimination

_____ (b) speaking clearly

_____ (c) directing sounds

- - - - - - - - - - - - - - - - -

(a)

12. In order to actually comprehend a word or phrase, however, children must also be able to <u>associate</u> it with an object, action, or situation. The discrimination and the association probably occur simultaneously and are part of the same process.

When a mother brings her baby a bottle, she will probably say something like: "Here's your bottle" or "Want your bottle now?" She might vary what she says from time to time, but certain words will recur: "bottle," "your bottle," or maybe a whole phrase— "Here's your bottle." The baby will gradually pick out some of these sounds as being distinctive in some way and as being associated with a particular object, action, or situation.

When psychologists say that a baby has learned to <u>comprehend</u> the word "bottle," what do they mean? (Check one.)

_____ (a) The baby can discriminate it from other sounds.

_____ (b) The baby associates it with an actual bottle.

_____ (c) The baby can both discriminate it from other sounds and associate it with an actual bottle.

- - - - - - - - - - - - - - - - -

(c)

13. We say that children comprehend a word or a group of words when they can both:
    1. discriminate the sound from other sounds
    2. attach some meaning to it (associate it with a particular object, action or situation)
    Most mothers play games like "pat-a-cake" (clapping hands) and "bye-bye" (pretending to go away) with their babies. When mothers take the time to play these repetitious games while talking to their

children, they are helping their children acquire <u>language comprehension</u>. Explain what the children are actually learning in terms of <u>discrimination</u> and <u>association</u>. _____

_____

_____

- - - - - - - - - - - - - - - - - -

The children are learning to discriminate certain groups of sounds and to associate those sounds with a particular action (or to give meaning to the sounds).

14. The comprehension of infants and young children cannot always be assumed to be like that of adults. The child who knows the meaning of "allgone" does not know that it is really two words, each of which has a separate meaning by itself. It is the group of sounds "allgone" that the child has singled out and given meaning to. The distinctive <u>unit of meaning</u> is "allgone."
    If a mother always uses the words "up we go" when lifting her baby, "eat it up" when feeding him, "beddie-bye" when putting him in his bed, can we assume the baby will learn the meaning of each of the separate words "up," "we," "go?" What will probably be the

child's distinctive <u>unit of meaning</u> in each case? _____

_____

- - - - - - - - - - - - - - - - - -

no; "up we go," "eat it up," "beddie-bye"

15. Similarly, children gradually refine their ideas of what words or units of meaning are actually associated with certain objects, actions, or situations. A child may at first think that "beddie-bye" stands for being lifted up, cuddled, kissed, read to, and so on. Eventually, the child learns to associate it with "going to bed."

When a mother brings a child a bottle and says "Here's your bottle," what are some of the things a child might associate with the word

"bottle"? _____

_____

_____

- - - - - - - - - - - - - - - - - -

_____

the mother's presence, smile, or closeness; the taste of the milk; the feeling of the nipple in his mouth (any of the things that might take place during the feeding situation)

16. Is young children's comprehension of the language like that of

    adults? Explain. _____

    _____

    _____

- - - - - - - - - - - - - - - - - -

Probably not; young children probably assign meaning to a different set of sounds than adults do; also their associations are probably different than those of adults.

17. It is possible to increase young children's comprehension of words by direct training. If nine-month-olds are shown simple objects and told the names of the objects, and if this procedure is repeated several times, some of them will eventually learn to comprehend the new words.

    Also, if children are allowed to have different experiences with objects and are given instructions on their use ("dress the doll," "pat the doll," "pick up the doll"), they will learn the names of the objects faster than children who have not had such experiences.

    From this evidence, which would you say is most likely? Reading to, and playing with, your child will: (Check one.)

    _____ (a) stimulate language comprehension

    _____ (b) retard language comprehension

    _____ (c) have no effect on language comprehension

- - - - - - - - - - - - - - - - -

(a)

18. As noted before, it is not always easy to get an accurate estimate of language comprehension just from listening to children speak. Children understand more language than they use. They can, however, be directly <u>tested</u> for comprehension of specific words or phrases. For example, children can be shown a series of pictures and instructed

"Show me _____."* If they can point to the correct picture we assume they know the word.

(a) If children can correctly identify a sofa, can we assume that

they are able to use the word in conversation? Why? _____

_____

(b) Language production can be easily studied just by listening to a child's speech for a certain length of time. What can we do to

study a child's comprehension? _____

_____

- - - - - - - - - - - - - - - - - -

(a) No; because children understand more language than they actually use
(b) Test the child on specific words and phrases, or ask the child to identify a picture of the word

19. The study of language production starts with babies' first sounds. All babies <u>babble</u> from a very early age on. These early babbling sounds are natural and spontaneous, and at first seem to be made for the sheer pleasure of making them and hearing them.

Would you say then that babies' early babbling noises are learned or

innate? _____

- - - - - - - - - - - - - - - - -

They seem to be innate.

20. Once children begin to utter sounds, however, parents and others around them <u>reinforce</u> the babbling by smiling, cuddling, repeating the sounds, and so on. This reinforcement causes children to con-tinue or even increase the babbling; more reinforcement is given, and so on, until babbling is a well-established response. Studies of infants raised in orphanages and institutions show what happens to the babbling response in a situation in which it is not reinforced. In many such institutions there are not enough caretakers to spend time with the babies. While the babies start off crying and babbling normally, after a few months, the babbling response dies out and

_____

*The word doesn't have to be a noun (as in, "Show me the <u>cat</u>"). You could say "Show me <u>running</u>" (a verb), "Show me <u>happy</u>" (an adjective), and so on.

the babies lie there listlessly and make few sounds.

What is apparently missing in the institutional setting that is needed in order for the response to continue? _____

_____

- - - - - - - - - - - - - - - - - - -

reinforcement, or the absence of people who reinforce the babbling responses

21. The reinforcement that babies receive for the sounds they make is differential reinforcement. That is, some sounds are reinforced more than others. Take two of the sounds commonly made by babies —cooing sounds and fretful sounds. Parents love to hear their babies make cooing sounds and usually respond to them by smiling, talking, cuddling, or other reinforcing actions. Mildly fretful sounds, however, are usually not responded to by parents (unless the sounds become insistent and turn into cries).

If, indeed, cooing sounds are more often reinforced than fretful sounds, which would you expect the child to make more often—cooing or fretful sounds? _____

- - - - - - - - - - - - - - - - - -

cooing sounds

22. The sounds that infants make are: (Check one.)

_____ (a) all equally reinforced

_____ (b) differentially reinforced

- - - - - - - - - - - - - - - - -

(b)

23. A psychologist named Routh was able to show that infants aged two to seven months could be conditioned to use certain kinds of sounds more than others. Babies were conditioned to use vowels more than consonants, or consonants more than vowels. The reinforcement was smiling, a series of "tsk" sounds, and a light stroking of the stomach.

Explain how Routh would be able to get one group to produce more consonants and another group to produce more vowels.

- - - - - - - - - - - - - - - - -

One group would be reinforced every time consonants were produced; the other group would be reinforced only for vowels.

24. There is another way, besides reinforcement, in which children are encouraged to produce certain sounds. Mothers often repeat a particular word, hoping that their babies will <u>imitate</u> it and thus increase their vocabulary. For instance, a mother, while feeding her child, repeats the word "daddy" again and again. At some point the baby may attempt to imitate the mother and may make a sound such as "dada."

In this case, the child's production of the word "dada" was due to: (Check one.)

_____ (a) imitation

_____ (b) reinforcement

_____ (c) both imitation and reinforcement

- - - - - - - - - - - - - - - - -

(a) (Remember that a sound cannot be <u>reinforced</u> until it has occurred. Imitation is the means by which particular sounds can be elicited.)

25. Obviously, reinforcement and imitation work together to influence children's language production. When a child imitates something his or her mother has said, the mother usually smiles, rubs the child's cheek, or utters pleased and happy sounds. In this way she is

_____ the sound the child has imitated.
imitating/reinforcing

- - - - - - - - - - - - - - - - -

reinforcing

26. Two factors that influence a child's language production are

_____ and _____ .

- - - - - - - - - - - - - - - - -

reinforcement; imitation

27. By the time a child is three or four years, the imitation game takes on a new twist. Through the technique of _expansion_, mothers gradually increase children's language skills and help them move closer to correct language usage.

    The following dialogue is an example of how expansion works:
    Child: Kitty meow.
    Mother: Yes, the kitty goes meow.
    The mother _expands_ on what the child has said; she does not imitate the child's utterance exactly, but adds to it and makes it more like adult speech. In the process, she provides the child with a model for a more advanced level of speech.

    Why is this process called expansion? _____

    _____

- - - - - - - - - - - - - - - - - -

    because the mother _expands on_ what the child has said

28. Expansion is a process by which the mother: (Check one.)

    _____ (a) imitates what the child has said

    _____ (b) adds to what the child has said

    _____ (c) neither of the above

- - - - - - - - - - - - - - - - - -

    (b) (The mother's expansion of her child's speech is probably also reinforcing to the child.)

29. Let's see how the child might typically react to the mother's expansion:
    Child: Kitty meow.
    Mother: Yes, the kitty goes meow.
    Child: Kitty go meow.
    (a) What has the child added to the statement as a result of the mother's expansion? _____
    (b) Is the child's statement now an exact imitation of the mother's?

    _____

- - - - - - - - - - - - - - - - -

    (a) the word "go"; (b) no

30. When a mother expands on her child's speech, the child typically: (Check one.)

_____ (a) repeats her "corrected" statement exactly

_____ (b) does not change his statement at all

_____ (c) brings his statement to a slightly more advanced level of speech

- - - - - - - - - - - - - - - - - -

(c)

31. In which of the following mother-child conversations is the mother using the technique of expansion?

_____ (a) Mother: Johnny, come here.
Child: Me playing.
Mother: No, you come right here.

_____ (b) Child: Go car.
Mother: Shall we go in the car?
Child: We go in car.

_____ (c) Mother: That's a nice farm.
Child: See horsie.
Mother: Shall we stop and see the horse?
Child: We stop and see horsie.

_____ (d) Child: Me throw ball.
Mother: Throw it to me.
Child: O.K.

- - - - - - - - - - - - - - - - - - -

(b) and (c) are expansions. In the other two cases, the mother is telling the child to do something, not adding to something the child has said.

32. How does the process of expansion help a child acquire a more advanced language level? (In your own words.) _____

_____

_____

_____

_____

- - - - - - - - - - - - - - - - - -

The mother takes what the child has said and expands on it or adds to it. The child then expands his or her own statement by bringing it closer to adult speech.

33. Not all of children's language acquisition can be explained in terms of imitation and reinforcement, however. After children have learned the basic sounds and phrases, they very quickly begin to generate their own phrases and word combinations, some of which they may never have heard before. These new word combinations therefore are not direct imitations, and they have never been reinforced.

    For example, an 18-month-old child who has learned the sound of "allgone" in connection with food may begin using it in combination with many other words such as "Allgone watch," "Allgone Mommy," or "Allgone boat." These new combinations have never been heard before and yet they are used in a situation in which the meaning is correct.

These new constructions (two-word sentences) are probably the result of: (Check one.)

_____ (a) direct imitation

_____ (b) direct reinforcement

_____ (c) both

_____ (d) neither

- - - - - - - - - - - - - - - - -

(d)

34. A psychologist named Braine asked two mothers to write down all the "spontaneous utterances" of their children over a period of several months. That is, they noted <u>only</u> those word combinations that were not direct imitations of something the children had heard. (The children were at the stage where they were combining two words.) Braine found that there were systematic regularities to the children's speech. The children used certain key words again and again in different word combinations, but the key words were always used in the same way.

    In frame 33 we saw examples of these regularities in their two-word sentences (for example, "allgone watch" or "allgone Mommy"). "Allgone" is always used in the same way and in the same position in the sentence. Similarly, a child might use "see" in many different combinations, but would always place it in the same position, and make it serve the same function (for example, "see horsie," "see dog," or "see boy"). The combinations "allgone see" or "see allgone" never occurred, even though the child knew and could say both words.

Based on these results, which of the following statements would you say is probably true of children's early language?

_____ (a) Children's early sentences show certain systematic regularities.

_____ (b) Children's early sentences are unsystematic and appear to have no real structure to them.

- - - - - - - - - - - - - - - - - -

(a)

35. In fact, because of these regularities in children's two-word sentences, Braine concluded that even young children are using very specific, if simplified, <u>rules</u> in constructing their sentences. It is as if the children are saying to themselves: "Allgone" must always come first in a sentence and be followed by a certain kind of word (usually a noun). The sentences "allgone see" and "see allgone" do not fit that rule; therefore those sentences never occur.

Children use the word "big" only in front of a noun ("big car," "big man," "big dog"), and never in front of a verb ("big go," "big see," "big take"). This demonstrates that they: (Check one.)

_____ (a) prefer nouns to verbs

_____ (b) are using some grammatical rule

_____ (c) prefer big things to little things

_____ (d) do not use grammatical rules

- - - - - - - - - - - - - - - - - -

(b)

36. What is the evidence that even young children are applying rules in the construction of their two-word sentences? (In your own words.)

_____

_____

_____

- - - - - - - - - - - - - - - - -

Their two-word sentences show certain systematic regularities; certain words are always used in the same way; certain combinations of words never occur, even though the child knows both words (for example, "allgone see").

37. A set of rules for combining words is called a <u>grammar</u>. Would you say that even young children have a grammar? Explain your answer.

_____

_____

- - - - - - - - - - - - - - - - - - -

Yes, because they seem to be applying rules when they combine words to make up new sentences.

38. Braine says that children's earliest grammar consists of <u>pivot</u> and <u>open</u> words. A <u>pivot</u> is a key word that can be used in many combinations. It is a particular word that has been singled out to occupy a specific position in a sentence and to which a number of words can be attached. All the rest are <u>open</u> words.

In the examples in frames 33 and 34, which, according to Braine, are pivot words and which are open words?

_____

- - - - - - - - - - - - - - - - - - -

Pivot: allgone, see; Open: watch, Mommy, boat, horsie, dog, boy

39. Regardless of how one analyzes the speech of young children, it is obvious that it is not like the speech of adults. Children's speech is not governed by adult grammar. Children's earliest grammar is, of course, very simple. It is as if children are not yet ready to deal with the complexities of adult language, and so make up their own set of rules as a sort of stop-gap measure.

Young children's rules are almost always simpler than adult rules, almost a streamlined version of adult grammar. Look back at frame 29: Even when the mother expands on the child's speech, the child does not simply imitate the mother's speech.

Would you say that the new grammar produced by the child is simpler than the mother's, more complex, or equally complex? _____

- - - - - - - - - - - - - - - - - - -

simpler

40. When adults supply young children with a correct grammatical statement, the children apparently:

_____

_____ (a) grasp the rules immediately

_____ (b) ignore the rules involved

_____ (c) streamline and simplify the rules to suit their own needs

- - - - - - - - - - - - - - - - - -

(c)

41. Try getting a very young child (around 2-1/2 or 3 years of age) to repeat: "Let me go to the store." The child might say: "Me go store." Then try: "Suppose we go to the bakery." The child will probably say: "We go bakery."

(a) If the child were asked to repeat: "What if we go to the circus?"

What would the child probably say? _____

(b) Describe how the child has altered the adult's grammar.

_____

_____

_____

- - - - - - - - - - - - - - - - - -

(a) "We go circus." (b) The child dropped out the complicated additions to the verb ("Let me," "suppose," "what if," and the article "the"); the child has simplified the adult's grammar.

42. Eventually, the child learns correct, that is, adult, grammatical rules. Jean Berko, in an ingenious study, demonstrated that by age four, all children have mastered most fundamental rules of adult grammar. She designed a game which gave children a chance to demonstrate their knowledge of: 1. possessive and plural endings; 2. different verb forms; and 3. comparatives and superlatives of adjectives.

For example, the children are shown a picture of an animallike creature and are told: "This is a wug. Now there are two of them. There are two _____."

(a) What should children answer to demonstrate their knowledge of plural endings? _____

(b) According to Berko's study, by what age have children mastered most fundamental rules of adult grammar? _____

- - - - - - - - - - - - - - - - -

(a) wugs; (b) age four

43. By using nonsense syllables instead of actual words, Dr. Berko could be sure that the child actually understood the grammatical rule and was not simply imitating a word heard before. Children had never heard the word "wugs" before and had certainly never used it.

    Suppose she had asked the question this way: "Here is a bug. Now there are two _____." If children answered "bugs," could she be sure that they actually understood the rule for forming plurals?

    Explain. _____

    _____

- - - - - - - - - - - - - - - - -

    No, because they might be simply imitating something they had previously heard.

44. Why does the use of nonsense syllables insure that children were not simply imitating, but had actually learned a rule?

    _____

    _____

- - - - - - - - - - - - - - - -

    Because the children had never heard the word "wugs" before and therefore could not be imitating it; they must have learned a rule for forming plurals.

45. Strangely enough, children's early grammatical errors also demonstrate that language acquisition is a process of rule-learning rather than word-learning, or simple imitation of adult speech. An analysis of children's errors reveals that children often overgeneralize a rule they have learned, and apply it in cases where it is not correct.
    When children say: "I goed to the store" or "I digged a hole," they are not imitating adult speech. In fact, they have probably never heard the words "goed" or "digged" before. By using these words, they are demonstrating that they understand a rule for forming the past tense of a verb.

    If children always used correct speech, would psychologists be able to tell whether they were learning rules of grammar? Explain.

    _____

    _____

    _____

- - - - - - - - - - - - - - - -

    _____

No; because their speech would always sound like imitation of adult speech; there would be no way of knowing whether children were just imitating adult speech or applying a rule.

46. Children who are just learning to talk often have trouble with plurals. They might say: "I saw two mans" or "There are three sheeps in that field."

   Explain how these errors demonstrate that children do not just imitate specific words from adult speech, but actually learn rules of grammar. _____

   _____

- - - - - - - - - - - - - - - - - - -

   Children have never heard these words from adults; therefore they could not be simply imitating them from adult speech. (From these particular errors, we would probably guess that the rule being applied is: to make a plural, add "s" to the singular.)

47. In your own words, trace the development of children's speech from their first babbling sounds to simple sentences. Show how this development is affected by imitation, reinforcement, and expansion.

   _____

   _____

   _____

   _____

   _____

   _____

   _____

   _____

- - - - - - - - - - - - - - - - - - -

   Children's earliest babblings are selectively reinforced; some sounds—generally those close to adult speech—are reinforced more than others. Babies also try to imitate adult speech and are probably reinforced when they do it successfully. When children get older, their parents usually use the technique of expansion to bring their children's speech closer to adult speech. Mothers expand on what the children say, and the children in turn expand on their original utterance. For example, if a child says: "me go," the mother might say: "you want to go to the store?" The child might answer: "Me go store."

48. We have seen that, especially in early speech sounds, imitation and reinforcement play a part in language acquisition. We have also seen that expansion of a child's speech by the mother can aid language development.

But how can we account for the fact that children learn and apply rules of grammar, and that they master many of the complexities of adult grammar at such an early age (around age four)? Many psychologists who study young children's acquisition of language believe that children are born with a mechanism or device that is capable of processing all the language sounds around them. This innate mechanism is sometimes called a language acquisition system or language acquisition device. Language acquisition, say these psychologists, is possible only because children are programmed to analyze language data in a certain way.

Psychologists who postulate a language acquisition system or device believe that the ability to understand and speak language is

_____.

learned/innate

- - - - - - - - - - - - - - - - - -

innate

49. What this language acquisition device (LAD)* actually does, psychologists say, is to filter all incoming speech and come up with a theory of how speech is constructed. A diagram is often used to demonstrate this process:

Linguistic data ⟶ [box] ⟶ Grammatical competence

In the above diagram, what should the "filter" (the box in the middle) be labeled? _____

- - - - - - - - - - - - - - - - - -

LAD, or language acquisition device

_____

*LAD is the term used by Noam Chomsky, a linguist at MIT. Chomsky's study of "transformational grammar" has had a profound effect on the way psychologists look at language acquisition.

50. Not everyone believes that children are innately programmed to analyze linguistic data in a certain way. Some psychologists still argue that reinforcement and imitation can account for all language acquisition. However, most psychologists now agree that, as a part of their intellectual makeup, most people do look for regularities in their environment and do formulate rules to account for these regularities.

If people are given three buttons to push and told that some of the time they will be rewarded and some of the time they will not, people automatically try to figure out what the "gimmick" or rule is. They might ask: do I start from left to right to press the buttons, or right to left? Do I press each one once, twice, or more times in succession? And so on.

The preceding example illustrates that: (Check one.)

_____ (a) People naturally try to apply rules to new situations.

_____ (b) People are not smart enough to learn a discrimination task.

_____ (c) People learn by imitation and reinforcement.

- - - - - - - - - - - - - - - - - -

(a)

51. This <u>rule-applying</u> tendency is general, however, and does not seem to be limited specifically to language rules. Therefore, perhaps LAD should be labeled instead: (Check the most appropriate.)

_____ (a) a language device

_____ (b) rule-applier

_____ (c) reinforcement device

- - - - - - - - - - - - - - - - - -

(b)

52. Most people today believe that children _____ attempt to apply
                                              do/do not
rules to incoming language data.

- - - - - - - - - - - - - - - - - -

do

53. (a) What is a grammar? _____

_____

(b) Do young children show evidence that they are using a simple grammar in their earliest two-word sentences? _____

- - - - - - - - - - - - - - - -

(a) a set of rules for combining words; (b) yes

54. Is this earliest grammar the same as an adult grammar? Explain.

_____

- - - - - - - - - - - - - - - -

No, it is simpler. (According to some psychologists, it contains only two classes of words—pivot and open words.)

55. (a) How did Jean Berko's study show that children do not learn grammatical rules simply by imitation of specific words they have heard? _____

_____

(b) How do children's <u>errors</u> also show this? _____

_____

_____

- - - - - - - - - - - - - - - -

(a) Jean Berko's study used nonsense words which children had never heard or used before; therefore the correct forms were not learned by imitation. (b) Children sometimes produce incorrect forms by applying rules (example, "he goed"). They have not heard these incorrect forms from adults.

USES OF LANGUAGE

56. When asked to name the primary function of language, most people say "communication." Interestingly enough, there has been relatively little research on the communication aspects of language. Jean Piaget in Switzerland and Dorothea McCarthy in the United States are perhaps the only developmental psychologists to study in any detail the developmental changes in children's communication. The basis of communication is that two people are:
    1. talking about the same subject
    2. being influenced by what the other person says about the subject

Let's hear how this works. Ralph and Harry think they are communicating about politics. Let's listen in:

Harry: I just met the guy who is running for Senator.

Ralph: I think all politicians are crooked.

Harry: Did I ever tell you that I once considered running for office?

Ralph: I wouldn't trust a politician as far as I could throw him.

Harry: (Musing) Maybe someday when the kids are older...

Ralph: I wonder if they'll ever pin anything on that member of Congress who was involved in the housing scandal....

According to our definition, have Ralph and Harry communicated?

Explain. _____

_____

- - - - - - - - - - - - - - - - - -

No, because neither was influenced by what the other was saying. (It might even be argued that they were not really discussing the same subject, but we'll take their word for that.)

57. Two children are playing together and talking. Again, let's listen in:

Sarah: I'm carrying sand in my truck.

Jan: See how I mess up the dolly's clothing?

Sarah: This sandbox is a beach and I'm driving along the beach.

Jan: Now the dolls are all sitting down to supper.

Sarah: Oh, my truck's going to crash over the edge, bang!

(a) Are Jan and Sarah talking about the same subject? _____

(b) Is either one influenced by what the other is saying or feeling?

_____

(c) Are they communicating? _____

- - - - - - - - - - - - - - - - - -

(a) no; (b) no; (c) no

58. In one of the following conversations there is real communication between the two children. Which conversation is it? Explain your choice.

Conversation A Jean: This is how you work the lever.

Hal: You pull this part down, then...what?

Jean: Then you push in the button.

Hal: Yeah. I get it now.

Conversation B Russ: First the lever goes up, then down.
Ian: I'm playing with a car.
Russ: It's a pick-up truck...picks up toys.
Ian: My car is going to crash into the wall.
Russ: Now the man is driving the truck to the dump.

_____

_____

_____

- - - - - - - - - - - - - - - - - - -

Conversation A; because the children are talking about the same
subject, and each is influenced by what the other says. (Jean
explains, Hal acknowledges; Hal asks a question, Jean explains,
Hal acknowledges.) The two children in Conversation B are
neither talking about the same subjects, nor are they influenced
by what the other is saying.

59. For two people to be really communicating according to our definition, what must they be doing?

1. _____

2. _____

- - - - - - - - - - - - - - - - - -

1. talking about the same subject
2. being influenced by what the other person is saying

60. Piaget has a term for speech that does **not** communicate. He refers
to it as <u>egocentric</u> speech. When Piaget says that much of the speech
of four-year-olds is egocentric, what does he mean? (Check one.)

_____ (a) Four-year-old children are selfish.

_____ (b) When four-year-old children talk, they often do not
communicate.

_____ (c) The speech of four-year-old children is speech that
communicates.

- - - - - - - - - - - - - - - - -

(b)

61. Piaget found that, as children grow older, they use speech more and
more to exchange ideas and information. This kind of speech—speech

that actually communicates something—is often called <u>sociocentric</u>
speech.

In frame 58, for example, Jean is showing Hal how to work a
lever. She listens to Hal's question and is able to furnish the additional information Hal needs. There has been a real exchange of
information between the two.

Speech used in this way, to exchange ideas and information, is called
what kind of speech? _____

- - - - - - - - - - - - - - - - -

sociocentric

62. (a) In the beginning, children's speech is _____.

                                    egocentric/sociocentric

(b) Gradually, children learn to use speech as _____.

                                    play/communication

- - - - - - - - - - - - - - - - -

(a) egocentric; (b) communication (Later research has suggested
that young children's speech is not so egocentric as Piaget described
it. There is no question, however, that children's ability to communicate and to exchange ideas improves with age.)

63. Explain the age changes that occur in children's communication.

_____

_____

_____

- - - - - - - - - - - - - - - - -

At first, children's speech is egocentric—that is, there is no real
exchange of ideas or information. Gradually, the child learns to
use sociocentric speech—speech that communicates.

64. A second way in which children can use language is to regulate and
control their behavior. Let's look at an example that demonstrates
how this works. In one experiment, children are shown a red light
and a green light and instructed to press a rubber bulb when the red
light comes on, but not to press it when the green light comes on.
Children's natural tendency is to press the bulb <u>any</u> time a light
comes on. What they must do is inhibit the pressing response whenever the green light comes on.

In this experiment the children must regulate their actions by:

_____ (a) teaching themselves to respond to the lights

_____ (b) stopping themselves from responding to one of the lights

- - - - - - - - - - - - - - - - -

(b)

65. It was shown that language aided children in performing this task. Children who could say to themselves: "Don't press on the green light" did better on this task than children who did not use language in this way.

Thus, this experiment demonstrates that: (Check one.)

_____ (a) Children find it harder to respond to a red than to a green light.

_____ (b) Children's use of language is not at all related to their behavior.

_____ (c) Children can use language to regulate and control their own actions.

_____ (d) Children's natural tendency is not to press the bulb whenever a light comes on.

- - - - - - - - - - - - - - - - -

(c)

66. As you might expect, children's ability to use language to regulate their behavior increases with age. The Russian psychologist who did the above experiment, A. R. Luria, found that both three-year-olds and older children could repeat the instructions at the beginning of the experiment. Both groups of children showed evidence of understanding the instructions. The three-year-olds did not, however, "tell themselves" out loud, during the task, to stop responding. The older children would remind themselves of the instructions and would act accordingly. Consequently, the three-year-olds had more trouble with the task.

(a) Did both the three-year-olds and the older children understand

the instructions? _____

(b) Which children used the instructions to regulate and control their behavior? (Check one.)

_____ the younger children

_____ the older children

_____ both older and younger children

- - - - - - - - - - - - - - - - - - - -

(a) Yes, they seemed to understand. (b) the older children
(Other research has shown that, <u>with training</u>, even three-year-old
children can use language to help them in this task.)

67. Does children's ability to use language effectively in regulating and
controlling their own behavior increase with age? _____

- - - - - - - - - - - - - - - - -

yes

68. Name two ways in which language can be used by children.

_____ , _____

_____ .

- - - - - - - - - - - - - - - - -

to communicate; to regulate and control their actions

69. Let's look a little more closely at how language works in regulating
and controlling behavior. Some psychologists say that language is
itself a response. When an 18-month-old child sees a dog, the
child's response might be to approach the dog, or pat it, or pull its
hair. A child of three years, who has learned the word "dog" might
respond instead by saying "doggie," or "doggie bites." In each
case, the child has made a <u>response</u> to the sight of the dog. Which
of the two responses is a <u>language response</u>?

_____

- - - - - - - - - - - - - - - - -

the three-year-old's response ("doggie" or "doggie bites")

70. Say, for example, the child's natural tendency is to pat the dog or to
pull its tail, or to touch it in some way. Suppose that after saying
"doggie bites," the child stops himself from touching the dog, or
withdraws his hand. Would you say that the <u>language response</u> has
had an effect on his behavior? Explain your answer.

- - - - - - - - - - - - - - - -

Yes; it seemed to help the child regulate and control his behavior; that is, it caused the child to inhibit the other response

71. When a verbal or language response intervenes somehow between the stimulus and response, it is called a verbal mediator. This verbal response mediates, or alters in some way, the person's behavior. Explain how in the previous example the verbal mediator—"doggie bites"—altered the child's behavior in that situation.

- - - - - - - - - - - - - - - -

Instead of patting or touching the dog, the child held back, or withdrew his hand.

72. In the following diagram, where would the verbal mediator come in?

| Stimulus | → | Response | → | Reinforcement |

_____ (a) before the stimulus

_____ (b) between the stimulus and the response

_____ (c) between the response and the reinforcement

_____ (d) after the reinforcement

- - - - - - - - - - - - - - - -

(b)

73. A verbal mediator is a verbal _____ that has an effect on
                                          stimulus/response
a person's behavior.

- - - - - - - - - - - - - - - -

response

74. Verbal mediators can be spoken out loud (overt) or they can be spoken by a child to himself (covert). Either way, these responses have an

effect on the child's behavior.

Let's say that two four-year-old children both know that stoves are hot and can burn them. One of the children says aloud every time he passes by the stove: "The stove can burn me." The other child says the same thing to himself each time he is near the stove.

For which of the children will the verbal mediator ("The stove can burn me") have an effect on the ultimate behavior?

_____ (a) the child who says it out loud

_____ (b) the child who says it to himself

_____ (c) probably both children

- - - - - - - - - - - - - - - - -

(c) probably both children

75. (a) What is a verbal mediator? _____

_____

(b) Is a verbal mediator overt or covert? _____

- - - - - - - - - - - - - - - - -

(a) It is a verbal response that has an effect on a person's ultimate response (or action or behavior).
(b) It can be either overt or covert.

76. As children get older, more and more of their verbal mediators become covert. That is, when older children "tell" themselves what the instructions are, how to behave in certain sit   ns, or how to

solve a problem, they usually do it _____.
                                        aloud/to themselves

- - - - - - - - - - - - - - - - -

to themselves

77. Because of the obvious and profound effect that language (in the form of verbal mediators) has on problem-solving, some psychologists have theorized that thinking is nothing more than inner speech. At first, they say, children solve problems by literally "telling themselves" aloud how to respond. Eventually they "tell themselves" silently, or covertly; at this point, speech actually becomes thought.

According to this view, thought is a: (Check one.)

_____ (a) covert verbal stimulus

_____ (b) covert verbal response

_____ (c) overt verbal stimulus

_____ (d) overt verbal response

- - - - - - - - - - - - - - - - - - -

(b)

78. Let's look at some of the implications of this view. If thought is
nothing more than inner speech, then deaf children who are severely
deficient in language skills should be severely limited in their ability to think.
    In fact, this is not the case. Hans G. Furth, a psychologist who
has done much research on deaf children, has found that the thinking
processes of deaf and hearing children are very similar. He also
found that deaf children do as well on most problems as hearing
children.

These results _____ the view that thought is nothing
                 support/do not support
more than inner speech.

- - - - - - - - - - - - - - - - - -

do not support

79. There is no doubt that language aids in thinking and problem-solving.
(If you wish, review Chapter Three for a discussion of the relationship between language and problem-solving.) Many problems, however, can be solved without the use of language. Remember
Lucienne's solution to the matchbox problem* in Chapter Three. Do
you think language was used in solving that problem? Explain.

_____

_____

- - - - - - - - - - - - - - - - -

·Lucienne was too young to use language to help her; she appeared
to represent the problem in terms of an <u>action</u> (opening and closing
her mouth).

_____

*In trying to figure out how to open a matchbox, Lucienne suddenly
opened and shut her mouth several times; then, as if she had thus "solved"
the problem, she promptly opened the box.

80. Piaget speaks of different modes of representing a problem. He demonstrates how children "think" differently, depending on which mode they use to solve a problem. Symbolic representation, or representation in terms of language, comes fairly late in a child's development.

Which of the following statements do you suppose best reflects Piaget's view of how language and thinking are related?

_____ (a) Thought is nothing more than inner speech.

_____ (b) Language is an aid to thought but not essential to it.

- - - - - - - - - - - - - - - - - -

(b) (Certainly Piaget agrees that language allows us to solve in-creasingly abstract problems. He does not, however, believe that thought is simply inner speech.)

LANGUAGE AND SOCIAL CLASS

81. Recently, because of the current interest in cultural enrichment pro-grams for disadvantaged children, there has been much research into social class differences in language development. Middle-class children consistently do better in school and on intelligence tests than lower-class children. Much of their superior performance can be traced directly to superior language capability. One of the goals of the Head Start program is to prepare disadvantaged* children to do as well in school as middle-class ("advantaged") children.

Which of the following activities would probably be most successful in reaching that goal, preparing disadvantaged children for school?

_____ (a) working on math concepts

_____ (b) developing their motor skills

_____ (c) improving their language skills

Explain your answer. _____

_____

- - - - - - - - - - - - - - - - -

_____

*Much of the research on language and social class has, at least in part, used financial status as a class indicator; hence the term "lower class." For purposes of this discussion, the terms "lower class" and "disadvantaged" will be used interchangeably.

(c); because much of the school success of middle-class children is due to their superior language ability.

82. The differences in the language development of middle- and lower-class children fall into two categories:
    1. differences in <u>vocabulary</u> (Middle-class children know more words than lower-class children.)
    2. differences in the <u>use</u> of language (Middle-class children use language more effectively than lower-class children.)

    (a) If children are not able to make themselves understood when they try to explain something, even though they know all the right words, we say that the children have difficulty in:

    _____ vocabulary

    _____ using language effectively

    (b) If a three-year-old child cannot identify simple household objects on an intelligence test, we say that the difficulty is in:

    _____ vocabulary

    _____ using language effectively

- - - - - - - - - - - - - - - - -

(a) using language effectively; (b) vocabulary

83. Lower-class children have more difficulty in two aspects of language skills than middle-class children. Those two aspects of language are

_____ and _____.

- - - - - - - - - - - - - - - - -

vocabulary; using language effectively

84. Let's look at possible reasons for the lower vocabulary level of lower-class children. Think back to the discussion on how children learn language comprehension:
    1. They must experience many new objects and situations in their environment.
    2. These objects must be labeled appropriately for them.

    Therefore, which of the following might cause lower-class children difficulty in learning language comprehension?

    _____ (a) They lack experience with many new objects and situations.

    _____ (b) They have not had objects and experiences appropriately labeled for them.

_____ (c) Either or both of the above reasons might be causing the difficulty.

- - - - - - - - - - - - - - - - - -

(c)

85. There does seem to be evidence that lower-class mothers spend less time talking with their babies and young children than middle-class mothers. Middle-class mothers play vocabulary "games," even with young infants: "I see your <u>toes</u>" (pointing), "I see your <u>fingers</u>," "I've got your <u>nose</u>," and so on. All babies, of course, eventually become aware of their toes, fingers, nose and other parts of their bodies; games like this, however, help them to associate those parts of their body with specific words.

(a) When a mother plays this kind of game with her child, which is she providing?

_____ new objects in the child's environment

_____ labels for objects in the child's environment

(b) Which mothers apparently spend more time talking with their babies and young children?

_____ middle-class mothers

_____ lower-class mothers

- - - - - - - - - - - - - - - - -

(a) labels for objects in the child's environment; (b) middle-class mothers

86. While there is not clear evidence one way or the other, many psychologists and educators have in the past assumed that disadvantaged children do not experience as many new objects and situations as middle-class children do. They have assumed that disadvantaged children are more limited in their activities and contacts with the community and do not have as many toys or household gadgets around to experience and learn from.

Many nursery schools focus on making stimulating toys, puzzles, games, and objects available to children, and on taking field trips to the zoo, museums, bakeries, farms, the fire station, and so on.

This kind of nursery school is mainly concerned with:

_____ (a) providing labels

_____ (b) providing new objects and situations

- - - - - - - - - - - - - - - - - -

(b)

87. Many preschool programs for disadvantaged children have adopted
this model. They emphasize enrichment of experience in helping
children comprehend language better. There is evidence, however,
that this type of program by itself is not very successful. In any
program for disadvantaged children it appears to be more important
to emphasize labeling—that is, to make a specific point of teaching
new words for new experiences. The actual number of experiences
is less important to a child's language learning than the accuracy
and quality of the labels applied to these experiences.

Which of the following activities might be added to the above enrichment program to provide specific vocabulary teaching? (Check one.)

_____ (a) The children would, as a group, discuss what they had
done or learned each day.

_____ (b) The children would be drilled on the names of all the objects in the room.

_____ (c) The parents would be included in some of the activities
and encouraged to discuss them with their children.

_____ (d) All of these activities would aid the children in labeling.

- - - - - - - - - - - - - - - - - -

(d)

88. Which type of language program seems to be more effective in helping disadvantaged children improve their language skills?

_____ (a) providing new objects and experiences

_____ (b) providing labels for objects and experiences

- - - - - - - - - - - - - - - - - -

(b)

89. Since children are with their parents more than they are in a preschool program, many programs are now emphasizing parent
involvement. The attempt is to increase the actual amount of talking,
specifically labeling activities, between children and parents. Some

programs focus on mothers and their infants, theorizing that this kind of verbal interaction is best begun very early.

Which of the following activities are probably the most effective in improving disadvantaged children's language skills? (Check two.)

_____ (a) experiencing many new objects and situations

_____ (b) learning to label objects and situations

_____ (c) encouraging parents to talk with their preschool children

- - - - - - - - - - - - - - - - - - -

(b) and (c)

90. Now let's look at specific social class differences in the use of language. Generally, psychologists and linguists agree that the language of the middle-class is more complex than language used by lower-class children and adults. Sentence structure is more varied, conditional phrases are used more often, and so on. Lower-class sentence structure is simpler and more direct. Sentences are short and their structure varies little.

Look at the following two passages, both written by ten-year-old children.
(a) "Our trip to the zoo"
Today we went to the zoo. Because we all like animals, we enjoyed the trip very much. While the lions and tigers were very nice to see, we really enjoyed watching the polar bear. He played in the water just like a child. We hated to leave at the end of the day because we had so much fun.
(b) "Our trip to the zoo"
We went to the zoo. It was fun. We saw lions and tigers. We saw a polar bear. The polar bear swam in the water. Then we came home. It was fun.
Which would you say was probably written by a middle-class child and which by a lower-class child? Explain your answer.

_____

_____

_____

- - - - - - - - - - - - - - - - - -

(a); because the language is more complex, or sentence structure is more varied, or there are more conditional phrases.

91. Lower-class language structure is _____ than
                                          simpler/more complex
    middle-class language structure.

- - - - - - - - - - - - - - - - - -

    simpler

92. In addition, lower-class language is more <u>concrete</u>. Much of the
    time it is used to communicate directly about facts, things, or ac-
    tions. It tends to be <u>immediate</u> and <u>direct</u>. Middle-class parents
    tend to use language in a more abstract way to express concepts,
    ideas, and relationships such as similarities and differences.

    Two men are discussing a sports car they have just seen. One
    discusses the way it handles, the acceleration, its fuel injection
    system, and its double overhead cam. The other compares the
    experience of driving it to that of flying an airplane, speculates on
    why Italian sports cars are better made than American sports cars,
    and points out the progress that has been made in the auto industry
    in the past twenty-five years.

    Which person is probably using a middle-class pattern of language?

    Explain. _____

    _____

    _____

- - - - - - - - - - - - - - - - -

    The second person; because he talks in a more abstract way about
    the car; he uses comparisons and abstract ideas more than the first
    person. (This example points out samples of two different <u>patterns</u>
    of language; it should in no way be taken as implying that a person's
    social class can be deduced from one brief segment of conversation.)

93. What are some differences between middle-class and lower-class

    patterns of language? _____

    _____

- - - - - - - - - - - - - - - - -

    Middle-class language tends to be abstract and complex; lower-class
    language is more concrete and simple in structure.

94. Since most school subjects are biased in favor of a middle-class
    language "style," it follows that lower-class children are penalized

for their language pattern. Middle-class patterns of language prepare a child for doing well in most school-related situations.

When psychologists speak of using language <u>effectively</u>, then, they
generally mean: (Check one.)

_____ (a) using language that is simple and concrete

_____ (b) using language that is complex and abstract

- - - - - - - - - - - - - - - - - -

(b)

95. An English educational sociologist, Basil Bernstein, made a study of
the language patterns used by middle-class and lower-class parents
in talking with their children. He found that lower-class parents tend
to use language to communicate rules of behavior to their children.
They discuss, explain, and reason less than middle-class parents do.
Also, their speech tends to restrict discussion or choice and to con-
vey authority—"You do it like this."
     Middle-class parents, on the other hand, tend to <u>explain</u> why
things should be done a certain way. They use discussion and reason
in talking with their children, and elaborate more when explaining
how things work or how things should be done.
     Bernstein labeled each of these patterns of language interactions
between parents and children. He refers to one as a <u>restricted code</u>
and the other as an <u>elaborated code</u>.

On the basis of the descriptions above, which pattern would you guess
represents a <u>restricted</u> code, and which represents an <u>elaborated</u>

code? _____

_____

- - - - - - - - - - - - - - - - - -

The lower-class pattern uses a restricted code; the middle-class
pattern uses an elaborated code.

96. Read the following two samples of conversation between parents and
children.

Conversation A   Mother: Hold on tight.
                 Child: Why?
                 Mother: Hold on tight.
                 Child: Why?
                 Mother: You'll fall.
                 Child: Why?
                 Mother: I told you to hold on tight, didn't I?

Conversation B Mother: Hold on tightly.
Child: Why?
Mother: If you don't, you will be thrown forward
and you'll fall.
Child: Why?
Mother: Because if the bus suddenly stops, you'll
jerk forward onto the seat in front.
Child: Why?
Mother: Now hold on tightly and don't make such
a fuss.

(a) Which parent would you say is using an elaborated code and which
one is using a restricted code?

_____

(b) Which is probably the middle-class parent?

_____

- - - - - - - - - - - - - - - - - - -

(a) The parent in Conversation B is using an elaborated code; the
parent in Conversation A is using a restricted code. (b) the parent
in Conversation B

97. (a) A restricted code of communication is used to communicate

_____.
rules/reasoning

(b) An elaborated code is based on _____.
authority/discussion

- - - - - - - - - - - - - - - - - - -

(a) rules; (b) discussion

98. Two American psychologists, Hess and Shipman, did a study which
supports Bernstein's results. They studied three groups of parents
and children: a middle-class group, a blue-collar working class
group, and a group of parents and children on welfare. They had
the parents explain three simple tasks to their children; they then
analyzed the patterns of language used in the explanations.

Hess and Shipman found that the sentences used by the middle-
class parents were more subtle and complex grammatically, and
that their explanations were both more organized and more abstract
in content.

Does this American study support the results obtained by Basil

Bernstein in England? Explain your answer. _____

_____

_____

_____

- - - - - - - - - - - - - - - - -

Yes; Bernstein found that middle-class parents spend a lot of time
explaining and reasoning, rather than communicating rules. They
elaborate more in their explanations and instruction. This study
supports those findings.

99. Hess and Shipmen concluded that lower-class and middle-class parents teach different <u>uses</u> of language through the way they communicate with their children. In a subtle way, lower-class parents teach
their children that language is basically for communicating rules
and facts. On the other hand, middle-class parents, by the example
they set, teach their children how to use language for thinking and
problem-solving.

(a) How do parents go about teaching language use to their children?

_____

(b) Which parents generally teach the problem-solving use of

language? _____

- - - - - - - - - - - - - - - - -

(a) through the way they communicate with their children;
(b) middle-class parents

100. Results of the studies by Bernstein and by Hess and Shipman show
that middle-class parents teach their children to use language in a
way not taught by lower-class parents.

Lower-class parents do <u>not</u> teach their children to use language for:
(Check one.)

_____ (a) communicating

_____ (b) problem-solving

_____ (c) relating concrete facts and details

- - - - - - - - - - - - - - - - -

(b)

101. In what two ways are middle-class children generally better in language ability than lower-class children? _____

_____

- - - - - - - - - - - - - - - - - - - -

They have a larger vocabulary; they make more effective use of language.

102. Describe what Hess and Shipman concluded about what middle-class parents teach their children about language use?

_____

_____

_____

- - - - - - - - - - - - - - - - - - -

Middle-class parents tend to teach their children how to use language for thinking and problem-solving. Lower-class parents tend to teach that language is for communicating facts and rules of behavior.

103. Recently, Bernstein's conclusions have been criticized because he did not distinguish in his research between language <u>performance</u> (production) and language <u>competence</u> (comprehension). There is some evidence that lower-class children can, if necessary, use the elaborated code, even though they do not do so in everyday speech.

   In one study, lower-class boys were asked to write both a <u>formal</u> and an <u>informal</u> letter. The informal letter was written in the way the children usually spoke; the formal letter was written in a middle-class "style"—that is, the letters could not be distinguished from those written by middle-class children.

The study just described demonstrates that lower-class children

_____ use the same pattern of speech in formal and informal
do/do not
situations.

- - - - - - - - - - - - - - - - - -

do not

104. The study above shows that lower-class children can use middle-class patterns of speech when the situation demands it. This suggests that: (Check one.)

_____ (a) Their language performance is probably better than their language competence.

_____ (b) Their language competence is probably better than their language performance.

_____ (c) There is no difference between their language competence and their language performance.

- - - - - - - - - - - - - - - - - -

(b)

105. The issue of the relationship between language and social class is still not resolved. Perhaps lower-class children are not as linguistically "deprived" as researchers have assumed; perhaps they can use language just as effectively—that is, in an abstract and complex way— as middle-class children if the situation is right. It may simply be that researchers have not been able to get disadvantaged children to perform up to their capacity. In any event, based on the evidence to date, it cannot be naively assumed that lower-class children's school-related difficulties can be solved by teaching them the "standard" or middle-class language patterns.

It has been shown that the vocabulary of disadvantaged children can be improved by providing labels for objects and experiences and encouraging children to use them. Is there as yet any agreement on how to help lower-class children use language more effectively? Explain.

_____

_____

_____

_____

_____

- - - - - - - - - - - - - - - - - -

No; because the relationship between social class and language use is not clear. It is possible that lower-class children can use language in a more effective way than they do in everyday speech—that is, that they can use language that is more abstract and complex.

SELF-TEST

This Self-Test is designed to show you whether or not you have mastered this chapter's objectives. Answer each question to the best of your ability. Correct answers and review instructions are given at the end of the test.

1. Explain the difference between language comprehension and language production. Why is it important to distinguish between the two?

    _____

    _____

    _____

    _____

    _____

    _____

2. Trace the development of children's speech from their first babbling sounds to simple sentences. Show how this development is affected by imitation, reinforcement, and expansion.

    _____

    _____

    _____

    _____

    _____

    _____

    _____

    _____

    _____

3. Explain how children's speech errors often suggest the use of a grammatical rule.

    _____

    _____

4. How did Jean Berko demonstrate that four-year-old children have mastered most fundamental rules of grammar?

5. Do all psychologists believe that language acquisition is simply the result of imitation and reinforcement? Explain.

6. Explain the age changes that occur in children's communication.

7. Explain how verbal mediation helps children regulate their behavior.

8. Some psychologists maintain that thought is nothing more than inner speech. Explain why research with deaf children does <u>not</u> support this theory.

9.   In what two ways is the language of middle-class children different
     from that of lower-class children?

     _____

     _____

     _____

10. If you were designing a program to increase children's vocabulary,
     what activities would you include?

     _____

     _____

     _____

     _____

     _____

     _____

11. Compare the characteristics of middle-class and lower-class speech.

     _____

     _____

12. Discuss the apparent differences in the way middle- and lower-class
     parents use language.

     _____

     _____

     _____

     _____

     _____

Answers to Self-Test

Compare your answers to the questions on the Self-Test with the answers
given below. If all of your answers are correct, you are ready to go on
to the next chapter. If you missed any questions, review the frames indicated in parentheses following the answer. If you miss several questions, you should probably reread the entire chapter carefully.

1.   Language comprehension refers to how much a child actually under-
     stands of language; language production is the language he or she
     actually uses in everyday speech. It is important to make the

distinction between the two because children's comprehension is always greater than their production. It would be misleading to assume that a child only "knows" those words he or she uses. (Frames 2—4)

2. Children's earliest babblings are selectively reinforced; some sounds —generally those close to adult speech—are reinforced more than others. Babies also try to imitate adult speech, and are probably reinforced when they do it successfully. When children get older, their parents usually use the technique of expansion to bring their children's speech closer to adult speech. The parent expands on what the child says, and the child in turn expands on his or her original utterance. For example, if a child says: "me go," the mother might say: "You want to go to the store?" The child might answer: "Me go store." (Frame 47)

3. When children use an incorrect grammatical form, the listener can be fairly sure that they are not simply imitating adult speech. If the word used appears to follow a grammatical rule (for example, "goed" or "thinked"), the child using it probably knows and is applying a grammatical rule. (Frames 45, 46, 55)

4. Jean Berko used nonsense words and asked the children to give the correct form of the word. For example, she would say: "This is a wug. Now there are two of them. There are two _____." If the children say "wugs," they apparently know a rule for forming the plural. (The use of nonsense syllables assured her that the children were not simply imitating a word they had heard before.) (Frames 42—44, 55)

5. No, some believe that children have a built-in language processing system—a language acquisition device—that allows them to process and understand all the sounds in their language environment. (Frames 48—49)

6. At first children's speech is egocentric—that is, there is no real exchange of ideas or information. Gradually, the child learns to use sociocentric speech—speech that communicates. (Frame 63)

7. If children can "tell themselves," either overtly or covertly, to do something, it helps them to respond appropriately. (Frames 64—65, 75)

8. Inner speech occurs when children gradually learn to regulate their behavior by "talking to themselves." Research has shown that the thinking processes of deaf and hearing children are very similar. Deaf children do as well on most problems as hearing children. Therefore, thought cannot be only represented by speech; speech is probably only one mode of representing a problem. (Frames 78—80)

9. Middle-class children generally have a better vocabulary than lower-class children, and they use language more effectively—that is, they use more complex and abstract speech. (Frames 82, 93)

10. The program would include practice in labeling objects and experiences. Perhaps the children might go on field trips, then discuss or list and describe the things they had seen. Together, the class might write a story about the trip. Essentially, the program would emphasize labeling, rather than just providing a wide variety of experiences. Parents would also be encouraged to participate and to talk with their children about the activities. (Frames 88, 89)

11. Middle-class speech tends to be abstract and complex. Lower-class speech tends to be simple and direct. (Frames 89—93)

12. According to Bernstein, middle-class parents use an elaborated code when talking with their children, and lower-class parents use a restricted code. That is, middle-class parents tend to use language to discuss, explain, and reason. Lower-class parents tend to restrict discussion to communicate rules of behavior. (Hess and Shipman found similar results.) (Frames 95—105)

SELECTED BIBLIOGRAPHY

The acquisition of language

Braine, M. D. S. The ontogeny of English phrase structure: The first phrase. Language, 1963, 39, 1-13.

Chomsky, N., and Weir, R. H. Syntactic Structures. The Hague: Mouton, 1957. Very technical; for those who want to study transformational grammar in depth.

Ervin-Tripp, S. M., and Slobin, D. I. Psycholinguistics. Annual Review of Psychology, 1966, 17, 435-474. A general introduction to the study of psycholinguistics.

McNeill, D. The development of language. In P. Mussen, ed., Manual of Child Psychology. New York: Wiley, 1977. A good overview.

Solbin, D. Imitation and grammatical development in children. In N. Endler, L. Boulter, and N. Osser, eds. Contemporary Issues in Developmental Psychology. Discusses the role of imitation and expansion in language development.

Weir, R. H. Language in the Crib. The Hague: Mouton, 1962. A delightful glimpse into the language and thought of children.

Egocentric speech

Piaget, J. The Language and Thought of the Child. London: Routledge & Kegan Paul, 1926.

Language and thought

Furth, H. G.   Research with the deaf: Implications for language and
cognition. Psychological Bulletin, 1964, 62, 145–164.

Uses of language

Luria, A. R., and Yudovich, F. Speech and the Development of Mental
Processes in the Child. London: Staples (MacGibbon & Kee), 1959.

Language as a verbal mediator

Kendler, T. S. Development of mediating responses in children. In
J. C. Wright and J. Kagan, eds. Basic cognitive processes in
children. Monographs of the Society for Research in Child
Development, 1962, 28, no. 2, 33–52.

Language and social class

Bernstein, B. Social structure, language, and learning. In J. P.
DeCecco, ed.   The Psychology of Language, Thought, and Instruction.
New York: Holt, Rinehart, & Winston, 1967, pp. 89–103.

Ginzburg, H. The Myth of the Deprived Child. Englewood Cliffs, N.J.:
Prentice-Hall, 1972.

Hess, R. D. and Shipman, V. C. Early experience and the socialization
of cognitive modes in children. Child Development, 1965, 36, no. 4,
869–886.

CHAPTER SIX
The Development of Sex Differences

By the age of twelve or so, boys and girls differ in a wide variety of measures and traits. In these days of rapid change, both men and women are seriously questioning how these differences develop. How many sex differences are biologically determined and how many are culturally determined?

Related to this question are questions about our sex-role stereotypes. Do they influence children's development as much as the women's movement claims they do? If so, has the influence been a good or a bad one?

In this chapter, we will look at some of the differences that do exist between boys and girls and will try to determine how these differences probably develop. We will look at some of the factors involved in the development of sex-role identity in children, including imitation, reinforcement, and cultural stereotypes.

OBJECTIVES

When you complete this chapter, you will be able to

- summarize the differences between boys' and girls' personality traits and intellectual abilities;

- discuss the role of genetic factors and learning in the development of each of these differences;

- describe some of the differences in initial response tendencies of boy and girl infants;

- identify the three ways in which sex-role identity is often defined;

- discuss how Freud and the social learning theorists differ in their view of how children come to identify with one or the other of their parents;

- show how a child's understanding of maleness-femaleness changes with age;

- demonstrate how cultural stereotypes influence children's own sex-role identity;

- define cross-sex typing and describe some of its effects.

OBSERVING SEXUAL DIFFERENCES

Personality Differences

1. One of the more interesting questions in the field of child psychology is why psychologists have for so long ignored the study of sex differences. Time and time again, researchers have published their results on studies, only to add as an afterthought: "...these results hold for boys but not for girls." Or: "Girls performed differently on this task than boys." Or: "For girls, the results are in the opposite direction." There are very noticeable differences in the way boys and girls respond in a wide variety of situations. Only recently, however, have child psychologists come to study these differences in detail.

   In the area of <u>personality</u>, one of the main observable differences between boys and girls is in the amount of aggressiveness shown. Boys consistently show more physical aggression than girls, starting at a very young age. At the preschool and nursery school level, they are more likely than girls to hit out, to·get into fights, or to

engage in <u>negative attention-getting</u>. Moreover, this difference persists as children get older.

Following are a nursery school teacher's notes on ten-minute
observations of two children in the class.

Observation 1: Child A enters classroom with friend. Picks up
clay and pounds it several times on table. Grabs
friend's cookie cutter to use with clay. Begins
making a horse. Says "I need more clay" and takes
some from neighbor's pile. Neighbor cries and
tries to grab it back. Teacher intervenes to break
up fight.

Observation 2: Child B enters classroom and approaches puzzle
table. Asks to help neighbor with puzzle. They begin to work together. Another child approaches and
messes up their puzzle. Child B says "That's not
nice" and begins to put pieces together again.

Based on what you know of sex differences in aggression, which
child is exhibiting aggressive behavior usually associated with boys?

_____

- - - - - - - - - - - - - - - - -

probably child A   (Of course, individual behavior varies widely—in
this case, for example, child A might be a girl, but the behavior
exhibited by child A is more often observed in boys than girls.
Later we will discuss some of the reasons why this might be so.)

2.   (a) Even at a very young age, boys show _____ physical aggres-
                                          more/less
         sion than girls.

     (b) This difference _____ as children get older.
                          persists/does not persist

- - - - - - - - - - - - - - - - -

     (a) more; (b) persists

3.   Physically aggressive behavior is often labeled <u>antisocial</u> aggression,
     while indirect, nonphysical aggression—such as verbal hostility and
     sarcasm—is labeled <u>prosocial</u> aggression. Psychologists have found
     that, while boys nearly always score higher than girls on antisocial
     aggression, girls generally score higher than boys on prosocial ag-
     gression. Aggression is apparently channeled differently for boys
     than for girls.

(a) When we say that a girl has a biting tongue, we mean that she is

showing verbal, or _____ aggression.
                    antisocial/prosocial

(b) Boys are generally _____ than girls in prosocial
                        higher/lower

aggression.

- - - - - - - - - - - - - - - - - -

(a) prosocial; (b) lower

4. Another difference between boys and girls is that girls show more
    guilt over aggressive behavior than boys do. When boys act out ag-
    gressively—hitting, kicking, wrestling, quarreling—they show
    relatively little guilt about their behavior. Girls, however, from
    a very early age, label all aggressive behavior (including, apparently,
    prosocial aggression) as "bad." Consequently, they experience anx-
    iety and guilt about their aggressive tendencies.

    Two nursery school children, John and Sarah, get into a hairpulling
    and wrestling match over who is going to use the red truck. Which
    child is likely to feel more guilty over this aggressive behavior,

    John or Sarah? Explain. _____

    _____

- - - - - - - - - - - - - - - - -

    Sarah; because girls generally show more guilt over aggressive
    behavior than boys do.

5. If girls are loath to express aggression because of guilt feelings, will
    they be more likely to show aggression if their guilt can be lessened
    in some way? While research with children has not dealt directly
    with this question, results from a study on adult aggression suggest
    that the answer is yes.
        Two psychologists, Rapoport and Chammah, decided to find out
    how much aggression female subjects would show toward another per-
    son if the other person could not see or identify them. To do this,
    they used a variation of the "Prisoner's Dilemma" game. In this
    game, two "prisoners" are accused of the same crime, and are held
    and questioned separately. It is to each prisoner's personal advan-
    tage to "confess" (the confessing prisoner receives more money);
    however, the nonconfessing prisoner receives a more severe sentence.
    It is to the prisoners' mutual advantage if neither of them confesses,
    although each stands to gain less by cooperating. The game attempts

to discover how much cooperation will be shown by the "prisoners" under conditions of anonymity.

The experimenters found that, in this game, women showed significantly less cooperation than men. Female prisoners behaved more aggressively with other females than male prisoners behaved with other males.

Based on the evidence from this study, which of the following statements is probably true?

_____ (a) In some situations, females behave more aggressively than males.

_____ (b) Males always behave more aggressively than females.

- - - - - - - - - - - - - - - - - -

(a) (Remember that this study was done with adults as subjects; we cannot be sure that children would react in the same way. The results do suggest, however, a very direct relationship between aggressive behavior and guilt over aggression.)

6. How did the experimenters attempt to make the situation less guilt-producing than it might otherwise have been?

_____

- - - - - - - - - - - - - - - - - -

They arranged the experiment so that the two "prisoners" could not see each other.

7. We see then that boys express their aggression much more directly than girls, and generally do so without guilt. Do they also have a higher level of aggression than girls?

Let's look at the evidence: from a very early age, boys generally score higher than girls on most measures of aggression—behavior ratings, self-reports, projective tests, and fantasy-aggression measures. Most of these measures (perhaps with the exception of behavior ratings) claim to tap the child's inner level of aggression.

From boys' and girls' performances on these tests, which would you conclude? (Check one.)

_____ (a) Boys are probably higher in aggressive motivation than girls.

_____ (b) Girls are probably higher in aggressive motivation than boys.

_____ (c) There is probably no difference between boys and girls in amount of aggressive motivation.

- - - - - - - - - - - - - - - - - -

(a)

8. To summarize: write either "boys" or "girls" in each space below.

   (a) _____ generally show more antisocial (physical) aggression.

   (b) _____ generally show more prosocial (verbal) aggression.

   (c) _____ generally experience more guilt over aggression.

   (d) _____ are probably higher in aggressive motivation.

- - - - - - - - - - - - - - - - - -

(a) boys; (b) girls; (c) girls; (d) boys

9. One of the stereotypes we hold about boys and girls is that girls are more dependent than boys. Many studies support this conclusion. However, if we look at a breakdown of the data by age, we find that, initially, boys and girls are equally dependent; by age 12, however, girls score higher on most dependency measures than boys. This difference persists into adulthood.

   Here's the breakdown:

   Nursery school: No differences observed in dependent behavior (attention-seeking, clinging, asking for help, and so on); no projective tests used.

   Ages 6-10: Little data available; results are variable, depending on the measure used.

   Ages 12-adult: Females generally score higher in dependency than males on behavior ratings and on self-report and projective measures of dependency (these indicate that females are less self-sufficient and independent than males).

   Based on this data, which of the following conclusions would you draw about the relationship between sex and dependency? (Check one.)

   _____ (a) Girls are by nature more dependent than boys.

   _____ (b) Girls and boys start off equally dependent, but differences develop over time.

- - - - - - - - - - - - - - - - -

(b)

What causes this later difference in dependency, since boys and girls appear to start off at the same level? The reason could be one of the following:

1. The girls show more dependent behavior as they grow older.
2. The boys show <u>less</u> dependent behavior as they grow older.
3. Both girls and boys become less dependent, but boys drop their dependency behavior at a faster rate.

Actually, what seems to happen is summarized in the following figure:

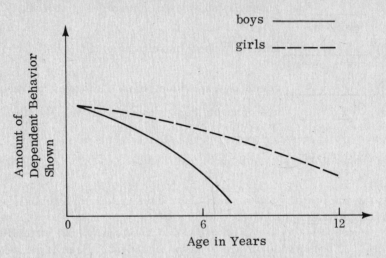

Study this figure carefully. Which of the above three statements does this figure support? _____

_____

- - - - - - - - - - - - - - - -

Statement 3: Both girls and boys become less dependent, but boys drop their dependency behavior at a faster rate. (A little later, we will discuss possible reasons for this pattern of development.)

11. As far as the <u>trait</u> or motive of dependency is concerned, it is impossible to tell if differences exist in very young children. Measures of dependency during preschool and early school years are essentially <u>behavior</u> ratings. There are no measures of dependency motivation, as such. All we can say for sure is that young girls do not show more dependent <u>behavior</u> than boys.

However, look back at frame 9: by what age can we be fairly sure that girls have higher dependency <u>motivation</u> than boys? Explain.

_____

_____

- - - - - - - - - - - - - - - - - -

By age 12; because by age 12, some of the measures being used are self-report and projective measures—that is, they attempt to measure dependency motivation.

12. A third personality variable on which boys and girls have been found to differ is the need for achievement. We know, of course, that actual achievement is lower for women than for men. For example, women underachieve in all occupations. There are more men than women in professional and managerial positions; men advance faster and make more money than women. Women are becoming aware that job discrimination by companies and employers is responsible for a large part of women's underachievement, and they are taking legal action to remedy the situation.

However, psychologists have also found that women consistently score lower on tests of achievement motivation than men. In other words, even given equal opportunity, they generally do not have the same desire to succeed as men do. *

J. W. Atkinson, a psychologist interested in achievement motivation, says that the difference he finds between males and females in achievement motivation is "...perhaps the most persistent unresolved problem on need achievement."**

Describe the "difference" Atkinson is referring to. How do men and women differ in achievement motivation?

- - - - - - - - - - - - - - - - -

Women consistently score lower on tests of achievement motivation than men; women apparently do not have the same desire to succeed as men.

---

*Of course, this is a generalization; many women are highly motivated to succeed. In fact, it is often said that, because of the discrimination that exists, women in business and the professions must be more highly motivated than their male counterparts in order to succeed.

**J. W. Atkinson, ed. Motives in Fantasy, Action, and Society (Princeton: Van Nostrand, 1958).

13. Again, let's look at whether these differences exist in very young children. There are few such studies of very young children. One nursery school study, however, which observed many dimensions of behavior, found that boys and girls differed on all the variables studied except achievement efforts. However, girls tended, more than boys, to lack confidence in their work, and looked more to adults for help and approval. They tended to anticipate failure more than the boys did.

(a) According to the study just described, do boys and girls in nursery school show the same amount of achievement behavior?

_____

(b) Do they show the same amount of confidence in their work?

    Explain. _____

- - - - - - - - - - - - - - - - -

(a) yes; (b) No; girls are less confident than boys.

14. Studies of first, second, and third grade children, using projective tests as a measure of achievement motivation, show similar results. That is, boys and girls score equally high on tests of achievement motivation, but girls tend to lack confidence in their ability.

By the age of 12 or so, however, boys generally score higher on achievement motivation than girls. This change is probably due to a combination of factors. Social success is very important to both boys and girls; for girls, however, social success usually means giving up "achievement success."* Since girls have consistently had more doubts about their abilities than boys, the pressures are probably very great on girls to "give up the fight."

In your own words, summarize the above hypothesis as to why adolescent girls are generally lower on achievement motivation than

adolescent boys. _____

_____

_____

_____

- - - - - - - - - - - - - - - - -

_____

*Margaret Mead has suggested that in our culture boys are "unsexed" by failure, and girls by success.

Girls have consistently had less confidence than boys in their work; at adolescence, they are more concerned with social success than achievement, so it is more comfortable to give up the desire to achieve. (This explanation is highly speculative, of course. Interestingly enough, however, Matina Horner, president of Radcliffe College, believes that "fear of success" is an important motive for women, but not for men.)

15. (a) In the area of personality boys and girls have been found to differ in what three types of behavior? _____ ,

   _____ , and _____ .

   (b) Explain what is known about differences in the underlying

   motivation in these three areas of behavior. _____

   _____

   _____

   _____

   _____

   _____

   _____

- - - - - - - - - - - - - - - - - - -

(a) aggression, dependency, and achievement behavior;
(b) Aggression: from a very early age, boys appear to be higher in aggression than girls. Dependency: by age 12 at least girls score higher on measures of dependency motivation. Achievement motivation: there appears to be no difference between boys and girls until around age 12.

Intellectual Differences

16. Let's turn now to differences in intellectual abilities. In overall IQ scores, boys and girls are nearly equal at all ages. The IQ tests are deliberately designed to minimize any sex differences. That is, during the development of the tests, the subtests were changed until, at any given age, the overall scores of boys and girls came out to be nearly equal.

   However, boys and girls have different patterns of abilities. That is, girls might be higher than boys in the vocabulary and information subtests, whereas boys might score higher than girls on mathematical problem-solving and copying designs.

Which of the following statements about sex differences in IQ scores are true, and which are false?

_____ (a) Boys and girls have the same patterns of abilities on IQ tests.

_____ (b) Boys' and girls' IQ scores are nearly equal at all ages.

- - - - - - - - - - - - - - - - -

(a) false; (b) true

17. Three areas of ability often studied are number ability, verbal ability, and spatial ability. Number ability involves computation and arithmetical reasoning. Spatial ability involves performance on formboards, puzzles, and other tasks involving form discrimination. Verbal ability involves many areas of language: vocabulary, fluency, spelling, articulation, reading skills, listening skills, use of grammar, and so on.

Tell whether the following tests are probably measuring number ability, verbal ability, or spatial ability.

_____ (a) Children are asked to repeat words and sounds as the examiner says them.

_____ (b) Children are asked to figure out how far a train would go in three hours if it traveled at 60 miles per hour.

_____ (c) Children are given incomplete sentences and asked to fill in the correct verb form.

_____ (d) Children are asked to pick out the figure that is not like all the others in the row.

- - - - - - - - - - - - - - - - -

(a) verbal ability; (b) number ability; (c) verbal ability;
(d) spatial ability

18. Let's look first at how boys and girls differ on number ability. Because they mature earlier than boys, girls learn to count earlier, and therefore score higher than boys on early tests of number ability. These early results may not be very significant because they involve simply the ability to count, rather than a real understanding of arithmetical reasoning. During the middle school years, there are no consistent differences between boys and girls on numerical skills, either computation or arithmetical reasoning. From high school age,

however, males consistently score higher than females on tests of numerical ability.

Which of the following statements best describes the relationship between sex differences and number ability?

_____ (a) Boys are consistently better than girls in number ability.

_____ (b) Boys score higher than girls at a very young age, and girls excel from high school age on.

_____ (c) Girls score higher than boys at a very young age, and boys excel from high school age on.

_____ (d) Girls are consistently better than boys in number ability.

- - - - - - - - - - - - - - - - -

(c)

19. During the middle school years there _____ significant
                                          are/are not
    differences in number ability between boys and girls.

- - - - - - - - - - - - - - - - -

are not

20. At what age do boys consistently score higher than girls on tests of
    number ability? _____

- - - - - - - - - - - - - - - - -

by high school age

21. On spatial tasks—putting puzzles together, putting forms in form-boards, working with mechanical toys—boys are generally better than girls, once their physical maturation has reached a certain level. During the preschool years, boys are not as physically mature as girls, and there appear to be no sex differences on spatial tasks. Beginning with the first grade, however, and continuing through college, boys consistently do better than girls on tasks of spatial ability.

    The stereotype of the "typical boy" includes reference to his mechanical ability, his ability to fix things, assemble model cars and planes, and so on. Girls, it is believed, are not generally as proficient at these activities. Based on the evidence of boys' and girls' spatial ability, does this stereotype have some basis in fact?

Explain. _____

_____

- - - - - - - - - - - - - - - - - -

Yes; boys are generally better on spatial tasks than girls.

22. In the area of verbal ability, as in spatial ability, differences
between boys and girls are fairly consistent throughout the
school years, only in the reverse direction. That is, girls appear
to start off better than boys and maintain a slight superiority in
most areas. Girls begin talking earlier, as might be expected from
their earlier rate of maturing; in addition, however, they are consistently more fluent, more articulate, better in spelling and
grammar, and less likely to have reading problems than boys.
These differences in verbal ability persist at least through adolescence and possibly beyond.

(a) At most ages, _____ score higher on tests of verbal ability.
             boys/girls

(b) This difference in verbal ability is _____ throughout
                              constant/variable
the school years.

- - - - - - - - - - - - - - - - - -

(a) girls; (b) constant

23. To summarize:
(a) In what three areas of personality are sex differences generally
found? _____

_____
(b) In what three areas of intellectual functioning are sex differences
usually found? _____
(c) Which of the above differences are fairly constant throughout the
school years? _____

_____

- - - - - - - - - - - - - - - - - -

(a) aggression, dependency, and achievement motivation;
(b) number, spatial, and verbal ability; (c) differences in
aggression, spatial ability, and verbal ability.

HOW DO THESE SEX DIFFERENCES DEVELOP?

24. The developmental psychologist, of course, must ask, "How do these sex differences develop?" We know that much of a child's development is the result of learning. We have seen that if a certain behavior is reinforced, it tends to recur. We also know that some aspects of development are the result of maturation; that is, genetically, a child is in some way <u>programmed</u> to grow or change or act in certain ways.

   In this section we will present some evidence suggesting innate differences between the sexes and some evidence pointing to environmental effects on the development of sex differences. The suggestion will be made that perhaps the two factors interact in complex ways to produce later sex differences.

   First of all, what is the evidence that males are genetically more <u>aggressive</u> than females? For one thing, field observations of 3 to 6-year-old children in six different cultures have shown that, in all the cultures studied, boys show significantly more physical aggression than girls.

   That these sex differences persist across cultures suggests that specific cultural and child-rearing practices:

   _____ (a) probably cause the higher aggression in males

   _____ (b) probably have little effect on the aggression level of males

- - - - - - - - - - - - - - - - -

   (b)

25. Observations of male and female monkeys in Harry Harlow's Wisconsin Primate Lab give further support to the theory of early sex differences in amount of aggressive behavior. Very young male monkeys engaged in more rough and tumble play, threatened other monkeys more, and initiated play with other monkeys more than did young female monkeys. Field studies of monkeys by other researchers show similar results.

   While there are obvious problems in applying evidence from primate studies to human behavior, these studies lend additional support to the hypothesis that:

   _____ (a) There may be innate sex differences in amount of aggression.

   _____ (b) There are probably no innate sex differences in amount of aggression.

- - - - - - - - - - - - - - - - -

(a)

26. In another study with primates, a male sex hormone (androgen) was injected into pregnant monkeys, thereby producing "masculinized" female offspring. The behavior of two of these masculinized female monkeys was compared with the behavior of two untreated monkeys for twenty minutes a day, five days a week, beginning at the age of two months.

    Results of hundreds of observations show that the treated females initiated play, threatened the other females, and engaged in rough and tumble play more frequently than the untreated females. This difference in behavior persisted well into the third year of life.

    This study _____ the theory that males are in-
            supports/does not support
    nately more aggressive than females.

- - - - - - - - - - - - - - - - -

    supports

27. Finally, we know that boys tend to have higher activity levels than girls. By itself, this tendency can be either positive or negative, depending largely on the situations in which the highly active children find themselves. Very possibly, however, a high activity level will lead to higher physical aggression; boys are simply "on the move" more than girls and have more chance to come into contact with other children and to get into trouble. Boys are also more likely to react to frustration by overtly physical aggression.

    In a typical kindergarten classroom, which children are more likely to show physical aggression—active or passive children? Explain.

    _____

    _____

    _____

- - - - - - - - - - - - - - - - -

    Active children; they are more likely to come into contact with other children. They are more likely to react to frustration by overtly physical aggression.

28. Boys' higher levels of aggression cannot be entirely explained, how-ever, by innate or genetic factors. Learning and reinforcement also play a part. Sears, Maccoby, and Levin, in their famous study of patterns of child-rearing, found that parents in their study allowed

boys to show more aggression than girls. Generally, boys were allowed to show aggression toward both parents and other children, and were in fact often encouraged to "fight back" if attacked. Girls, on the other hand, were praised for "good" behavior. Physical aggression was frowned upon.

This study suggests that:

_____ (a) Sex differences in aggression are entirely innate.

_____ (b) Sex differences in aggression may be partly a matter of learning and reinforcement.

_____ (c) Sex differences in aggression are entirely the result of learning and reinforcement.

- - - - - - - - - - - - - - - - - -

(b)

29. Explain how the principles of reinforcement might work to cause boys to become more aggressive than girls, referring to the study described in frame 28. (In your own words.)

_____

_____

_____

_____

_____

_____

- - - - - - - - - - - - - - - - - -

If boys are rewarded for aggressive behavior (which they appear to be), that behavior will increase. If girls are not rewarded for aggressive behavior (as they appear not to be), that behavior will tend to drop out. Therefore, boys will tend to be more aggressive than girls.

30. At this point psychologists do not agree whether there are innate sex differences in aggression, although certainly the evidence suggests biological factors play a part. They all agree, however, that reinforcement and learning play a significant part in creating the observed differences between boys and girls.

Look at the following three statements. One should be labeled "true," one "false," and one "maybe." Write in the correct label.

_____   (a) Sex differences in aggression are probably the re-
                       sult of both innate factors and reinforcement.

_____   (b) Sex differences in aggression are entirely innate.

_____   (c) Sex differences in aggression are entirely the re-
                       sult of reinforcement.

- - - - - - - - - - - - - - - - - -

(a) true; (b) false; (c) maybe

31. Let's look at how sex differences in dependency probably develop.
     Remember that there are no differences between very young children
     on amount of dependency shown. Among older children, however,
     girls fairly consistently show more dependency than boys. From this
     would you suspect that there are <u>innate</u> sex differences in amount of
     dependency between boys and girls? Explain your answer.

     _____

     _____

     _____

- - - - - - - - - - - - - - - - - -

No; because in the beginning there are no differences; if dependency
were an innate trait, it would probably be present from birth.

32. Can you develop a hypothesis to explain the fact that older girls are

     more dependent than older boys? _____

     _____

     _____

- - - - - - - - - - - - - - - - - -

Reinforcement may explain this difference in dependency. Parents
may reward dependency for girls, but not reward it for boys.

33. The development of sex differences in achievement motivation prob-
     ably also stems in part from differential reinforcement by parents
     and society. It is clear that contemporary American society does
     not encourage the development of achievement motivation in girls.
     Studies of school textbooks, children's books, and children's televi-
     sion programs have repeatedly shown the following stereotypes:
     males are depicted as the achievers, the ones who travel, work,
     have adventures, and tackle the "important" issues of life; females

are the ones who stay at home, take care of the house, and applaud the males' achievements. Furthermore, in these stories, boys aspire to become doctors, lawyers, pilots, and so on; girls dream of becoming nurses, secretaries, or wives. (Boys never aspire to become husbands!)

What have surveys of children's literature and television programs shown regarding society's attitude toward male and female achievements and achievement motivation? _____

_____

- - - - - - - - - - - - - - - - - -

Male achievement and achievement motivation are encouraged; female achievement and achievement motivation are not.

34. Parents also play an important role in encouraging (or discouraging) achievement motivation in girls. Interestingly enough, high-achieving girls have a different relationship with their mothers than high-achieving boys.

    There is evidence from at least two studies that girls who achieve well academically have mothers who are not very warm or nurturant. For boys to achieve in school, however, it seems to be crucial that they have warm nurturant mothers.

Results of the above studies demonstrate that:

_____ (a) Warmth and nurturance on the part of mothers is essential to children's academic achievements.

_____ (b) Mothers' warmth and nurturance have different effects on boys' and girls' school achievement.

_____ (c) Boys have warmer, more nurturant mothers than girls.

_____ (d) Academic achievement is unrelated to the warmth and nurturance of the mother.

- - - - - - - - - - - - - - - - -

(b)

35. Various hypotheses have been advanced to account for these differences. One that makes sense on the basis of the research results to date is a cross-sex support model. Girls, it is hypothesized, receive their emotional support from their fathers; boys, from their mothers. Fathers apparently make more achievement demands on their sons than on their daughters; therefore boys can "use all the help they can get" from their mothers. Girls, on the other hand, need less

nurturance from the mother; in fact, in order to make any achievement efforts, they need <u>pressure</u> from the mother, since the father
makes few "success" demands.

(a) According to the cross-sex support model, which is the emotionally supportive parent for girls? _____

(b) Why must mothers apply more pressure to achieve on girls than
on boys? _____

_____

- - - - - - - - - - - - - - - - - -

(a) the father; (b) because otherwise girls would get very little
pressure to succeed; fathers make more demands on sons than on
daughters

36. Explain the maternal relationships that are associated with high
achievement in boys and in girls. _____

_____

_____

_____

- - - - - - - - - - - - - - - - - -

Mothers of high-achieving boys are warm and nurturant (give a lot
of emotional support). Mothers of high-achieving girls are not so
warm and nurturant (make achievement demands on their daughters).

37. Research on sex differences in intellectual functioning has so far failed
to establish the <u>cause</u> of these differences. Some psychologists, including Eleanor Maccoby at Stanford, thought that perhaps boys' superior performance in spatial ability was due to their being allowed more
freedom of action. It was hypothesized that because they spent more
time in active, manipulative play, they would develop better spatial
ability than girls, whose play is quieter and less adventurous. This
hypothesis has not been supported. Psychologists do not yet know
the reason for sex differences in spatial ability.

Similarly, it is not clear why boys generally do better on tests
of number ability (at least in the older grades). Parents have long
expressed the idea that girls quickly develop a "block" against math,
and that anxiety, rather than lack of ability, causes their poor performance in mathematics. Again, however, there is no evidence to
support this belief. In general, very little is known about the factors

that are associated with number ability.

n the area of language ability, however, there may be some
evidence as to why sex differences exist. Studies have shown that
four-month-old boy and girl infants produce the same amount of
babbling. However, mothers apparently react differently to the
sounds produced by boy babies and girl babies. They are apparently more likely to imitate the babbling sounds of their four-month-
old <u>daughters</u> than of their four-month-old <u>sons</u>. When a mother
imitates an infant's babbling, she is reinforcing the babbling response—that is, making it more likely to occur again.

On the basis of learning theory, what will probably be the result
of differential reinforcement of boys' and girls' early speech

sounds? _____

_____

- - - - - - - - - - - - - - - - - -

Girl infants will gradually produce more speech sounds than boy
infants.

38. It is known that girls mature physically earlier than boys. Many
differences in performance at a very young age may be attributed
to this difference in rate of maturity. If one child begins acquiring
a skill at an earlier age than another child the first child will have
had more opportunity to <u>practice</u> that skill by, say, age five.

Explain how this principle might work in the case of language skills.
(Remember that girls acquire language skills earlier than boys;
girls are consistently better in language skills than boys.)

_____

_____

_____

_____

- - - - - - - - - - - - - - - - - -

If girls acquire language skills earlier than boys, they will have a
longer period of time in which to practice those skills. Therefore
girls would be expected to do better than boys at any given age.

39. Let's assume for now that girls are not genetically programmed to
be better in language than boys (since there is no direct proof of
this). What are two factors that might account for girls' superiority

in language ability? _____

_____

_____

_____

- - - - - - - - - - - - - - - - - -

Mothers reinforce the babbling of girl infants more than that of boy infants; and girls mature earlier than boys, acquire language skills earlier, and therefore have more time to practice them.

40. Let's look now at differences between boys and girls which appear in infancy and which may affect <u>many</u> areas of development.

Several studies have shown that female infants are more responsive to stimuli from their environment than are male infants. For example, if a jet of air is directed at the abdomen of newborn infants, more pressure is required to cause a reaction from male infants than from female infants. Similarly, female babies react more to the removal of a covering blanket than do male infants.

These studies show that one sex difference present in very young infants is: (Check one.)

_____ (a) responsiveness to physical stimulation

_____ (b) visual ability

_____ (c) ability to hear stimuli in the environment

- - - - - - - - - - - - - - - - - -

(a)

41. Two mothers take their young babies out for a stroll on a windy day. One of the babies becomes very agitated as the wind hits its face. This infant blinks, moves around in the carriage, and begins to cry. The other baby sleeps through the whole trip and does not seem to be bothered by the wind.

Which of the babies is showing a typically female pattern of reactivity?

Explain. _____

_____

- - - - - - - - - - - - - - - - -

The first baby; because female infants are more responsive to physical stimulation than male infants.

42. Related to this differential responsiveness to bodily stimulation is a differential responsiveness to <u>visual</u> and <u>auditory</u> stimulation. Six-month-old girls show greater attention to patterns of lights and film pictures than six-month-old boys do. In another study, six-month-old girls preferred to listen to novel or complex patterns of sounds, while boys of the same age preferred a simple repetitive tone.

If we assume, as most psychologists do, that sustained attention and a preference for novel stimuli represent a more <u>mature</u> ability, which would you say are probably the more mature—six-month-old boys or six-month-old girls? _____

- - - - - - - - - - - - - - - - -

six-month-old girls

43. In what ways are girl infants more responsive and mature than boy infants? _____

_____

_____

_____

- - - - - - - - - - - - - - - - -

Girl infants are more responsive to physical stimulation (a puff of air to the abdomen, removal of a covering blanket); they are more attentive to visual stimuli (lights, pictures); and they prefer novel patterns of sounds, whereas boys do not.

44. Eventually, these early sex differences may be related directly to later differences in personality and intellectual abilities between boys and girls. For now, we can only speculate on the possible effects these early differences might have. It seems clear, how-ever, that there are two factors interacting to cause the development of sex differences in personality and cognitive development:
   1. built-in differences in responses or response tendencies be-tween boys and girls
   2. differential reinforcement of these responses by society—parents, teachers, and the media
The future task of child psychologists will be to trace how these two factors interact to product existing sex differences.

THE DEVELOPMENT OF SEX-ROLE IDENTITY IN CHILDREN

45. We know that sex roles are, at least in part, socially conditioned.
    Children get their ideas about appropriate sex-role behavior partly
    through their interaction with others. There is in the literature,
    however, some confusion as to the exact meaning of sex-role
    identity. Psychologists sometimes refer to feelings, sometimes to
    behavior, and sometimes to understanding when they use the term
    "sex-role identity." That is, they may mean that a child:
      Understands that he is either male or female.
      Behaves like others of the same sex.
      Feels like others of the same sex.

    So, when psychologists say that a little boy has developed a masculine
    sex-role identity, they could mean that he:

    _____ (a) behaves like a boy

    _____ (b) feels like a boy

    _____ (c) understands that he is a boy

    _____ (d) any of the above

- - - - - - - - - - - - - - - - -

  (d)

46. If a psychologist observes a child in nursery school and classifies the
    child's behavior as masculine or feminine, the observer is measuring:

    _____ (a) the child's understanding

    _____ (b) the child's behavior

    _____ (c) the child's feelings

- - - - - - - - - - - - - - - - -

  (b)

47. Which of the following three studies is measuring a child's
    understanding of sex-role identity; which is measuring masculine or
    feminine behavior; and which is measuring masculine or feminine
    feelings? Label each statement "understanding," "behavior," or
    "feelings."

    _____ (a) Children are shown a group of toys and
                              asked which toys they would prefer to
                              play with.

_____ (b) Children are shown a group of toys and asked which toys <u>boys</u> play with and which ones <u>girls</u> play with.

_____ (c) Children are given a group of toys and told they can play with them for the next half hour. An observer notes which toys they play with.

- - - - - - - - - - - - - - - - - -

(a) feelings; (b) understanding; (c) behavior

48. A child understands that she is a little girl, says she wants to be "just like Mommy" when she grows up, but prefers to play with boys' toys and is sometimes called a tomboy.

In what way would you say she has <u>not</u> developed feminine sex-role identity?

_____ (a) in the area of behavior

_____ (b) in the area of feeling

_____ (c) in the area of understanding

- - - - - - - - - - - - - - - - - -

(a)

49. When discussing the development of feminine sex-role identity, a psychologist might be referring to the area of:

1. _____

2. _____

3. _____

- - - - - - - - - - - - - - - - - -

1. behavior
2. feeling
3. understanding

50. As with any developmental issue, the question is asked: "How does sex-role identity develop?"

Sigmund Freud believed that children go through a biologically determined process of <u>identification</u>. Eventually, unless there are problems in the relationship between child and mother, or child and father, children inevitably come to identify with the same-sex parent.

(a) Freud's explanation of how sex-role identity develops stresses: (Check one.)

_____ learning

_____ biological factors

_____ chance

(b) According to Freud, unless there are child-parent problems,

children _____ identify with the same-sex
              always/sometimes/never
parent.

- - - - - - - - - - - - - - - -

(a) biological factors; (b) always

51. The name Freud gives to this biologically determined process is

_____ .
learning/identification

- - - - - - - - - - - - - - - -

identification

52. Social learning theorists, however, believe that sex-role identity develops as a result of imitation and reinforcement. Here's how it works. Remember that children can learn behavior (such as aggressive behavior) by observing a model. Later, when given the opportunity, they will imitate the model's behavior. Let's say that a little girl observes her mother rocking her baby sister. In this case, her mother is a model from whom she just learned a new behavior.

Is she likely to imitate her mother's behavior? Explain. _____

_____

_____

- - - - - - - - - - - - - - - -

Yes; children can learn behavior by observing a model; later, when given the opportunity, they will imitate the model's behavior.

53. In social learning theory, there is no reason to assume children imitate one sex more than the other. Let's assume that children's parents provide the first models and children see them both an equal amount of time. Who would the children probably imitate?

_____ (a) the mother

_____ (b) the father

_____ (c) both father and mother

- - - - - - - - - - - - - - - - -

(c)

54. Both little boys and girls like to dress like Mommy, try on her
    makeup, and so on. Also, they will both pretend to shave and to
    smoke daddy's pipe. Gradually, little girls stop smoking daddy's
    pipe, and little boys stop trying on mommy's clothes. Why do you
    think this happens? (Think in terms of reinforcement.)

    _____

    _____

    _____

- - - - - - - - - - - - - - - - -

Little girls are rewarded (reinforced) for acting like mommy, but
not for acting like daddy. The reverse is true for little boys. In
fact, boys are usually punished (ridiculed, scolded) for acting too
much like mommy.

55. According to social learning theory, two ways in which the present
    stereotyped sex-typing might be changed would be:
    1. to reinforce different sex-role behavior
    2. to change the role models
    For example, if the mother became more "masculine," the girl
    could imitate her and still not fit the current stereotype. Of if the
    family itself did not change, the parents could reinforce the girl's
    attempts to emulate her father.
       Look at the following situations:
       Situation 1   A nontraditional family in which girls are still rein-
                     forced for being like mommy; the mother works,
                     however, and the father stays home and cares for
                     the house and children.
       Situation 2   A traditional family in which the girl is consistently
                     rewarded for acting like her father and is not re-
                     warded for showing an interest in cooking, cleaning,
                     and so on.

    (a) In both of these cases, according to social learning theorists,
         would the girl's sex-typing probably be different from the current

stereotype? Explain. _____

_____

(b) In which situation is the pattern of reinforcement being changed? In which situation are the role models nontraditional?

_____

_____

- - - - - - - - - - - - - - - - -

(a) Yes; according to social learning theorists, she would probably show more "masculine" traits. (b) In the second situation, the pattern of reinforcement is nontraditional; in the first situation, the role models are nontraditional.

56. While children tend to be discouraged from imitating the behavior of the opposite-sex parent, <u>cross-sex imitation</u> does occur. That is, boys imitate certain of their mother's traits and behaviors, and girls imitate certain of their father's traits and behaviors.

Susan, age nine, likes to watch football games like her father, has many of his traits, and says she is going to be an engineer like him when she grows up. How is this an example of cross-sex imitation?

_____

- - - - - - - - - - - - - - - - -

She is imitating certain of her father's traits and behaviors.

57. What is cross-sex imitation? _____

_____

_____

- - - - - - - - - - - - - - - - -

A boy imitates certain of his mother's traits and behaviors, and a girl imitates certain of her father's traits and behaviors.

58. The question for learning theorists is: What determines the child's choice of a model? One thing which seems to influence which parent a child will imitate is "who has the power?"

If the father is seen as the more powerful parent, both male and female children will tend to imitate him more often than the mother. If the mother is seen as more powerful than the father, both male and female children will tend to imitate her more often than the father.

Ron and his sister Harriet come from a family in which the father is dominant and sets the rules for the family. Which of the following statements would be true?

_____ (a) Both Ron and Harriet would imitate the father more than the mother.

_____ (b) Both Ron and Harriet would imitate the mother more than the father.

_____ (c) Ron would imitate the father, and Harriet the mother.

_____ (d) Ron would imitate the mother, and Harriet the father.

- - - - - - - - - - - - - - - - - -

(a)

59. According to social learning theorists, children of both sexes tend to imitate the parent who has greater _____.

- - - - - - - - - - - - - - - - - -

power

60. To summarize:
(a) Which parent did Freud believe a child normally identified with?

_____ the most powerful parent

_____ the same-sex parent

_____ the opposite-sex parent

(b) Which parent do the learning theorists believe a child identifies with?

_____ the most powerful parent

_____ the same-sex parent

_____ the opposite-sex parent

(c) According to Freud, what causes the development of sex-role identity?

_____ imitation

_____ reinforcement

_____ biological determination

(d) According to learning theorists, what causes the development of sex-role identity?

_____ imitation

_____ reinforcement

_____ biological determination

- - - - - - - - - - - - - - - - - -

(a) the same-sex parent; (b) the most powerful parent;
(c) biological determination; (d) imitation and reinforcement

61. It might be said that the Freudian view of the development of sex-role identity stresses the <u>feeling</u> aspect of sex-role identity. The Freudian view is concerned with what goes on inside the child, how closely the child identifies emotionally with the parent.

The social learning view stresses <u>behavior</u>—how much a child <u>acts</u> like one parent or the other.

Lawrence Kohlberg, a developmental psychologist, has a third theory of how sex-role identity develops. This theory stresses the <u>understanding</u> aspect. A little boy first understands that he is a boy, usually because people tell him he is. He then adjusts his behavior to fit his understanding of the concept "boy."

In Kohlberg's view, which comes first, the <u>understanding</u> of what a boy is and does, or the <u>learning</u> of appropriate behavior?

_____

- - - - - - - - - - - - - - - - -

the understanding of what a boy is and does

62. (a) The social learning theory stresses the importance of

_____.
feeling/behavior/understanding

(b) Kohlberg's theory stresses the importance of

_____.
feeling/behavior/understanding

(c) Freud's theory stresses the importance of

_____.
feeling/behavior/understanding

- - - - - - - - - - - - - - - - -

(a) behavior; (b) understanding; (c) feeling

63. According to Kohlberg, a child's understanding of what it means to be a boy or a girl changes with age and cognitive development. As a child begins to think more abstractly and develops reasoning ability, the child <u>understands</u> his or her sex-role identity at a more mature level.

Which child would have the more mature understanding of his or her sex-role identity? Explain.

_____ (a) a child in the stage of formal operations

_____ (b) a child in the stage of concrete operations

_____

_____

- - - - - - - - - - - - - - - - - -

(a); because the stage of formal operations involves the ability to think abstractly and to reason logically.

64. Kohlberg found that at first (one to two years), children only "know" that they are male or female because they are so labeled. (That labeling begins at birth, by the way; in some hospital nurseries, boy infants are wrapped in blue blankets, and girl infants in pink blankets!) Later, they learn to use other cues in making the judgment of maleness-femaleness.

If a two-year-old child is asked: "How do you know that you are a boy?" which is he most likely to answer?

_____ (a) I like to play boys' games.

_____ (b) My mommy told me so.

_____ (c) I look different from my sister.

- - - - - - - - - - - - - - - - - -

(b)

65. Kohlberg found that, from about the age of two to about the age of seven, children use various social and cultural cues in understanding the concept of sex-role identity. Two items that children of this age often use to define maleness or femaleness are <u>clothes</u> and <u>hair length</u>. They are, of course, aware that biological and genital differences exist between boys and girls; they simply do not use these differences as a basis for sex identification. Only when they can use logic and reason can they understand the concept that sex identity is based on biological and genital differences.

(a) When a four-year-old child says: "I can't tell whether they are boys or girls because they have no clothes on," you assume the child's concept of maleness and femaleness is based on

_____ differences.
clothing/biological and genital

(b) At what point do children use biological and genital differences as the basis for sex identification?

_____

- - - - - - - - - - - - - - - - -

(a) clothing; (b) when they can use logic and reason

66. According to Kohlberg, children's concept of maleness and female-

ness changes with age and _____ development.
                              emotional/cognitive

- - - - - - - - - - - - - - - -

cognitive

67. Until children reach the stage where they can understand the con-
ceptual basis for sex identity, their concept of maleness-femaleness
appears to be based almost entirely on cultural stereotypes of what
males and females are like. The child's conceptualizing is apparently
influenced very little by his home situation, his parents' values and
teachings, and specific child-rearing practices.

We have seen, for example, that children use clothes and hair
length as bases for differentiating males from females. If you ask a
five-year-old what the difference is between a boy and a girl, the
child is likely to say: "Boys wear pants and girls wear dresses."
Or: "Girls have long hair, boys have short hair. (Although this
stereotype is fast changing, children as yet have not caught up to the
change!)

If that same five-year-old child had a mother who wore slacks or
jeans all the time and an older brother with shoulder-length hair,
would the child be likely to give a different answer to that question?

Explain. _____

_____

- - - - - - - - - - - - - - -

Probably not; because the child's concept of maleness-femaleness is
apparently influenced very little by the home situation.

68. By the age of seven, children "know" that men do not cry, even
though they may have seen their father cry on numerous occasions,
and their parents have always stressed that "men have feelings too."

If a seven-year-old child were asked: "Do men cry?" and "Do
women cry?" what would the child probably answer? Explain.

_____

_____

_____

- - - - - - - - - - - - - - - - - -

The child would probably say no to the first question and yes to the
second question. Children's ideas about what men and women do are
influenced more by cultural stereotypes than by their own family
situation.

69. According to Kohlberg, children first learn the stereotype, then ad-
just their behavior to match it. They feel "good" when engaging in
the stereotyped sex-role behavior and "bad" when engaging in
"deviant" sex-role behavior. Obviously, the more rigid and nar-
rowly defined the cultural sex-role stereotypes, the less freedom
children have to try out or sample the wide range of possible
behaviors and find out which one seems right for them.

If Kohlberg is right in his estimate of the importance of sex-role
stereotypes in determining children's sex-typed behavior, what
would probably happen if the stereotypes were less rigid, limited,
and well-defined—if men and women were seen by children as doing

pretty much the same things? _____

_____

- - - - - - - - - - - - - - - - - -

Children would probably be free to try out a wider range of behaviors.

70. Despite the importance of sex-role stereotypes (and the instant
availability of such stereotypes through books, movies, and television), parents still play an important role in their children's
sex-role development.

As the learning theorists have shown, parents can to some extent
influence the amount of children's sex-typed behavior through the
principles of imitation and reinforcement (although perhaps less than
psychologists have in the past thought). They can influence, though
perhaps only slightly, children's understanding of sex-role identity

by attempting to control (limit or increase) their exposure to certain cultural stereotypes. That is, they can purchase books and encourage the watching of television shows that present the image they would prefer their child to have. (Parents have in the past done this to some extent unconsciously; some are now rather consciously doing it.)

Finally, parents can provide children with the emotional support necessary to help them accept their own <u>feelings</u>, even when those feelings do not match the cultural stereotype. If, for example, a boy can express, rather than deny, feminine feelings ("I wish I were a girl because girls get more attention than boys") and find they are accepted by his parents, he will be less likely to feel that they are "deviant" or "bad."

Parents probably have at least some influence over what aspects of sex-role identity?

_____ (a) behavior

_____ (b) understanding

_____ (c) feeling

- - - - - - - - - - - - - - - - -

all three—(a), (b), and (c)   (Of course, they can also work actively to change the sex-role stereotypes as presented in the media.)

71. More and more it is becoming obvious that many so-called masculinity-femininity scores really represent a child's <u>understanding</u> of what is appropriate for boys and girls to do or feel, rather than what they themselves actually do or feel.

In other words, many of these tests measure a child's awareness of

cultural sex _____.
                stereotypes/feelings

- - - - - - - - - - - - - - - - -

stereotypes

72. At a fairly young age (maybe as young as three or four), children can tell you "what boys do" and "what girls do." As soon as they know these things, they will tend to give the "right" answers on masculinity-femininity tests—they will show you that they understand what the stereotypes are.

For example, many tests of masculinity-femininity ask a child to choose between two activities—a traditionally male activity and a traditionally female activity. The question is usually something like:

"Which would you rather do—play baseball or play house?" In reality, however, the child may be <u>answering</u> as if the question were: "Which would boys rather do—play baseball or play house?"

If a ten-year-old girl is asked whether she would rather play hockey or bake a cake, she will probably answer "bake a cake." Can we be sure that she is actually responding in terms of her own preference? Explain. _____

_____

_____

- - - - - - - - - - - - - - - - - - -

No; she may simply be showing that she knows what the sex-role stereotypes are; she may be answering the question: "Which would girls rather do—play hockey or bake a cake?"

<u>Note</u>: Interestingly, girls are more likely to say that they "prefer" boys' toys or activities than is the reverse; that is, boys almost never state a preference for "female" toys or activities. Some psychologists believe this to be due to stronger pressures on boys than on girls to conform to sex-role stereotypes. On the other hand, perhaps boys' toys and activities are simply more interesting than girls'.

73. Children of ten generally have stronger same-sex sex-role identities than children of four. This probably due to:

_____ (a) a higher level of cognitive development

_____ (b) the fact that the ten-year-olds have received more reinforcement for same-sex behavior than have four-year-olds

_____ (c) both (a) and (b)

- - - - - - - - - - - - - - - - - -

(c)

CROSS-SEX TYPING

74. In most of the studies on sex-role identity there is an underlying assumption of something inherently "good" and "desirable" in a strong identification with one's own sex—whether sex-role identity is defined in terms of feelings, understanding, or behavior. There is evidence, however, that strong same-sex identification may not

be so desirable. For example, high IQ is correlated with high "masculinity" scores for <u>girls</u> and high "femininity" scores for <u>boys</u>. That is, the more "masculine" a girl's interests, the higher her IQ; the more "feminine" a boy's interests, the higher his IQ.

In addition, young children's IQ scores were found to be positively correlated with interest in games and activities of opposite-sex children. That is, girls with high IQ scores tend to be interested in what are traditionally considered boys' games. Similarly, boys with high IQ scores are often interested in "girls" activities.

The above studies seem to indicate that:

_____ (a) IQ is related to masculine identification.

_____ (b) IQ is related to feminine identification.

_____ (c) IQ is related to masculine identification in women and feminine identification in men.

- - - - - - - - - - - - - - - - - -

(c)

75. This tendency to take on the interests and preferences of the opposite sex is called <u>cross-sex typing</u>.

Which of the following children are showing cross-sex typing?

_____ (a) John enjoys baseball in the summer, football in the fall, and hockey in the winter.

_____ (b) Susan is the best pitcher on her Little League team.

_____ (c) David saves bits of cloth from his grandmother's sewing box and uses them to design clothes for his sister's dolls.

_____ (d) Veronique got a Suzy Homemaker oven for Christmas, and she often makes desserts on it for her father.

- - - - - - - - - - - - - - - - - -

(b) (Susan) and (c) (David) are showing cross-sex typing.

76. A girl is demonstrating cross-sex typing when she enjoys

_____ games and activities.
masculine/feminine

- - - - - - - - - - - - - - - -

masculine

77. Cross-sex typing is associated with _____ IQ scores.

                                       high/low

- - - - - - - - - - - - - - - - - - -

    high

78. Another positive characteristic associated with cross-sex typing is high creativity and originality. Girls scoring high in masculinity and boys scoring high in femininity are both more fluent in generating hypotheses. They are original in their thoughts, ideas, and manner of expressing themselves.

    Some psychologists have hypothesized that the higher creativity and originality of the highly masculine girls and highly feminine boys may be due to the absence of repression. They suggest that people have both feminine and masculine sides to their natures. If a girl scores high in femininity, she has had to work very hard at repressing the masculine side of her nature (the reverse would be true for boys). A person who is using repression as a mechanism could not be original, fluent, responsive, impulsive—in short, creative.

(a) In addition to high IQ scores, what is another positive or desirable trait association with cross-sex typing?

    _____

(b) Explain how cross-sex typing might be associated with absence of repression. _____

    _____

    _____

    _____

    _____

- - - - - - - - - - - - - - - - - -

    (a) creativity and originality; (b) This explanation assumes that people have both feminine and masculine sides to their natures. Girls who score high in femininity, it is hypothesized, repress their masculine side; the reverse is true for men. Repression is not associated with creativity. (This is a highly speculative argument. Psychologists, however, are coming to believe that an exaggerated conformity to stereotyped sex-roles is not a healthy thing.)

79. So, although boys generally identify with other boys, and girls with other girls, it is not true that the stronger the same-sex identity,

the healthier the child. We are only beginning to question and to learn about the real sex differences as opposed to the stereotyped. In the meantime, people are beginning to question whether conformity to established sex roles is necessarily a healthy thing. Future research in the field of sex differences and sex-role identity may clarify this issue further.

One of my five-year-old daughter's favorite stories is about a little girl who always gets preferential treatment by insisting on "ladies first."* In the end, the girl, who is a "real little lady" (You can tell by her matching ribbons and dress, her shiny black patent leather shoes, "...and I always put just a dab of perfume behind each ear!"), gets eaten by a band of hungry tigers because, even as they are heating the cooking pot and eyeing all their prisoners, she keeps insisting on "ladies first!"

The moral of this story is:

_____ (a) Conformity to established sex roles is not necessarily a healthy thing.

_____ (b) Sometimes five-year-olds show good taste.

_____ (c) Sometimes tigers show good taste.

- - - - - - - - - - - - - - - - - -

Perhaps (a), (b), and (c) are all true! At any rate, some studies on cross-sex typing show that strong same-sex identity is not necessarily a healthy thing.

*From Free to Be...You and Me. Developed and edited by Carole Hart, Letty Cottin Pogrebin, Mary Rodgers, and Marlo Thomas (New York: McGraw-Hill, 1974).

SELF-TEST

This Self-Test is designed to show you whether or not you have mastered this chapter's objectives. Answer each question to the best of your ability. Correct answers and review instructions are given at the end of the test.

1. By the age of twelve or so, boys and girls differ in many areas of personality and intellectual abilities. Name some of these differences.

_____

_____

_____

_____

2. Summarize what is known about how these traits develop.

_____

_____

_____

_____

_____

_____

_____

_____

_____

_____

_____

_____

_____

3. What are some of the known sex differences in response tendencies between three- and four-month-old infants?

_____

_____

_____

4. When psychologists speak of sex-role identity, they may be referring
    to any one of three different aspects of this identity. What are those

    three aspects? _____

5. Which aspect of sex-role identity is Freud referring to in his theory
    of identification? Explain that theory.

    _____

    _____

    _____

6. Which aspect of sex-role identity do social learning theorists deal
    with? Explain how they differ from Freud in their explanation of the
    identification process.

    _____

    _____

    _____

    _____

7. Describe Kohlberg's cognitive theory of the development of sex-
    role identity. Does he believe that parents play as important a
    role in that development as Freud and the learning theorists do?

    _____

    _____

    _____

    _____

    _____

    _____

8. Anais Nin has said that all human beings have both masculine and
    feminine sides to their nature; in order to develop their full potential
    as human beings, men must acknowledge and cultivate their feminine
    traits and women must acknowledge and be allowed to develop the
    masculine side of their nature. Show how this point of view is sup-
    ported by the data and theory on cross-sex typing.

_____

_____

_____

_____

Answers to Self-Test

Compare your answers to the questions on the Self-Test with the answers
given below. If you missed any questions, review the frames indicated
in parentheses following the answer. If you miss several questions, you
should probably reread the entire chapter carefully.

1. In personality, there are differences in amount of aggression,
    dependency, and achievement motivation. (Boys are higher in ag-
    gression and achievement motivation; girls, in dependency.) In
    intellectual abilities, there are differences in verbal, spatial, and
    number ability. (Boys are better in number and spatial ability;
    girls, in verbal ability.) (Frames 15—23)

2. Your answer should include the following points.
    Aggression: Differences in both aggressive behavior and aggressive
    motivation are present at a very early age. Some evidence that
    males may have an innate predisposition to be more aggressive than
    girls. (You may have included that girls express more prosocial
    aggression and more guilt over aggression than boys.)
    Dependency: Girls do not initially show more dependent behavior
    than boys; both boys and girls become less dependent, but boys drop
    their dependency behavior at a faster rate than girls.
    Achievement motivation: Initially no differences in achievement or
    achievement motivation. Girls less confident of their ability, how-
    ever, than boys. Differences in achievement motivation probably
    culturally determined. (You might have added that high-achieving
    boys tend to have warm, nurturant mothers; high-achieving girls do
    not.)
    Number ability: Boys' superiority in number ability develops during
    middle school years. Cause of differences unknown.
    Spatial ability: No early differences. Reason for boys' later supe-
    riority not known.
    Verbal ability: Fairly consistent differences; may be due to mothers'
    differential reinforcement of boys' and girls' earliest babbling sounds.
    (Frames 24—39)

3. Differential responsiveness to physical (bodily) stimulation, visual
    and auditory stimulation (girls more responsive to all of these).
    (Frames 40—44)

4.   feeling, behavior, understanding (Frames 45—49)

5.   Feeling; Freud believed that, unless there are problems in the re-
     lationship, children always identify with their same-sex parent. He
     believed the process to be biologically determined. (Frames 50—51)

6.   Behavior; they believe that children can identify with either parent
     (based, in part, on which parent is the most powerful). According
     to them, children develop appropriate sex-role behavior through
     imitation and reinforcement. (Frames 52—60)

7.   Kohlberg believes that children's understanding of their sex-role
     identity increases according to advances in their cognitive develop-
     ment. Children gradually learn the cultural sex-role stereotypes
     and then adjust their behavior accordingly. According to Kohlberg,
     cultural stereotypes play a more important role in the development
     of sex-role identity than parental imitation and reinforcement.
     (Frames 61—73)

8.   Cross-sex typing is associated with high IQ scores, and with cre-
     ativity and originality. Adherence to rigidly defined sex-roles is
     probably not a healthy thing. There is one theory that children who
     score high on same-sex identification have repressed the "other-
     sex" side of their nature. Repression is not conducive to creativity
     and originality. (Frames 74—79)

SELECTED BIBLIOGRAPHY

Sex differences in dependency and aggression

Kagan, J., and Moss, H. A. Birth to Maturity. New York: Wiley, 1962.
Sears, R. R., Maccoby, E. E., and Levin, H. Patterns of Child-Rearing.
     Evanston, Ill.: Row, Peterson, 1957.

Sex stereotypes

Harrison, B. G. Unlearning the Lie: Sexism in School. New York:
     Liveright, 1973.
NEA. Sex-role Stereotyping in the Schools. Washington, 1973.

An overview of sex differences

Bardwick, J. M. Psychology of Women. New York: Harper & Row, 1971.
Maccoby, E. E., ed. The Development of Sex Differences. Stanford:
     Stanford University Press, 1966.

A book for parents and children to share

Hart, Carole, Pogrebin, Letty Cottin, Rodgers, Mary, and Thomas, Marlo,
     eds. Free to Be...You and Me. New York: McGraw-Hill, 1974.

Additional Readings in Child Psychology

Textbooks:

Johnson, Ronald C., and Medinnus, Gene R. Child Psychology: Behavior and Development, second edition. New York: John Wiley & Sons, Inc., 1969. Introduces basic factors in development, then studies the effect of family and society on individual development.

Kennedy, Wallace A. Child Psychology, second edition. New Jersey: Prentice-Hall, Inc., 1975. A basic text requiring only a minimal background in psychology; also presents and discusses some journal articles, such as Harlow's "The Nature of Love."

McCandless, Boyd R., and Evans, Ellis D. Children and Youth: Psychosocial Development. Hinsdale, Ill.: The Dryden Press, 1973. Stresses the interaction between the physical, cognitive, and social-emotional development of children. A very readable text that nevertheless presents solid research data.

Mussen, Paul H., Conger, John J., and Kagan, Jerome. Child Development and Personality, fourth edition. New York: Harper and Row, 1974. This book covers all areas of development and is broad in scope; gives an up-to-date and fairly complete picture of what is known about children and their development. A good blend of description and back-up data.

Stone, Lawrence J., and Church, Joseph. Childhood and Adolescence: A Psychology of the Growing Person, third edition. New York: Random House, 1973. An easy-to-read book with many anecdotes and examples; not much emphasis on research.

Weiner, Irving B., and Elkind, David. Child Development: A Core Approach. New York: John Wiley & Sons, Inc., 1972. A brief introduction to the basic facts and issues in child development; includes a list of readings.

Books of selected readings:

Rebelsky, Freda G., and Dorman, Lynn (eds.). Child Development and Behavior, second edition. New York: Alfred A. Knopf, 1973.

Weiner, Irving B., and Elkind, David (eds.). Readings in Child Development. New York: John Wiley & Sons, Inc., 1972.

Final Exam

Chapter 1

1. As children get older, their behavior changes as a result of what two factors? _____

_____

2. In which of the following learning situations would <u>level of maturation</u> interfere with learning? Explain.

_____ (a) An 8-year-old girl learning to play baseball.

_____ (b) A 3-year-old boy learning to ride a bike.

_____

_____

3. You are a child psychologist and you want to know whether 7-year-old children will learn a vocabulary list better if it is presented orally or in written form. What method of study would you use to answer this question?

_____ (a) experiment

_____ (b) cross-sectional study

_____ (c) longitudinal study

_____ (d) natural experiment

4. Which of the four methods of study listed in question 3 give descriptive data? _____ Which give explanatory data? _____

5.   In which of the methods of study in question 3 are control groups used? _____

· 6.   We have posed the question: Will 7-year-old children learn a written or an oral vocabulary list better? To answer this question you might make a list of ten words and ask one group of children to learn them from a written list and one group to learn them from the teacher's oral presentation. You would then compare the average number of words learned by each group. In this experiment which would be the dependent variable and which would be the independent variable?

_____

_____

7.   Match the following:

_____ (a)   personality and social development

_____ (b)   perceptual development

_____ (c)   language development

_____ (d)   cognitive development

_____ (e)   motor development

(1)   increase in muscular control and coordination

(2)   integration of sense impressions

(3)   growth of patterns of interactions with others

(4)   growth of language skills

(5)   changes in the processes of thinking, conceptualizing, reasoning

8.   Consider the example of a child learning to climb stairs for the first time. Analyze this learning situation in terms of stimulus, response, motivation, reinforcement, and the connection that is learned.

_____

_____

_____

Chapter 2

9.   Which of the following best describes how a child's perceptual system works?

_____ (a)   It works like a camera; it takes an exact picture of scenes, objects, and events in the environment.

_____ (b) It works like an artist's brush; it sketches incomplete
scenes, and often distorts objects and events.

10. Name five important factors which influence our "sense impressions"
and help to determine how we perceive objects and events in our environment. _____

_____

_____

11. When two people are asked to describe the events at the scene of an
accident, they often focus on entirely different aspects of the situation
and thus give quite different descriptions of what happened. Why is it
that people cannot see or hear everything that goes on in such a situation? What do we call the perceptual mechanism which limits our

visual and auditory input? _____

_____

_____

12. Explain how a form discrimination test differs from a recognition

test. Give an example of each kind of test. _____

_____

_____

13. In the course of perceptual development, changes occur in attention,
scanning, and organization and interpretation. Describe those

changes. _____

_____

_____

14. What does the "visual cliff" experiment demonstrate about infant

perception? Describe that experiment. _____

_____

_____

_____

15. Older children need less visual "information" to recognize familiar pictures and objects than younger children do.   Explain why this is so.

_____

_____

_____

16. What does "MBD" stand for? Describe some of the symptoms of MBD.   _____

_____

_____

17. What activities might be included in a remedial program for MBD?

_____

_____

_____

Chapter 3

18. As children grow older, their problem-solving ability increases as a result of changes in: (a) problem-solving strategies; and (b) "mental representation" of problems. Describe these changes.

_____

_____

_____

19. Psychologists generally recognize five steps in the problem-solving process. Name these five steps and describe the developmental changes that occur in each step. _____

_____

_____

20. How does Piaget differ from the learning theorists in his ideas about children's intellectual development and "rule-learning"?

_____

_____

21. Below are four descriptions, each corresponding to one of Piaget's "stages" of cognitive development. Name the "stage" described by each.

_____ (a) This stage is characterized by the ability to deal with relationships between abstract ideas, symbols, and concepts.

_____ (b) In this stage, children represent problems in action terms.

_____ (c) In this stage, children tend to rely on visual encoding in solving problems.

_____ (d) At this stage the child is capable of "decentration."

22. What does "IQ" stand for? Give the formula for computing an IQ.

_____

_____

23. What are some of the environmental factors influencing IQ scores?

_____

_____

Chapter 4

24. In the following chart, fill in:

(a) the element of personality that is formed at each age.

Element of personality formed: self-esteem
                                ability to love
Important parental behaviors: a sense of identity

(b) the parental behaviors that are most important at each age.

Important parental behaviors: clarifying basic values
                              "mothering"
                              using reward more than punishment

Age	Element of per-sonality formed	Important parental behaviors
Infancy		
Early and middle childhood		
Adolescence		

25. Harry Harlow took baby monkeys from their real mothers and raised them with different kinds of "mother-substitutes." These mother-substitutes were stylized figures made of either wire-mesh or terry-cloth.

   Which kind of figure did the baby monkeys prefer—the wire-mesh or the terry-cloth? Explain what this preference demonstrated regarding the role of <u>feeding</u> in early mother-child relationships.

   _____

   _____

   _____

26. How do children develop "high" or "low" self-esteem? (Answer in terms of positive or negative feedback.) _____

   _____

   _____

27. Answer true or false. Parents of "low-esteem" children:

   _____ (a) use reward more than punishment.

   _____ (b) use harsh and inappropriate punishment.

   _____ (c) threaten "loss of love" as a punishment.

   _____ (d) are warm and accepting towards their children.

   _____ (e) show an interest in the children's activities and opinions.

28. When psychologists refer to "personality," they refer to a collection of <u>traits</u>. In what ways are "traits" more stable than "behaviors"?

_____

_____

29. (a) According to many psychologists, what causes frustration?

_____

(b) According to the frustration-aggression hypothesis, frustration

_____ (sometimes/always) leads to aggressive motivation.

30. Robert Sears did an experiment in which the effects of low, medium, and severe punishment were studied. Summarize that experiment

and its results. _____

_____

_____

31. Name two other factors, in addition to frustration, that have been shown to affect the amount of aggressive behavior shown by children.

_____

32. (a) What is a "defense mechanism"? _____

_____

(b) Do only anxious people use defense mechanisms? _____

33. Behavior modification is a technique for influencing behavior.
    (a) Explain how behavior modification works. _____

_____

(b) Does behavior modification attempt to influence a child's under-

lying motivation or personality traits? _____

<u>Chapter 5</u>

34. Which of the following statements is true?

_____ (a) Children's language comprehension is greater than their language production.

_____ (b) Children's language production is greater than their language comprehension.

35. Explain how imitation and "selective reinforcement" interact to help children learn to speak. _____

_____

_____

36. Describe how the technique of "expansion" works to bring children's speech closer to adult speech. _____

_____

_____

37. Jean Berko devised a test to find out if young children know and can use correct grammatical forms. Explain how her test showed that children were not simply repeating words they had heard before, but were instead demonstrating knowledge of grammatical rules.

_____

_____

_____

38. What does "LAD" stand for? What does it do? _____

_____

_____

39. Do all psychologists agree that a "device" such as "LAD" exists?

_____

40. Psychologists have done research on the thinking processes and problem-solving ability of deaf children. How do deaf and hearing children compare in these two areas? _____

_____

_____

_____

41. Research on deaf children suggests that: (Check one.)

_____ (a) thinking is nothing more than "inner speech."

_____ (b) speech is probably only one "mode" of representing problems.

42. How do middle-class and lower-class children compare on:

(a) vocabulary. _____

(b) use of complex and abstract speech. _____

_____

Chapter 6

43. Summarize how adolescent boys and girls differ in the areas of verbal, spatial, and number abilities. Which of the three differences appears in very young (preschool) children? _____

_____

_____

44. Is there any evidence to suggest how these differences develop?

_____

_____

45. By adolescence, boys and girls differ on a number of personality traits. Name three of these traits and tell how boys and girls differ on them. _____

_____

_____

46. Are these sex differences in personality probably innate or learned? Explain. _____

_____

_____

47. Freud's explanation of the development of sex-role identity differs from that of the social learning theorists. What are some of the differences in the two explanations? _____

_____

_____

48. According to Kohlberg's "cognitive" theory of the development of sex-role identity, children's sex-role behavior is determined by: (Check one.)

_____ (a) their level of understanding of the "correct" sex role.

_____ (b) their degree of identification with the same-sex parent.

49. For each of the following statements, indicate whether that statement would probably be made by a social learning theorist, a follower of Freud, or a proponent of the "cognitive" theory of sex-role identity. (Write in "social learning," "Freud," or "cognitive.")

_____ (a) Children will tend to identify with the parent who is perceived as having the most power.

_____ (b) All normal girls identify with their mother.

_____ (c) "Identifying with" a parent means "acting like" that parent.

_____ (d) Cultural sex role stereotypes have a great influence on the development of sex role identity.

50. What is "cross-sex typing"? Is it correlated with <u>high</u> or <u>low</u> intelligence? _____

_____

_____

ANSWERS

1. Maturation and experience (1:5)
2. (b) A three-year-old boy has probably not matured enough physically to be able to ride a bike, no matter how hard he tries to "learn."
    (1: 7-9)

3. (a) experiment (1: 41-70)

4. A cross-sectional study and a longitudinal study give descriptive
    data; an experiment and a natural experiment give explanatory data.
    (1: 70)

5. Control groups are used in experiments and natural experiments.
    (1: 59-70)

6. The dependent variable is "average number of words learned by each
    group"; the independent variable is "method of presentation"—whether
    the list is presented orally or in written form. (1: 56-58)

7. (a) 3; (b) 2; (c) 4; (d) 5; (e) 1 (1: 13-24)

8. The stimulus would be the stairs, or the sight of the stairs; the re-
    sponse, lifting each foot in a certain way; the motivation might be the
    desire to achieve, or to explore, or to be independent, or to impress
    Mommy; the reinforcement might be the satisfaction of getting up-
    stairs without Mommy's help, or the parents' smiles of approval;
    what is learned is the connection between the sight of the stairs—
    the stimulus—and the response of lifting the feet in a certain way.
    (1: 25-40)

9. (b) (2: 1-33)

10. (a) Aspects of the stimulus itself (some objects are more easily per-
    ceived than others).
    (b) The condition of the receptors (some people hear or see better
    than others).
    (c) Selective attention (we attend to some aspects of the stimulus and
    ignore others).
    (d) Organization (we have a natural tendency to group stimuli to-
    gether).
    (e) Interpretation (we have a natural tendency to interpret stimuli as
    something known or familiar).
    (2: 1-33)

11. Our perceptual system is limited, and we can "take in" only so much
    information at a time. We call the perceptual mechanism which limits
    our visual and auditory input "selective attention." (2: 17-19)

12. In a form discrimination test, the child must perceive similarities
    and differences in the shapes of objects. (An example is the Embedded
    Figures Test.) (2: 35-37)
        In a recognition test, a child must name the shape or object pre-
    sented to him; a recognition test assumes that the shape or object is
    already familiar to the child. (An example would be an incomplete
    figure, with parts or lines missing; the child must "fill in" the gaps
    in order to recognize the object.) (2: 58-68)

13. Attention—Children attend more to parts or details of a stimulus as they get older.
Scanning—Their scanning pattern becomes more systematic.
Organization and interpretation—They are better able to organize and interpret stimuli, and therefore do better in recognition tasks.
(2: 34–68)

14. The visual cliff experiment shows that 6-month-old infants have depth perception. In this demonstration, 6-month-old infants were placed on a runway. On either side of the runway was a patterned surface; the pattern on one side was designed to give the illusion of depth (it looked like a "drop-off"). In nearly all the cases, the infants would not cross over the "drop-off" side, even when their mothers stood on the other side of it and called to them. (2: 72–74)

15. Older children have had more experience (are more familiar) with common pictures and objects. They have more information available "in their minds" about them, and therefore need less information from the stimulus itself. (2: 62–66)

16. MBD stands for "minimal brain dysfunction." Some of the symptoms are poor coordination, hyperactivity, problems in visual and auditory discrimination, frequent accidents, clumsiness, difficulty in hopping and skipping, etc. Also (in older children) reading difficulties, speech problems, possibly emotional problems. (2: 76–91)

17. You might include remedial reading and speech therapy; also practice in "fine-motor" and "gross-motor" activities. (The use of drugs is still highly controversial.) (2: 95–99)

18. (a) Their strategies become more systematic. (3: 20–25)
(b) They become increasingly capable of using symbolic representation; they progress from action images to visual images, to symbols. (3: 7–28)

19. Encoding, memory, induction, evaluation, deduction.
1. Encoding—As children grow older, they are able to represent information in more abstract or symbolic ways (from action images to visual images to symbols).
2. Memory—They are better able to transfer information from short-term to long-term memory.
3. Induction—It is not clear how this changes. Possibly, however, as children grow older, they are able to generate more hypotheses or possible solutions to a problem.
4. Evaluation—Children become more reflective with age; that is, they wait longer before deciding on an answer, and make fewer errors.
5. Deduction—As children grow older, they learn from experience more rules that can always be applied in specific situations.
(3: 50)

20. The learning theorists believe that children learn rules simply by being rewarded for the right response; the "rule" is the learned stimulus-response connection. Piaget believes that children's rule learning ability is affected by the way in which they "encode" problems. (3: 51-53)

21. (a) stage of formal operations; (b) sensori-motor stage; (c) pre-operational stage; (d) stage of concrete operations (3: 53-75)

22. IQ stands for "intelligence quotient." The formula for IQ is:
$$\frac{\text{Chronological age}}{\text{Mental age}} \times 100, \text{ or } \frac{CA}{MA} \times 100 \quad (3: 88\text{-}95)$$

23. IQ scores are affected by past learning and experience, language ability, and motivation. (You may have named other related factors, such as training, cultural factors, etc.) (3: 83, 102-104)

24.

Age	Element of personality formed	Important parental behaviors
Infancy	ability to love	"mothering"
Early and middle childhood	self-esteem	using reward more than punishment
Adolescence	a sense of identity	clarifying basic values

(4: 4, 6-14, 24-41)

25. The baby monkeys preferred the terry-cloth figures, even when the terry-cloth figures did not "give milk" and the wire-mesh figures did. This preference demonstrated that feeding is probably not the most important element of the early mother-child relationship; warmth, softness, comfort—these are very important factors. (4: 10-13)

26. High self-esteem children probably experience a lot of positive feedback, both from parents and society; low self-esteem children experience a lot of negative feedback. (4: 24-34)

27. (a) false; (b) true; (c) true; (d) false; (e) false (4: 24-29)

28. They are more stable over time and across situations. That is, shy children tend to be shy adults, though the way in which they show their shyness changes from age to age. Also, an aggressive child might show his aggression in different ways, depending on the situation; the amount of underlying aggression, however, remains the same from situation to situation. (4: 50-53)

29. (a) being blocked from a goal
    (b) always
    (4: 71)

30. Sears looked at amount of aggression shown by three groups of boys.
    The parents of the three groups of boys differed in amount of punish-
    ment normally given for aggression (high-, medium-, or low-punish-
    ment). He found that both the high- and low-punishment groups were
    low in amount of aggressive behavior shown in a nursery school situa-
    tion. When he tested the boys later, however, on a measure of "fan-
    tasy aggression" (aggression shown in a doll-play situation), the
    "high-punishment" group scored higher than either of the other two
    groups on amount of aggression shown. Sears concluded that punish-
    ment for aggression decreases aggressive behavior, but increases
    aggressive motivation. (4: 94)

31. imitation and reinforcement (4: 84)

32. (a) A defense mechanism is a technique for lessening anxiety.
    (b) No, we all use defense mechanisms to some extent.
    (4: 114)

33. (a) Behavior modification is a technique by which the desired behavior
    is rewarded, and the "undesirable" behavior is not rewarded. The re-
    warded behavior tends to increase in frequency, and the unrewarded
    behavior tends to disappear. (4: 110-114)
    (b) No. (4: 112-114)

34. (a) is true (5: 4)

35. Babies and young children try to imitate adult speech sounds, and
    those sounds are "selectively reinforced"; that is, parents tend to
    reinforce "correct" speech, and not to reinforce "incorrect" speech.
    In this way, the incorrect speech sounds gradually drop out. (5: 20-
    26, 47)

36. The mother often repeats what the child says, but with additions or
    corrections (she "expands on" what the child has said). In return, the
    child expands on his original utterance. For example: If a child says
    "me go," the mother might say, "You want to go to the store?" The
    child might then reply, "Me go store." (5: 27-32, 47)

37. Jean Berko used "nonsense" words and asked the children to give the
    correct form of the word. Because the words were not "real" words,
    she was sure that the children had not heard any form of the word be-
    fore; therefore, their replies were not based on simple imitation, or
    repetition, of words heard before. (5: 42-44, 55)

38. LAD stands for "language acquisition device." It is a built-in language
    processing system, which allows children to process and understand

all the sounds in their language environment. All psychologists do
not agree that people actually have such a built-in language processing
system. (5: 48-49)

39. No (5: 50)

40. Research has shown that the thinking processes of deaf and hearing
children are very similar. Furthermore, deaf children do as well
on most problems as hearing children. (5: 78)

41. (b) (5: 78)

42. Middle-class children generally have a better vocabulary than lower-
class children, and they use language more effectively—that is, they
use more complex and abstract speech. (5: 82, 93)

43. Verbal ability—Girls are better than boys in most areas—word usage,
fluency, grammatical usage, reading, etc.
Spatial ability—Boys are better than girls.
Number ability—Boys are better than girls.
(6: 16-22)

44. In the areas of number and spatial ability, no. In the area of verbal
ability, research has shown that there are no differences in amount
of early babbling. However, mothers reinforce the babbling of their
girl babies more than that of their boy babies. Possibly, then, girls'
superiority in verbal abilities is due to this selective reinforcement
(and the resulting fact that girls would have more chance to practice).
(6: 37-39)

45. The traits are: aggression, dependency, and achievement motiva-
tion.
Boys are higher in achievement motivation.
Boys are higher in aggression.
Girls are higher in dependency. (6: 15)

46. The differences in achievement motivation and dependency are probably learned. Initially boys and girls are equally dependent and
achievement-motivated. Apparently parents and society diffentially
reinforce boys and girls for these traits.
    There may, however, be innate sex differences in aggression.
Boys consistently show more aggression than girls. Evidence from
research on monkeys also suggests innate sex differences (one example: female monkeys, injected at birth with male hormones, show
more aggression than other female monkeys). (6: 24-33)

47. Your answer should include the following points. (1) Social learning
theory emphasizes behavior; Freud's theory emphasizes feelings.
(2) Freud's theory states that children are "biologically determined"

to identify with the same-sex parent; according to social learning theory, children can identify with either parent, depending on environmental factors.   (6: 50-51)

48.   (a)   (6: 61-69)

49.   (a)   social learning   (6: 58)
      (b)   Freud   (6: 50)
      (c)   social learning   (6: 61)
      (d)   cognitive   (6: 67)

50.   Cross-sex typing is showing an interest in, and a preference for, the activities and interests generally associated with the opposite sex.   (For example, a girl who prefers baseball to dolls.)   It is correlated with <u>high</u> intelligence.   (6: 74-77)

Index